Transnational Women Writers in the Wilmot Coterie, 1798–1840

Studies in the Eighteenth Century
ISSN: 2398-9904

This major series from Boydell & Brewer, published in association with the British Society for Eighteenth-Century Studies, aims to bring into fruitful dialogue the different disciplines involved in all aspects of the study of the long eighteenth century (c.1660–1820). It publishes innovative volumes, singly or co-authored, on any topic in history, science, music, literature and the visual arts in any area of the world in the long eighteenth century and particularly encourages proposals that explore links among the disciplines, and which aim to develop new cross-disciplinary fields of enquiry.

Series editors: Ros Ballaster, University of Oxford, UK; Matthew Grenby, Newcastle University, UK; Robert D. Hume, Penn State University, USA; Mark Knights, University of Warwick, UK; Renaud Morieux, University of Cambridge, UK

Previously published

Material Enlightenment: Women Writers and the Science of Mind, 1770–1830, Joanna Wharton, 2018

Celebrity Culture and the Myth of Oceania in Britain, 1770–1823, Ruth Scobie, 2019

British Sociability in the Long Eighteenth Century: Challenging the Anglo-French Connection, edited by Valérie Capdeville and Alain Kerhervé, 2019

Things that Didn't Happen: Writing, Politics and the Counterhistorical, 1678–1743, John McTague, 2019

Converting Britannia: Evangelicals and British Public Life, 1770–1840, Gareth Atkins, 2019

British Catholic Merchants in the Commercial Age, 1670–1714, Giada Pizzoni, 2020

Lessons of Travel in Eighteenth-Century France: From Grand Tour to School Trips, Gábor Gelléri, 2020

Political Journalism in London, 1695–1720: Defoe, Swift, Steele and their Contemporaries, Ashley Marshall, 2020

Fictions of Presence: Theatre and Novel in Eighteenth-Century Britain, Ros Ballaster, 2020

Ephemeral Print Culture in Early Modern England, Tim Somers, 2021

The Geographies of Enlightenment Edinburgh, Phil Dodds, 2022

Changing Pedagogies for Children in Eighteenth-Century England, Michèle Cohen, 2023

Transnational Women Writers in the Wilmot Coterie, 1798–1840

Beyond Borders and Boundaries

Alexis Wolf

THE BOYDELL PRESS

Published in association with

© Alexis Wolf 2024

All Rights Reserved. Except as permitted under current legislation no part of this work may be photocopied, stored in a retrieval system, published, performed in public, adapted, broadcast, transmitted, recorded or reproduced in any form or by any means, without the prior permission of the copyright owner

The right of Alexis Wolf to be identified as the author of this work has been asserted in accordance with sections 77 and 78 of the Copyright, Designs and Patents Act 1988

First published 2024
The Boydell Press, Woodbridge

ISBN 978 1 78327 788 9

The Boydell Press is an imprint of Boydell & Brewer Ltd
PO Box 9, Woodbridge, Suffolk IP12 3DF, UK
and of Boydell & Brewer Inc.
668 Mt Hope Avenue, Rochester, NY 14620-2731, USA
website: www.boydellandbrewer.com

A CIP catalogue record for this book is available
from the British Library

The publisher has no responsibility for the continued existence or accuracy of URLs for external or third-party internet websites referred to in this book, and does not guarantee that any content on such websites is, or will remain, accurate or appropriate

For Neill

Contents

	List of Illustrations	viii
	Acknowledgements	x
	List of Abbreviations	xii
	Note on the Text	xiii
	Introduction: Beyond Borders and Boundaries	1
1.	Women's Views of Revolutionary Europe	29
2.	Literary and Material Sociability at Home and Abroad	62
3.	Women's Networks of Knowledge	93
4.	Collaborative Women's History	131
5.	Women Writers and the Transnational Imagination	174
	Conclusion	207
	Bibliography	211
	Index	227

Illustrations

1. Portrait of Katherine Wilmot (1773–1824) by Unknown Artist, c. 1803–08. Private Collection. Photograph produced with funding by the Women's History Network. Reproduced by the kind permission of owner and photographer. — 3

2. Portrait of Martha Wilmot (1775–1873) by Unknown Artist, c. 1803–08. Private Collection. Photograph produced with funding by the Women's History Network. Reproduced by the kind permission of owner and photographer. — 4

3. British Library Add MS 31911, f.259r; Russian Passport © The British Library Board. — 13

4. Blair Adam House Collection, Wilmot Box 3, 'Original journals of "Kitty" Wilmot'; binding. © Blair Adam House. — 31

5. Royal Irish Academy MS 12 L 32, 'Letters of Katherine Wilmot from France-Italy 1801–03', Moscow, 1805; endpaper detail, n.d. © Royal Irish Academy. — 51

6. Royal Irish Academy MS 12 L 24 'Ms in English, 1821–22, Martha Bradford (née Wilmot): Letters from Russia, April 1803–October 1806 (Copied by her mother)', p. 123. © Royal Irish Academy. — 87

7. Royal Irish Academy MS 12 L 34, 'Note-book of Katherine Wilmot, Moscow, 1806', p. 1. © Royal Irish Academy. — 94

8. Royal Irish Academy MS 12 L 20, 'Ms in English, 1803–08, Martha Bradford (née Wilmot): Journal of stay in Russia', p. iii: 'A Perisloff Merchants Wife [sic]'. © Royal Irish Academy. — 96

9. Royal Irish Academy MS 12 L 29.1, 'Letters of Martha Bradford (née Wilmot) and Katherine Wilmot', p. 47: 'Song on the subject of the Offerings made to the Dead, by the Russian Peasants'. © Royal Irish Academy. — 118

10	British Library, *Memoirs of Princess Daschkaw*, vol. I, frontispiece. © The British Library Board.	144
11	British Library, *Memoirs of Princess Daschkaw*, vol. II, frontispiece. © The British Library Board.	145
12	British Library, *Memoirs of Princess Daschkaw*, vol. I, n.d., recto: autograph letter to Mrs. Wilmot. © The British Library Board.	149
13	British Library, Add MS 31911, f.007r. © The British Library Board.	165
14	British Library, Add MS 31911, f.047r. © The British Library Board.	169
15	British Library, *Memoirs of Princess Daschkaw*, vol. II, p. 211. © The British Library Board.	184

The author and publisher are grateful to all the institutions and individuals listed for permission to reproduce the materials in which they hold copyright. Every effort has been made to trace the copyright holders; apologies are offered for any omission, and the publisher will be pleased to add any necessary acknowledgement in subsequent editions.

Acknowledgements

I first encountered the papers of the Wilmot sisters as a young person abroad with an interest in women's literary history. The palpable story of their lives and writings spanned countless journals, letters and travelogues, and I noted their own considerable efforts to write about other women's lives. I felt a kinship with them that has remained over the years I've spent reading their words.

This book would not be what it is without the generosity of many mentors and readers. Luisa Calè and Emily Senior provided this project with indispensable attention and knowledge. Early encouragement from Marianne Wichmann Bailey and Trevor Speller was profoundly important. I am grateful to Gillian Dow and Markman Ellis for their meticulous reading and belief in the value of this work, as well as other important mentors including Sharon Ruston and Robert Jones. I am also grateful to my editors at Boydell & Brewer for their support, particularly Mari Shullaw and Elizabeth McDonald.

I am indebted to the many librarians and archivists who assisted my research in a number of public and private collections in Ireland, the United Kingdom and the United States. These include the staff past and present at the Royal Irish Academy Library, especially Siobhán Fitzpatrick, Bernadette Cunningham and Sophie Evans, along with the staff of the British Library's Manuscripts Reading Room, the Beinecke Rare Books Collection and the John Murray Archive at the National Library of Scotland. I am also grateful to Keith and Elizabeth Adam of Blair Adam House in Kelty, Scotland, for their willingness to share their family's history with me and for preserving the Wilmot sisters' papers.

I was lucky to have periods of time to work on this project during fellowships at Chawton House Library in Hampshire, the Wordsworth Trust in Grasmere, Cumbria, and at the Lewis Walpole Library in Farmington, Connecticut. Other small grants enabled me to carry out the research necessary to complete this project, including a Birkbeck-Wellcome Trust ISSF Postdoctoral Grant and the British Association for Romantic Studies' Stephen Copley Bursary. The Birkbeck School of Arts provided essential support through a Doctoral Studentship and gave me an early intellectual home. I am grateful to the women's History Network for awarding me an Early Career Fellowship, which provided essential research and childcare funding in the final stages of writing.

My own circle of literary friendship has also made this book possible. My thanks go to Grayson Del Faro, David Miller, Marianne Brooker, Robert Stearn, Lisa Climie and Lyndsey Jenkins, all of whom read and commented on my work at various stages. Flore Janssen, Leah Sidi, Hannah Petertil, Joshua James Amberson, Ariel Birks, Soody Ghoolamie, Rose Oliveira, Honor Rieley, Güneş Tavmen, Sasha Dovzhyk, Jessica Stacie, Hannah Morcos and Chloe Grimmett provided moral support.

I wish to thank my family for their support for my work, especially my parents Fred and Shelly, and my sister Amanda, even as my research took me (and kept me) very far from home. Thank you also to Sherry, Marius, Carole, Michael, Lucy, Martin and, of course, my sweet Alasdair.

My husband Neill has been a constant source of encouragement, believing in the importance of this book from the beginning. It is to him I dedicate it.

Abbreviations

Archival Collections

BAHC   Blair Adam House Collection
Beinecke Beinecke Rare Book & Manuscript Library
BL   British Library
NLS   National Library of Scotland
RIA   Royal Irish Academy

Texts

Memoirs   Ekaterina Dashkova and Martha Bradford, *Memoirs of the Princess Daschkaw, Lady of Honour to Catherine II: Empress of all the Russias Written by Herself: Comprising Letters of the Empress, and Other Correspondence*, 2 vols (London, 1840).

Note on the Text

I have used a short-title referencing system due to the length of the many eighteenth-century titles cited in this book. Where relevant, footnotes will contain the author, an abbreviated title, publication details and page numbers. Please see the bibliography for full reference details.

Earlier versions of parts of Chapter 1 previously appeared in articles in *European Romantic Review* (30:5–6, 2019) and *Journal for Eighteenth-Century Studies* (45:2, 2022); an earlier version of part of Chapter 2 previously appeared in *19: Interdisciplinarity Studies in the Long Nineteenth Century* (27, 2018).

Introduction: Beyond Borders and Boundaries

In 1808, Martha Wilmot prepared to sail home to Ireland. Following a residence of more than five years in Russia, and amidst the upheaval of the Anglo-Russian War, she was forced to take stock of the large amount of papers packed away in her trunks. The captain of her ship had been informed that the 'government had received intelligence that she was taking papers of consequence out of the country' and that the officials 'had a very suspicious eye on her'.[1] In response to the border guards' desire to find 'papers of consequence', Martha later wrote:

> Papers I certainly had, for I had the princess's memoir in her own handwriting, copies of the correspondence between her and Catherine the Second, besides some other papers, and several letters from different individuals in Russia to their friends in England.[2]

During her years in Russia, Martha lived as the guest of Princess Dashkova, a Russian noblewoman and statesperson under Catherine II. Martha encouraged and assisted Dashkova in writing her memoir. Following the arrival of Martha's sister Katherine Wilmot in Russia in 1805, both sisters created multiple copies and translations of the memoir, as well as other manuscripts intended to supplement the narrative, such as copies of the correspondence sent to Dashkova by Catherine II. Martha noted that she also carried 'a good many papers and letters, the collection of five years', an assemblage that included six volumes of her own diaries, as well as extensive fair copies of letters and travel literature written by the sisters (II, p. 280). Fearing that a search of the papers she carried could damage Dashkova's political standing in Russia and prevent her own departure, Martha took the decision to burn Dashkova's handwritten manuscript, along with some of her own personal correspondence. Burning the original manuscript was painful, but Martha took comfort in 'knowing that the copy I

---

[1] *Memoirs*, II, p. 277.
[2] *Memoirs*, II, p. 278.

had made was safely deposited in England' by Katherine the previous year (II, p. 286). The misfortune of burning a portion of her own private papers was also lessened by a similar act of collective transcription, which is not explicitly declared: the five years' worth of correspondence that she knew to have been collected, transcribed and circulated by her female relatives in Ireland in her absence. Finding nothing among her papers worthy of holding her, Martha was released by the Russian border guards following a five-day search and allowed to sail for England.

Martha's assemblage of original papers, as well as the 'copies' that she attempted to carry home from Russia, embody the key themes addressed in *Transnational Women Writers in the Wilmot Coterie, 1798–1840: Beyond Borders and Boundaries*, the first full study of the writing and networks of Irish sisters Katherine and Martha Wilmot (1773–1824; 1775–1873). The Wilmot sisters' remarkable lives show the possibilities and limitations faced by women writers and travellers of their day. Their manuscripts are distinctive for their capturing and reflecting on the era's political conflicts, including a flight from Ireland during the Irish Rebellion (1798), time spent in Paris during the Peace of Amiens (1801–03), and extended residences in Russia during the Napoleonic Wars (Martha from 1803 to 1808, and Katherine from 1805 to 1807). The sisters' voluminous surviving papers also reveal the late eighteenth transnational authorial practices of women editors and writers through their work on the posthumously published *Memoirs of Princess Daschkaw* (1840), edited by Martha, which also put writing by both sisters into print for the first time.

While the scope of the Wilmots' travels is remarkable enough to warrant biographical and scholarly attention, it is the ways in which they document their own attempts at self-education and networked literary practices abroad that makes their writing truly significant. During their travels, Katherine and Martha Wilmot participated in a startling range of intellectual and literary pursuits, including travel writing, biography, antiquarianism, early ethnographic observation, language acquisition, translation practices and editorial work. Their writings were collectively preserved by the women of their immediate family and social circle, and later circulated far beyond those connections.

Locating the Wilmots

The Wilmot sisters' opportunities to travel abroad sprang from their Irish Protestant family's participation in transnational sociability both within and beyond Ireland. They were brought up in County Cork. Their father

Figure 1 Portrait of Katherine Wilmot (1773–1824) by Unknown Artist, c. 1803–08. Private Collection. Photograph produced with funding by the Women's History Network. Reproduced by the kind permission of owner and photographer.

Figure 2   Portrait of Martha Wilmot (1775–1873) by Unknown Artist, c. 1803–08. Private Collection. Photograph produced with funding by the Women's History Network. Reproduced by the kind permission of owner and photographer.

Edward Wilmot, born in Derbyshire, was Port Surveyor of the Revenue Board, first at Drogheda and later at Cork. He was a retired Captain of the 40th Regiment of Foot, an Irish establishment. Their mother, Martha – also known as Mary within the family – was the daughter and co-heir of the Reverend Charles Moore, Rector of Innishannon. Katherine (b. 1773) was the eldest daughter and Martha (b. 1775) the second eldest among nine siblings.[3] Both were educated at home to a high standard for girls of their day.[4] The family possessed enough private means to keep a large estate in Glanmire, near Cork, and were active among Irish Protestant sociable and literary communities, often referred to in historical scholarship as Anglo-Irish circles. Yet the term 'Anglo-Irish' does not fully encompass the complexity of the position of families such as the Wilmots. Protestant Irish families of the eighteenth century may have had English roots extending as far back as the Anglo-Norman invasions of the twelfth century, or could alternatively be located among British colonisers in the sixteenth and seventeenth centuries. Others still had more recent connections to England in the eighteenth century. The Wilmots' heritage represented a blend of these categories, showing the indistinct qualities of the classification.[5] Katherine and Martha, in their letters, diaries and published travel writing, described themselves as both 'Irish' and 'British' in turn. These categories were often leveraged at moments specific to their context – usages that were linked not only to travel, but to the sisters' individual affinities. For instance, Katherine's description of herself as Irish in Napoleonic Paris during the Peace of Amiens (1801–03) spoke subtly to a relationship between Republican France and the waning revolutionarily minded interests of the United Irish communities with whom she had socialised on the fringes; while Martha's patriotic reference to herself as British positioned her identity as a foreign traveller loyal to her own country at the outbreak of the Anglo-Russian War (1807–12). What is clear throughout their surviving writing, however, is the vitally important role that their Irish sociable and literary communities

---

[3] The Wilmot children included six daughters and three sons.
[4] While it has often been suggested that no expense was spared in the sisters' education, such as by Lady Londonderry in her 'Introduction' to the *Russian Letters*, few factual details survive. Katherine and Martha were clearly well read and capable writers. However, they learned no foreign languages, as was common for young women of their day. This lack was a hindrance on their journeys, but also a rationale for travelling abroad in order to fill this gap.
[5] See Martha Wilmot and Catherine Wilmot, *The Russian Journals of Martha and Catherine Wilmot, 1803–1808 [With plates, including portraits]*, ed. by Edith Marchioness of Londonderry and H. Montgomery Hyde (London, 1934), p. xvi.

played in their sense of self, communities that supported their travels and encouraged their literary pursuits throughout both of their lives.[6]

This book concerns itself with the literary practices taken up by the Wilmot sisters, which are framed through the lens of foreign journeys and close relationships between women in the late eighteenth century. Katherine was the first of the two sisters to go abroad thanks to an invitation to travel as companion to Margaret King, Lady Mount Cashell on a family voyage to the Continent at the start of the Peace of Amiens in 1801. Katherine was a member of an extensive social and literary community in County Cork that included Mount Cashell and members of other prominent Irish Protestant women in the area, including the Chetwoods (connected to the Wilmots by marriage) and the Penroses, but which also extended to Dublin, including the salon circles of Lady Moira.[7] Commonplace books created by women of Katherine's wider circle in the 1790s and 1800s reveal an active community of literary exchange, particularly in the realm of poetry, as well as support for an interest in the United Irish cause in the years surrounding the 1798 Irish Rebellion.[8] Katherine was a frequent visitor to Lady Mount Cashell's home in the years leading up to their shared journey. Mount Cashell, a former pupil of Mary Wollstonecraft and member of the Irish Protestant aristocracy, maintained connections with her former governess' political ethos as well as her acquaintances. Katherine's journey as Mount Cashell's companion, therefore, brought her into contact with key intellectual and

---

[6] Much pioneering work has been done in recent years to illuminate the richness of Irish literary sociability of the late eighteenth and early nineteenth centuries, particularly in relation to women's writing. See, for example, *A History of Modern Irish Women's Literature*, ed. by Heather Ingman and Clíona Ó Gallchoir (Cambridge, 2018); Clíona Ó Gallchoir, *Maria Edgeworth: Women, Enlightenment and Nation* (Dublin, 2005); and *Irish Literature in Transition, 1780–1830*, ed. by Claire Connolly (Cambridge, 2020).

[7] Angela Byrne explores aspects of this literary network in relation to Irish revolutionary sympathies in her article, 'Life after Emmet's death: Sarah Curran's literary and friendship circle', *Irish Studies Review*, 30 (2022), 119–135; Amy Prendergast's excellent study of salon cultures in eighteenth century Ireland provides useful insight into this communities. See *Literary Salons Across Britain and Ireland in the Long Eighteenth Century* (Basingstoke, 2015).

[8] Surviving examples of commonplace books associated with members of the literary circle include: BAHC, Wilmot Box 1, Bundle 2, 2/6 'Commonplace book recorded as given by Alicia Wilmot to Dorothea, Cork', 1797–98; Senate House Library, MS 704, 'Commonplace book, written in the early 19th century, containing copies of poems by various authors, including Mrs. R. Wilmot', 1782–1816; For more on support for the Irish Rebellion in the circle, see Alexis Wolf, 'Identity and Anonymity in Lady Mount Cashell's 1798 Rebellion Broadside', *Journal for Eighteenth-Century Studies*, 45:2 (2022), 259–276.

literary figures of the day, ranging from the doomed United Irishman Robert Emmett to English and American radicals such as William Godwin and Thomas Paine, many of whom she wrote about in her letters and diaries. She captured these experiences in an epistolary travelogue addressed to her brother Robert, which was shared for years among the family's sociable circle in manuscript. In Paris, Katherine regularly attended the salon of Helen Maria Williams and formed a close friendship with John Hurford Stone, publisher of The English Press. After two years in the city, the Mount Cashell's travelling party continued to Italy, but their journey was cut short by the outbreak of new hostilities between England and France. Katherine made her way back to Ireland via London, arriving home shortly after her sister Martha's own departure abroad.

Martha travelled to Russia in 1803 as a solution to a period of low spirits. The death of her favourite brother Charles from yellow fever while commanding a sloop in the West Indies in 1802 had cast a depressive shadow over her. The family's concern for Martha's well-being led to the idea of a trip overseas, mirroring Katherine's experience. Martha's journey to Russia was made possible thanks to her family's pre-existing and intimate connection to Princess Dashkova. The noblewoman was a close friend of their father's cousin, Catherine Hamilton (n.d.–1805). The women had first met in 1770 in Spa and subsequently travelled together in France, Switzerland and Scotland. It was Catherine Hamilton's invitation that had brought Dashkova to Ireland, where she met Captain Wilmot during a tour of the country in 1779–80. Hamilton's own visit to Russia as Dashkova's guest in the early 1780s laid the groundwork for the Wilmot sisters' later journeys there, and the two elder friends arranged Martha's initial voyage between them. While Captain Wilmot at first resisted the idea of his daughter travelling alone to such a distant country, he was persuaded by Martha's eagerness as well as Dashkova's promises of protection. After a four-month voyage, Martha stayed with the Princess at her Troitskoe estate near Moscow, also travelling through St Petersburg and later to the noblewoman's feudal lands in Poland. She and Dashkova formed an intense and intimate bond, with the elder woman asking Martha to consider her as her Russian mother. As Dashkova's companion and protégée, Martha mingled with members of the Russian court and studied Russian language and culture alongside French and Italian, as well as art and music. Early on in the visit, Martha persuaded the noblewoman to reflect on her own personal and political life in writing, and aided in the composition of Dashkova's memoir as amanuensis. In 1805, Katherine joined her sister in Russia. The purpose of her visit was not only to explore the country as well, but to eventually bring Martha home to Ireland. Both sisters undertook literary work on Dashkova's memoir, acting as scribes, translators and editors of letters and manuscripts from Dashkova's extensive collection of documents amassed during her time as Director of the Imperial Academy of Arts and Sciences in St Petersburg under Catherine II. The sisters also generated a huge volume of their own life writing in the form of letters and journals, which were copied and circulated within and beyond the Wilmot family in Ireland and England. The labour carried out by the Wilmot sisters in Russia was intended not only to preserve Dashkova's legacy, but also to inscribe the intimacy of the transgenerational and transnational women's literary networks that produced it. Despite the memoir project's completion, Martha chose to remain with Dashkova in Russia rather than travel back to Ireland in 1807 with Katherine. The cold Russian climate did not agree with Katherine due to continuing issues with her health. Martha herself returned to Ireland the following year due to the emergence of hostilities between England and Russia as part of the on-going Napoleonic conflicts, a departure marked by the pain of separating from her 'Russian Mother'. On her return journey, she was shipwrecked twice, arriving in Harwich, England at the close of 1808 and reaching Cork in 1809.

Dashkova's death in 1810 cemented Martha's resolve to eventually publish the memoir. Efforts to do so would occupy Martha's attention intermittently for more than three decades, a process protracted both by resistance on the part of Dashkova's brother, Simon Woronzow, the former Russian Ambassador to England, as well as major flaws with the style and cohesion of the text itself. Martha's marriage to Reverend William Bradford, a rector in Storrington, Sussex, later brought her the opportunity to live abroad again in Vienna, when he was made Chaplain to the British Embassy there (1819–29). Katherine also returned abroad later in life, settling in France from 1817 due to ill health. She died in Paris in 1824. Martha's far-reaching editorial work on *Memoirs of Princess Daschkaw*, which was eventually published in 1840, included the memorialisation of her sister's writing and travels, along with a description of her own journeys, through the addition of lengthy supplements in the second volume. The work's publication and wide circulation not only gave Martha a literary identity late in life, but also inscribed the Wilmots as serious travellers and members of the republic of letters of the late eighteenth century. Following her husband's death in 1857, Martha returned to Ireland to live with her daughter Catherine Anne Daschkaw Brooke (1813–81), who, along with her sister Blanche Elizabeth Bradford (n.d.), took an interest in preserving their mother and aunt's literary remains following Martha's death in 1873.

By positioning the literary efforts of the Wilmot sisters at its core, what follows centres primarily on the activities of women writers of the middling rank, a social and historical-literary position that frequently evades scholarly notice and archival preservation, rather than their upper-class patrons and mentors. As such, what follows is an exploration of the literary opportunities afforded to women travellers without their own elite social status, or of an ill-defined middling class, who journeyed abroad and formed relationships as the companions of aristocratic women.[9] Painting a picture of middling women travellers and writers is not a simple matter. As Katherine Turner writes, 'the world of "women writing travel" has always been intersectional ... in terms of the writers' gender, sexuality, marital status, race, religion, national identity, class and profession.'[10] Historic studies of rank and class, particularly in relation to those of the 'middling sort', is further complicated by the fact that 'individuals do not live out their lives within neat, homogenous social categories.'[11] Recent scholarship on the Wilmot sisters has grappled with how to interpret their lives, writing and travels at the intersection of class and wealth, perhaps due to their obscurity as subjects. The Wilmot family has been described as 'wealthy and influential', and the sisters themselves as 'elite'.[12] Angela Byrne, with a deep historical understanding of the Wilmots' networks in Ireland, describes their family as middle-ranking.[13]

In their own papers and manuscripts, Martha and Katherine frequently highlight how a mix of social and family connections funded and enabled travels, and thus, indirectly, their literary pursuits. For instance, Katherine's Peace of Amiens journal, annotated at a later date by Martha, describes how 'a Legacy from our Grandmother ... too large to be spent in trifles

---

[9] Between the extremes of the aristocracy and the working class, Peter Earle famously states, 'were the middling people, who worked but ideally did not get their hands dirty'; Peter Earle, *The Making of the English Middle Class: Business, Society and Family Life in London 1660–1730* (Berkeley, 1989), p. 3.

[10] Katherine Turner, 'Women Writing Travel', *Forum for Modern Language Studies*, 59:2 (2023), 315–319; <https://doi.org/10.1093/fmls/cqad027> [accessed 21 April 2024].

[11] Alan Kidd and David Nicholls, 'Introduction: The Making of the British Middle Class?', in *The Making of the British Middle Class? Studies of Regional and Cultural Diversity Since the Eighteenth Century*, ed. by Alan Kidd and David Nicholls (Stroud, 1998), pp. xv–xl, p. xxv.

[12] Emma Gleadhill, *Taking Travel Home: The Souvenir Culture of British Women Tourists, 1750–1830* (Manchester, 2022), pp. 208; 237.

[13] Angela Byrne, 'Anonymity, Irish Women's Writing, and a Tale of Contested Authorship: Blue Stocking Hall (1827) and Tales of My Time (1829)', *Proceedings of the Royal Irish Academy: Archaeology, Culture, History, Literature*, 119C (2019), 259–281, p. 266; Byrne points out that Captain Edward Wilmot 'appears to have been well respected in the Cork area, making important connections with landowners like the Mount Cashells and the Penroses', p. 266.

and too small to be laid by as a fortune' allowed the elder sister to travel as Lady Mount Cashell's companion.[14] While Katherine's inheritance allowed her to comfortably sustain herself abroad, her friendship with Mount Cashell opened doors to her in Paris that may otherwise have been closed, including literary, political and social interactions. Martha's letters and diaries from Russia, as well as her later work on Dashkova's papers, record the noblewoman's frequent generous gifts and financial support, including large sums of money. An editorial postscript in *Memoirs of Princess Daschkaw*, for instance, highlights the Princess' gift of £5,000 to her young friend, which Martha notes was 'in addition to other very munificent obligations of a similar nature'.[15] At the same time, letters sent by Martha to her relation John Eardley Wilmot – a Member of Parliament and writer – reveal the complicated means by which several members of her own immediate and extended family, including her parents, brothers and cousins, funnelled money through complicated financial networks during the Napoleonic Wars to support her Russia travels.[16] Captain Edward Wilmot's letters – a few of which survive dating from the period of his daughters' travels in Russia – highlight the unexpected nature of Dashkova's patronage and affection across class, national and familial lines. 'I feel myself overwhelmed with gratitude to the truly munificent as well as motherly Princess for her multiplied kindnesses of every description that I literally am at a loss for words to convey an adequate idea of my sensation', Edward writes to Eardley Wilmot, describing Dashkova's gifts of money and offers of protection.[17] 'Nor is dearest Martha alone a sharer in her liberality and maternal kindness of every sort', he notes, highlighting the role of Dashkova's attention on the entire family, which 'is so like a dream, that I am lost in amaze when ever [sic] I contemplate on it'.[18] These varied contemporary records demonstrate that while the sisters did have significant financial backing from within their family, and might best be described as either middle or upper-middle class, it was in fact the class-status *connections*

---

[14] RIA 12 L 32, n.d. [endnote dedication]; for more on the Peace of Amiens travelogue, see Chapter 1.

[15] *Memoirs*, II, 207.

[16] See Beinecke OSB MS 54, Box 3, Folder 151: Wilmot, Martha. 33 ALS to John Eardley-Wilmot, October 1803–November 1810. These letters are fascinating for the detailed financial records they contain. John Eardley Wilmot plays a part in sending money to Martha from her immediate relatives, as well as sending her funds himself. These resources are later added to by Dashkova's gifts of money. On Martha's return to Britain, Eardley Wilmot discharges her of any of her remaining debts, underlining the strong networks of financial support she and her sister benefited from.

[17] Beinecke OSB MS 54, Box 3, Folder 148, Edward Wilmot, '2nd February 1806', 1v.

[18] Ibid.

and wealth of their patrons and companions that enabled them to join in the experience of elite tourists abroad, and which made a lasting impact on the provincial Irish Protestant family's evolving sense of identity through transnational friendship.

The starting point for revealing these connections can be found in the rich surviving archives holding the literary remains of the Wilmot sisters. Three central archival collections devoted to them are examined in relation to one another for the first time in this book: the Royal Irish Academy's Wilmot-Dashkova Collection; British Library Add MS 31911, containing Martha's scribal manuscript copy of Dashkova's *Memoirs* and other related papers; and a family archive at Blair Adam House in Scotland, which has been recently reconnected to their wider corpus.[19] Additional materials in the National Library of Scotland's John Murray Archive, the Beinecke Library's Eardley-Wilmot correspondence, and Senate House's collections provide further context for the Wilmot sisters' integration into the republic of letters in the late eighteenth and early nineteenth centuries. Each collection contributes vital material for understanding the full scope of the Wilmot's efforts. The strategic arrangement of these archives also creates a sense of legacy, whether for the sisters as individuals, or for their collective writings. Certain manuscripts have been altered to reveal or obscure information. The allocation of manuscripts within particular archival bodies sheds light on what writing the sisters and their descendants favoured for preservation, compared with that withheld from public attention. The Wilmots' archives offer a window into the important role that manuscript production and circulation played in both sociable and domestic settings for women in the late eighteenth and into the nineteenth centuries, while their later advances towards publication reveal strategies for engaging with the print marketplace taken up by interconnected groups of women in period.

The Royal Irish Academy Library's Wilmot-Dashkova Collection is the most abundant source of material on the sisters and their circle. The Royal Irish Academy collection comprises nearly two-dozen manuscripts, books and material objects accumulated by the sisters during their travels, including personal travel journals, loose correspondence and bound scribal volumes containing copies of their letters. The collection was passed down Martha's female line throughout the nineteenth century. It is composed of the finest and most complete examples of the Wilmots' life writing, travel

---

[19] Dublin, RIA, Wilmot-Dashkova Collection; London, BL Add MS 31911: Autobiographical Memoirs, in French, of Ekaterina Romanovna, Princess Dashkova (or Daschkaw), transcribed, in 1805, during a residence with the Princess, by Miss Martha Wilmot, afterwards Mrs Bradford, from the original draught; BAHC, Kelty, Perth, Scotland.

writing and ethnographic or antiquarian endeavours, apparently selected by Martha herself for careful preservation through inheritance. Several items note the line of inheritance in marginalia, which also highlight the role of Martha's daughters, Catherine and Blanche, in the collections' continued survival. Elizabeth Lecky (1842–1912), Martha's great niece by marriage, eventually donated the assemblage to the Royal Irish Academy Library in 1903, having inherited them from her late husband W. E. H. Lecky, a distant relation of the Wilmot family.[20] The holdings in the Wilmot-Dashkova Collection associate the Wilmots with narratives of transnational travel, literary production and intellectual engagement.

The bound volume held by the British Library contains the main copy of Dashkova's manuscript that was used to create *Memoirs of Princess Daschkaw*. The manuscript is copied out in Martha's hand with several instances of Dashkova's own writing present as well. The volume also includes a great deal of additional material relevant to Dashkova's life and connections, which also appeared in *Memoirs*, such as transcripts of speeches given while she served as President of the Imperial Academy of Arts and Sciences (1783); scribal transcripts of her correspondence with Catherine II, created by Katherine during her time in Russia; as well as letters from Dashkova to Martha and Katherine following their return from Russia. The collection was donated to the British Museum by Martha's daughters in 1882, and contains their prefatory statements attesting to the work's authenticity and praising Martha's editorial work. The manuscript shows the literary labour that Martha and Katherine undertook to help Dashkova write her memoir, as well as Martha's extensive editorial efforts to bring the work to a public audience. It has been strategically assembled to underline these connections; for instance, in the form of the Wilmots' original Russian passports, which are included towards the back of the tome. The passports lend proof to the sisters' claims as travellers in Russia and Dashkova's assistants, a theme that becomes literally bound up as a constitutive aspect of the manuscript of the memoir.

The Blair Adam House Collection provides a fascinating counterpoint to the two institutional archives noted above. This collection has only recently come to light through my archival research on the Wilmots, and therefore has not been discussed at length in relation to the other Wilmot materials. Its recovery enables me to answer questions raised by absences

---

[20] Elizabeth Lecky was a writer, suffragist and historian who also engaged in historical biography, publishing the posthumous works of her husband, the historian and theorist William Edward Hartpole Lecky. See Elisabeth Lecky and William Edward Hartpole Lecky, *A Memoir of the Right Hon. William Edward Hartpole Lecky, by his Wife* (London, 1909).

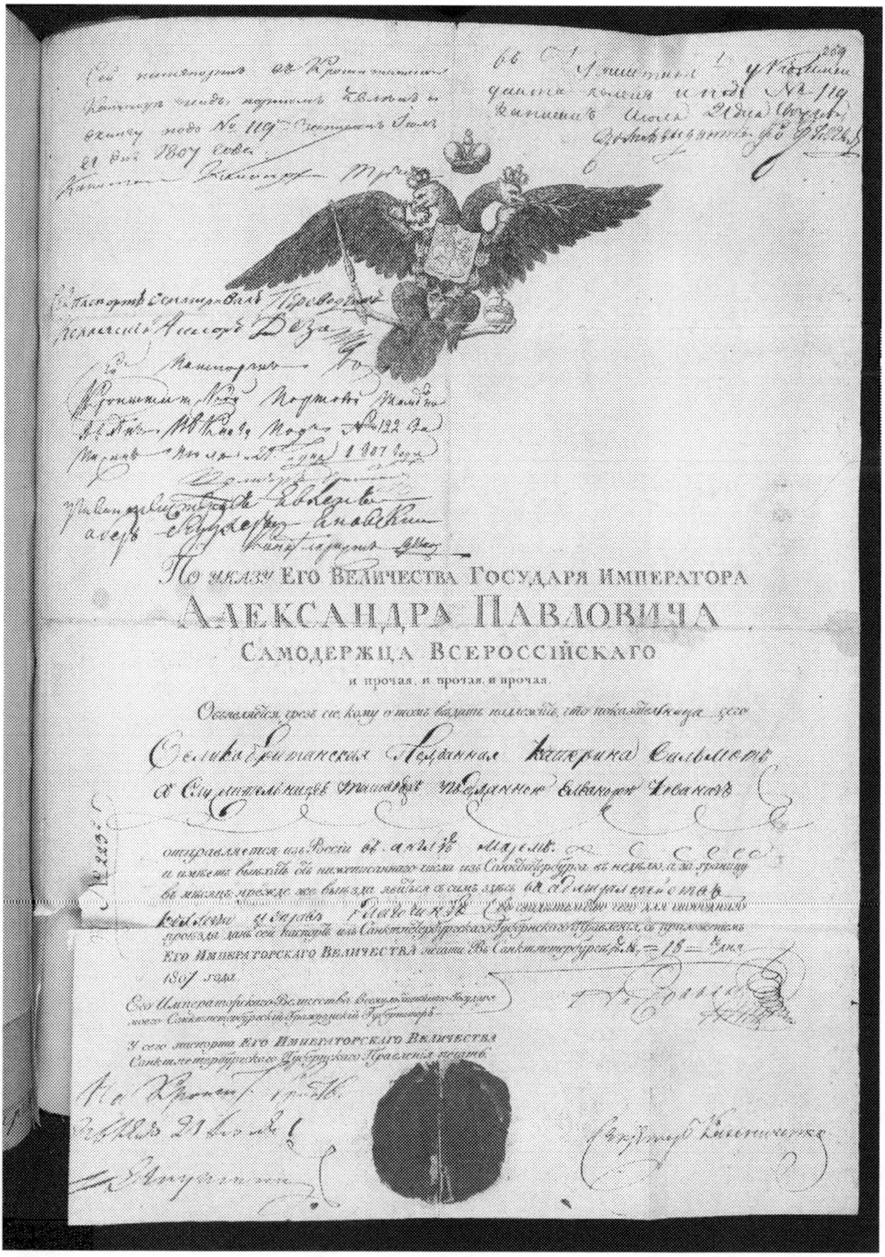
По указу Его Величества Государя Императора
Александра Павловича
Самодержца Всероссійскаго
и прочая, и прочая, и прочая

Figure 3 British Library Add MS 31911, f.259r; Russian Passport © The British Library Board.

in other archives; for instance, by definitively determining the provenance of the translation of *Memoirs*. The collection allows certain manuscripts to be reassessed due to the revelation of variant, earlier copies, including Katherine Wilmot's 1801–03 Peace of Amiens travelogue.[21] The Blair Adam archive also reveals entirely new facets of the Wilmots' textual histories, such as Martha's 1798 journal of the Irish Rebellion. The collection, which has been housed at least in part at Blair Adam since the first half of the twentieth century, was expanded through the enthusiastic efforts of the late Evelyn Marindin (née Wilmot-Chetwode) (1876–1954), an indirect descendant of the Wilmot sisters. The manuscripts in this collection may have been shielded from public view due to their draft-like and incomplete state. They are illuminating in that they seemingly represent what was deemed unworthy of inclusion in the other more formalised collections, and therefore may not have been considered able to secure a textual legacy for the Wilmots. In other places, these materials may have been deemed too personal or revealing to be included in public collections; for instance, Katherine's writing on her own depressive state during her stay in Paris, or Martha's revelation of the true identity of the translator of *Memoirs* in a private scrapbook volume containing supplemental material for the publication.[22] The materials in the Blair Adam House Collection give a distinctly different view of the Wilmots' lives and travels and the choices made by women writers in either presenting or obscuring their own literary efforts.

Circulating Between Spheres

Debate surrounding separate social spheres necessarily looms large over a book concerned with women's international travels, practices of textual production and circulation, and engagement with sociable networks in the late eighteenth century. Jürgen Habermas's exclusion of women from an active realm of public engagement through both the production of literature and political action in *The Structural Transformation of the Public Sphere* sparked a wave of feminist criticism.[23] The subsequent application of the theory of separate spheres to eighteenth-century women in Leonore Davidoff and Catherine Hall's *Family Fortunes* also ignited a heated debate

---

[21] See Chapter 1 for an extended discussion of variant versions of the travelogue, located in both the RIA and BAHC.
[22] See Chapters 1 and 4.
[23] Jürgen Habermas, *The Structural Transformation of the Public Sphere*, trans. by Thomas Burger (1989) (Cambridge, 1996); first edition 1962.

regarding women's historical place.[24] Scholarship in the ensuing decades has questioned the arbitrary separation of spheres by proving women's involvement in a wide variety of both public and sociable forums, and placing them at the centre of cultural exchange.[25] The work of many scholars on this topic has been invaluable to my study in their questioning of arbitrary boundaries of sociability between the sexes in the period. Karen O'Brien, for instance, insists that the 'sense of boundary between the domestic and the social realms was generally fluid and informal' for eighteenth-century writers, with women finding a forum of engagement in 'both informal and institutionalised settings'.[26] Amanda Vickery looks to 'women's own writing' as a means of rejecting the public/private binary, for these primary literary sites to recover 'women's own concerns'.[27] Clare Brant's application of the public/private debate to eighteenth-century epistolary correspondence leads her to endorse a 'third site', a 'personal' sphere that 'recognises the significance of letters to individuals and to relationships', given that letters and other life writing were 'composed in company, voluntarily circulated beyond the addressee and frequently found their way into print'.[28] This book contributes to and extends the debate by demonstrating the concrete ways in which women literally crossed the borders and boundaries of separate spheres to exist in a third site, whether 'personal', or perhaps, more accurately, the 'sociable'; for instance, by positing Katherine's participation in the Parisian salon of Helen Maria Williams and subsequent creation of a manuscript travelogue for circulation. Describing this as a 'sociable' sphere allows for a more nuanced understanding of how women's writing

---

[24] Leonore Davidoff and Catherine Hall, *Family Fortunes: Men and Women of the English Middle Class 1780–1850* (London, 1992).

[25] For a sampling of texts arguing against rigid separate spheres that have informed this study, see *Feminists Read Habermas: Gendering the Subject of Discourse*, ed. by Johanna Meehan (New York, 1993); Lawrence E. Klein, 'Gender and the Public/Private Distinction in the Eighteenth Century: Some Questions About Evidence and Analytic Procedure', *Eighteenth-Century Studies*, 29 (1995), 95–109; *Women, Writing and the Public Sphere, 1700–1830*, ed. by Elizabeth Eger, Charlotte Grant, Clíona Ó Gallchoir and Penny Warburton (Cambridge, 2001); *Women, Gender and Enlightenment*, ed. by Sarah Knott and Barbara Taylor (Basingstoke, 2005); Harriet Guest, *Small Change: Women, learning, patriotism, 1750–1810* (Chicago, 2000); Eve Tavor Bannet, *The Domestic Revolution: Enlightenment Feminism and the Novel* (Baltimore, 2000).

[26] Karen O'Brien, *Women and Enlightenment in Eighteenth-Century Britain* (Cambridge, 2009), pp. 11, 10.

[27] Amanda Vickery, *The Gentleman's Daughter: Women's Lives in Georgian England* (New Haven, 1998), p. 10.

[28] Clare Brant, *Eighteenth-Century Letters and British Culture* (Basingstoke, 2006), p. 5.

circulated in a forum of discourse that was neither public nor private, but rather intentionally invested in the realms in between. By occupying the space of the drawing room and the salon in performance and communal reading, as well as through postal transmission to recipients both at home and abroad in fair copy form – all of which the Wilmots did in Ireland, England, France and Russia – the 'sociable' sphere enabled literary women of the late eighteenth century to circulate their texts – whether letters, travelogues, ethnographic observations or historical biographies– with a wider audience beyond the intended reader.

Following the Wilmot sisters' literary activities from Ireland to France to Russia reveals how transnational forms of sociability took place through manuscript culture in the late eighteenth century. Significant scholarship has transformed how manuscript culture is interpreted in the context of late eighteenth-century literature and culture, with particular resonance for the interpretation of women's writing. Taking theoretical cues from ground-breaking studies of scribal practices in early centuries, such as Harold Love's *Scribal Publication in Seventeenth-Century England* and Margaret Ezell's *Social Authorship and the Advent of Print*, recent studies have shown the centrality and continued importance of manuscript authorship and circulation in the late eighteenth century, concurrent to the emergence of mass print cultures throughout the century.[29] Michelle Levy's important work has expanded understandings of manuscript culture in the late eighteenth century and into the nineteenth century by arguing that these social and collaborative aspects of manuscript production and exchange had long provided an accessible pathway to discourse for women in particular.[30] Valuable research into manuscript culture in the period by Rachael Scarborough King, Hillary Havens, George L. Justice and Nathan Tinker, among others, has raised questions about the notion of the book itself, and led to a repriortisation of manuscript texts, such as the ones written and circulated by women including the Wilmots, among contemporary readers and writers.[31] A more inclusively framed republic of letters for eighteenth-century women writers offers 'an alternative way of mapping

---

[29] Harold Love, *Scribal Publication in Seventeenth-Century England* (Oxford, 1993); Margaret J. M. Ezell, *Social Authorship and the Advent of Print* (Baltimore, 2003).
[30] Michelle Levy, *Literary Manuscript Culture in Romantic Britain* (Edinburgh, 2021); *Family Authorship and Romantic Print Culture* (Basingstoke, 2008).
[31] Rachael Scarborough King, *After Print: Eighteenth-Century Manuscript Cultures* (Charlottesville, 2020); Hilary Havens, 'Manuscript Studies in the Eighteenth Century', *Literature Compass*, 16:7 (2019); *Women's Writing and the Circulation of Ideas: Manuscript Publication in England, 1550–1800*, ed. by George L. Justice and Nathan Tinker (Cambridge, 2002).

and interpreting the role of epistolary communication and manuscript production', privileging the literary practices of women authors, rather than bowing to a dominating focus on the rising technologies of print media.[32] Manuscript culture, I argue throughout this book, enabled women writers to produce, mediate and exchange new forms of writing across exciting and ever-expanding geographical, social and gendered contexts in the period.

Tracing the circulation of manuscript texts in this way leads to a new understanding of how women travellers and writers engaged with new formations of knowledge in the late eighteenth century. National institutions were founded in the late eighteenth century as a means of categorising antiquities both at home and abroad. In this book I consider the capability of women travellers to mediate antiquarian practices through their collecting practices, despite their gendered exclusion from institutional bodies of knowledge, as seen through the Wilmots observing, collecting, transcribing and circulating of Russian peasant folk songs and traditions. As Rosemary Sweet notes, 'eighteenth-century antiquaries regarded themselves as part of a Republic of Letters', an assertion that is embodied in the way that the Wilmots' collection and mediation practices in Russia reflect Enlightenment dialogues.[33] Noah Heringman tracks 'the late Enlightenment proliferation of "antiquities"' in the form of 'specimens of the ancient past' as the formative source for the nineteenth-century emergence of specialised modern prehistoric, classical, medieval and geological disciplines.[34] Antiquarian practices in the period focused on the study of textual relics and living folk tradition as a means for recovering and consecrating national identities. Yet the Wilmots' own mediation of antiquities and folk customs during their time in Russia, examined in what follows, is also dependent on their position as cosmopolitan travellers abroad. Their activities seem to exemplify Immanuel Kant's ideas of an emergent late eighteenth-century 'community among the peoples of earth', the 'cosmopolitan right' 'of a stranger not to be treated in a hostile manner by another upon his arrival on the other's territory'.[35] In applying the term cosmopolitanism to the

---

[32] Melanie Bigold, *Women of Letters, Manuscript Circulation, and Print Afterlives in the Eighteenth Century: Elizabeth Rowe, Catherine Cockburn, and Elizabeth Carter* (Basingstoke, 2013), pp. 16–17.

[33] Rosemary Sweet, 'Antiquaries and Antiquities in Eighteenth-Century England', *Eighteenth-Century Studies*, 34:2 (2001), 181–206, p. 192.

[34] Noah Heringman, *Sciences of Antiquity: Romantic Antiquarianism, Natural History, and Knowledge Work* (Oxford, 2013), p. 3.

[35] Immanuel Kant, *Towards Perpetual Peace, and Other Writings on Politics, Peace, and History* ed. by Pauline Kleingold, trans. by David L. Colclasure (New Haven, 2006), pp. 84, 85, 82.

Wilmot sisters' travels and writing, this book aligns itself with Cyrus R. K. Patell's understanding of cosmopolitanism as 'a perspective that regards human difference as an opportunity to be embraced rather than a problem to be solved', and that frequently does so through literary encounter and the observation of difference.[36]

Antiquarian and early ethnographic collecting practices, along with the act of travel writing itself – by both the Wilmots and other women travellers – show how the concerns of Empire are inextricably bound up with the concerns of travellers in the late eighteenth century. Even on the well-charted European Grand Tour, as Sutapa Dutta writes, travel presented vital opportunities for 'self-fashioning, with a conscious balance between observing and recording useful information for the individual and the state'.[37] When further afield, women travelled abroad not only as tourists or diplomats, but as political observers with a stake in imperial concerns, whether through travel writing that weaves in commentary furthering the goals of the British Empire abroad, or as critics observing foreign cultures and conflicts as a means of mediating change at home.[38] As long-term guests and protégées of Dashkova, a feudal landowner and member of the Russian court, the Wilmots were also uniquely positioned in terms of complex imperial and colonial relations; I argue that it is important to read their surviving writings in this context. Similar focus on arbitrating national identities and international relations arise in the supplements to Dashkova's *Memoirs*, which feature the Wilmots' travel writing. As such, all journeys taken by British women travellers – even those with a hybrid Irish-British sense of identity, such as the Wilmot sisters – 'can be seen to be ideologically inscribed' by seeking to solidify experience as a historical record.[39]

History as a genre and field of enquiry is increasingly studied as a fertile ground for women's literary and knowledge pursuits in the late eighteenth and early nineteenth centuries, including the emergence of women-authored historical texts and group biographies. Rosemary Ann Mitchell's influential recovery of a strong cohort of women actively publishing historical texts

---

[36] Cyril R. K. Patell, *Cosmopolitanism and the Literary Imagination* (Basingstoke, 2015), p. 4.

[37] Sutapa Dutta, 'Introduction', in *British Women Travellers: Empire and Beyond, 1770–1870*, edited by Sutapa Dutta (New York and Abingdon, 2020), pp. 1–18, pp. 2, 5.

[38] Travel abroad granted women writers a clear sense of authority, as explored in brilliant detail in Carl Thompson's special issue on 'Journeys to Authority'. See Carl Thompson, 'Journeys to Authority: Reassessing Women's Early Travel Writing, 1763–1862', *Women's Writing*, 24:2 (2017), 131–150.

[39] Dutta, p. 5.

in the early to mid-nineteenth century instigated a reappraisal of assumptions about women historians in the period, with their writing focusing on genres outside the mainstream such as biography, court history, editing and translation.[40] Yet Devoney Looser has pushed against reading the nineteenth century as the boundary for women publishing historical writing by seeking out the actual historiographical practices engaged in by women in the long eighteenth century as well, not only as readers but also as writers, and by observing women historians' ability to subvert the typical constraints of genres capable of historicity in order to place their historical writing in print, such as through the use of travel writing or sacred biography.[41] Pushing back against the second-wave feminist recovery project of 'herstory' by reinserting women writers as creators of *history* in their own contemporary contexts, the work of Mitchell and Looser, along with that of other scholars in the past two decades, Rohan Amanda Maitzen and Mary Spongberg among them, has renegotiated and redefined the methods of subversion adopted by generations of women historians writing around the edges of typical historical boundaries through the use of fiction, travel writing and other marginal genres.[42] Such associations were particularly strong in Ireland through the popular publications of late eighteenth century women novelists such as Maria Edgeworth and Sydney Owenson.[43] This book contributes to this emerging field of study by linking manuscript circulation of historical texts as intrinsic to the entrance of women into print marketplaces in the late eighteenth century. This can be seen clearly in the sisters' publication of Dashkova's *Memoirs*, an act that was only possible due to their long-term manuscript practices in Russia, Ireland and England. These activities were also contingent on diffuse networks of readers, and, often, respondents, who fed back on historical work-in-progress in manuscript form prior to publication in print.

Such literary practices are intrinsically linked with the sociable circulation enabled by late eighteenth century coteries, a form of open-ended yet

---

[40] Rosemary Ann Mitchell, '"The Busy Daughters of Clio": Women Writers of History from 1820 to 1880', *Women's History Review*, 7:1 (1998), 107–134.

[41] Devoney Looser, *British Women Writers and the Writing of History, 1670–1820* (Baltimore, 2000).

[42] See Looser, pp. 1–2; Rohan Amanda Maitzen, *Gender, Genre and Victorian Historical Writing* (New York, 1998); Mary Spongberg, *Writing Women's History Since the Renaissance* (Basingstoke, 2002); Mary Spongberg, *Women Writers and the Nation's Past 1790–1860* (London, 2018).

[43] See Claire Connolly, 'A Bookish History of Irish Romanticism', *Rethinking British Romantic History, 1770–1845*, ed. by Porscha Fermanis and John Regan (Oxford, 2014), pp. 271–296.

limited society founded on friendships and shared literary interests. The Wilmot sisters' international lives and writing practices are closely linked to the intimate relationships they shared with other, often more prominent, women, for whom they served as informal companions. The coterie as a concept has undergone substantial recuperation in recent decades as an eighteenth-century locus for cultural exchange, particularly for women authors. From new readings of the Bluestockings to the Shelley circle, the coterie is increasingly situated at the core of literary production in the period.[44] Julia M. Wright likens the coterie to the literary salon, in that it 'functions for a time in the interstices between public and private spheres through a fortuitous confluence of writers and concerns'; the coterie can similarly 'be maintained across decades and function as ... private and intimate', especially when contained within the boundaries of the family.[45] Gary Kelly subtly highlights the coterie's interstitial negotiation between public and private, this convergence of acquaintance, correspondence, and social/cultural/political interests evoking the idea of a third 'personal' sphere.[46] Betty Schellenberg describes a literary coterie as 'a relatively cohesive social group whose membership may undergo shifts over time, but that is held together as a continuous identifiable whole by some combination of kinship, friendship, clientage', focusing particularly on 'at least occasional geographical proximity'.[47] The Wilmot sisters' international travels away from the provincial family home seem to defy this proximity, instead functioning as a virtual coterie bound together by writing that is sent home. At the same time, their intimate relationship with Dashkova indicates irregularity across boundaries of class and nationality, rather than the formation of a 'cohesive social group' – disparities that somewhat echo Freya Gowrley's readings of the queer, intergenerational coterie situated around Horace Walpole's Strawberry Hill.[48] Yet shared identification between the participants in the geographically scattered community, the deep kinship and mentorship established between the Wilmots and Dashkova, and the group's shared

---

[44] Elizabeth Eger, *Bluestockings: Women of Reason from Enlightenment to Romanticism* (Basingstoke, 2010); Jon Mee, 'Coteries in the Romantic Period', *European Romantic Review*, 27:4 (2016), 515–521.

[45] Julia M. Wright, '"All the Fire-Side Circle": Irish Women Writers and the Sheridan Lefanu Coterie', *Keats-Shelley Journal*, 55 (2004), 63–72, p. 65.

[46] Gary Kelly, 'Politicizing the Personal: Mary Wollstonecraft, Mary Shelley, and the Coterie Novel', in *Mary Shelley in Her Times*, ed. by Betty T. Bennett and Stuart Curran (Baltimore, 2000), p. 148.

[47] Betty A. Schellenberg, *Literary Coteries and the Making of Modern Print Culture* (Cambridge, 2016), p. 9.

[48] Freya Gowrley, *Domestic Space in Britain, 1750–1840: Materiality, Sociability and Emotion* (London, 2022). See Chapter 5, pp. 177–222.

desire to create a lasting legacy all prove more prevailing than that which separates them. Friendships formed between the Wilmots and the women with whom they lived, travelled and created texts while abroad are consistently returned to in this book, as these alliances played an important role in enabling collective writing in manuscript and increasing both individual and shared agency through later publication. Similarly, the exchange of countless texts-in-progress between the sisters and their women relatives generated a body of familial literature that was intended to extend beyond the orbit of their private domestic enjoyment, and that underpins most of their surviving archives. This book places Martha and Katherine at the core of an informal literary circle, despite their involvement with more well-known, upper-class and aristocratic women, including Dashkova, Williams and Lady Mount Cashell.[49] By identifying the Wilmot sisters as the central figures within their own coterie or network, it is possible to get a new view of women writers, editors and travellers from the upper middling class.

Non-Canonical Voices

The canon of late eighteenth-century women's writing has expanded exponentially over the past five decades, with women's literature of the period reaching a near equal footing in university curricula. Yet much work remains in terms of recovering the voices of women writers active beyond mainstream categories that are valued in today's literary disciplines. 'Women writers of eighteenth-century Britain were not novelists, poets, or dramatists', notes Clare Brant. 'They were writers of letters, diaries, memoirs, essays – genres of sometimes uncertain status then and certainly liminal status now.'[50] Recent studies of women's non-canonical writings have pushed attention beyond conventional modes of authorial production in the late eighteenth and early nineteenth centuries. Scholars including Amy Prendergast and Susanne Schmid have compellingly placed informal coteries of literary sociability at the foreground, highlighting how women-led salons brought about new forms of transnational and collaborative cultural exchange across Ireland, England and Europe.[51] Joanna Wharton's *Material Enlightenments* similarly explores how family ties and networks

---

[49] For more on the wider and specifically Irish networks of which the Wilmot sisters were a part, see Byrne, 'Life after Emmet's death'.
[50] Clare Brant, 'Varieties of Women's Writing', in *Women and Literature in Britain: 1700–1800*, ed. by Vivien Jones (Cambridge, 2000), pp. 285–305, p. 285.
[51] Amy Prendergast, *Literary Salons*: Susanne Schmid, *British Literary Salons of the Late Eighteenth and Early Nineteenth Centuries* (New York, 2013).

of women writers and literary correspondence reshaped social politics and contributed to a new philosophy of the mind in the late eighteenth and early nineteenth century.[52] In *The Lady's Magazine*, Jennie Batchelor examines the influence of women's participation in the periodical press on eighteenth-century and Romantic culture, showing that supposedly lower forms of authorship in fact provided fertile ground for literary engagement among women.[53] Others such as Amy Culley, Daniel Cook and Susan Civale have pointed more directly to life writing as a means of the vitality of collaboration and circulation in the period, highlighting late eighteenth and early nineteenth-century women's writing as central to literary sociability at home and abroad in the period.[54]

Attention to the Wilmots' literary achievements has been surprisingly minimal, most likely due to the fact that their work largely occupies the 'liminal' spaces described by Brant. Yet the wide-ranging scope of their writing across both manuscript and print cultures, not to mention their extraordinary travels as the companions to illustrious figures and at important historical moments, clearly invites further study. The sisters' writing was initially collected in several twentieth-century publications geared towards a general readership. In 1924, Katherine Wilmot's epistolary travelogue based on her Continental travels during the Peace of Amiens was edited from one of several remaining scribal manuscript copies by Thomas Sadleir.[55] An Irish Heraldic scholar, Sadleir apparently took an interest in the narrative due to its indirect connection to Lord Mount Cashell, and inappropriately titled the publication *An Irish Peer on the Continent, 1801–1803, Being a Narrative of the Tour of Stephen, 2nd Earl of Mount Cashell, as Related by Catherine Wilmot*. While Katherine did travel as a member of Lord Cashell's family party as a companion to his wife, the narrative rarely mentions the Earl. Two subsequent publications afforded the Wilmots more authorial presence: *The Russian Journals of Martha and Catherine Wilmot, 1803–1808* (1934) and *More Letters from Martha Wilmot:*

[52] Joanna Wharton, *Material Enlightenment: Women Writers and the Science of the Mind, 1770–1830* (Woodbridge, 2018).

[53] Jennie Batchelor, *The Lady's Magazine (1770–1832) and the Making of Literary History* (Edinburgh, 2022).

[54] See Amy Culley, *British Women's Life Writing, 1760–1840: Friendship, Community and Collaboration* (Basingstoke, 2014); Susan Civale, *Romantic Women's Life Writing: Reputation and Afterlife* (Manchester, 2019); and *Women's Life Writing, 1700–1850: Gender, Genre, Authorship*, ed. by Amy Culley and Daniel Cook (Basingstoke, 2012).

[55] Catherine Wilmot and Thomas U. Sadleir, *An Irish Peer on the Continent, 1801–1803, Being a Narrative of the Tour of Stephen, 2nd Earl of Mount Cashell, as Related by Catherine Wilmot* (London, 1924); printed from a private collection manuscript copy not examined in this book, a near-duplicate of RIA 12 L 32.

Impressions of Vienna (1935).⁵⁶ The editors of these two publications, Lady Londonderry and H. Montgomery Hyde, were the first to examine and describe the papers in the Royal Irish Academy. Their generous biographical introductions to these volumes gave the Wilmots their first printed recognition as travellers since Martha's own editorial work on *Memoirs* nearly a century earlier. However, comparison of these volumes with the extant archives reveals editorial practices that frequently abridged archival sources, leaving out fascinating aspects of the Wilmots' experiences abroad. Elizabeth Mavor's *The Grand Tours of Katherine Wilmot* (1992) reproduced fragments from Katherine's Peace of Amiens Grand Tour as well as her journey to Russia as a trade book, redacting some of her more nuanced cultural observations and personal reflections.⁵⁷ Additionally, their work has been cited extensively as reference material on the women with whom they travelled and shared affective bonds: Katherine's Peace of Amiens travelogue letters were drawn on repeatedly in Edward McAleer's *The Sensitive Plant* (1958), a biography of Lady Mount Cashell.⁵⁸ Martha and Katherine's Russian letters and journals enhance scholarly and biographical representations of Dashkova's character as well as the final years of her life in A. Woronzoff-Dashkoff's *Dashkova: A Life of Influence and Exile* (2008), as well as in the introductions to twentieth-century retranslations of *Memoirs* by Kyril Fitzlyon and Jehanne M. Gheith (1958; 1995).⁵⁹

Scholarship dedicated to the Wilmots' work more specifically was sparse until quite recently.⁶⁰ The past decade, however, has seen a well-deserved and substantial increase of interest in the sisters in the context of both travel writing and women's literary history. Historian Angela Byrne has

---

⁵⁶ Martha Wilmot and Catherine Wilmot, *The Russian Journals of Martha and Catherine Wilmot*; Martha Wilmot, *More Letters from Martha Wilmot: Impressions of Vienna 1819–1829*, ed. by Edith Marchioness of Londonderry and H. Montgomery Hyde (London, 1935). Note, this second volume covers Martha's writing from the period that she lived in Vienna with her husband, who held the post of Chaplain to the British Ambassador there for more than a decade.

⁵⁷ Elizabeth Mavor, *The Grand Tours of Katherine Wilmot, France 1801–3 and Russia 1805–7* (London, 1992).

⁵⁸ Edward McAleer, *The Sensitive Plant: A Life of Lady Mount Cashell* (Chapel Hill, 1958).

⁵⁹ Ekaterina Romanovna Dashkova, *The Memoirs of Princess Dashkova [with plates, including portraits]*, trans. and ed. by Kyril Fitzlyon (London, 1958); Jehanne M Gheith, 'Introduction', in *The Memoirs of Princess Dashkova*, trans. and ed. by Kyril Fitzlyon, afterword by A. Woronzoff-Dashkoff (Durham NC, 1995).

⁶⁰ An article on eighteenth-century British interest in Russian traditional music by A. G. Cross featured a brief study of the Wilmots' Russian music collection practices, as read through their extant letters and journals; see A. G. Cross, 'Early British Acquaintance with Russian Popular Song and Music (The Letters and Journals of the Wilmot Sisters)', *The Slavonic and East European Review*, 66:1 (1988), 21–34, p. 22.

made significant contributions to the study of their time in Russia. Byrne's 2008 thesis on the Irish in Russia in the long eighteenth century devotes a chapter to the sisters' efforts at self-fashioning while residents of that country.[61] Two subsequent book chapters by Byrne helpfully survey the Royal Irish Academy's Dashkova-Wilmot Collection, and negotiate the ways in which the papers held by the Royal Irish Academy provide additional biographical material on Dashkova's later life.[62] Pamela Buck has addressed the role of both collecting and gift exchange as markers of cross-national affinity building in the Wilmots' travels, with a particular focus on Katherine's interest in souvenir representations of Napoleon.[63] Emma Gleadhill's interesting recent monograph similarly takes up study of the Wilmots' travels through the lens of material culture, with one chapter focusing on Katherine's interest in Napoleonic keepsakes, and another on the connection between Dashkova's gifts to Martha and international relations in the period.[64] Katherine's Parisian letters have also been used as broad descriptors of the salon of Helen Maria Williams and the atmosphere of Anglophone sociability in Napoleonic Paris by scholars including Deborah Kennedy and Gary Kelly.[65] Additionally, the Wilmots' experiences have begun to be used more broadly as representative of women travellers in Russia.[66]

[61] Angela Byrne, 'The Irish in Russia, 1690–1815: Travel, Gender and Self-fashioning' (unpublished doctoral book, National University of Ireland, Maynooth, 2008); Byrne's book based on her thesis is forthcoming at the time of writing.

[62] Angela Byrne, 'Princess Dashkova and the Wilmot Sisters', in *Treasures of the Royal Irish Academy Library*, ed. by Bernadette Cunningham and Siobhán Fitzpatrick (Dublin, 2009), pp. 248–255; Angela Byrne, 'Supplementing the Autobiography of Princess Ekaterina Romanovna Dashkova: the Russian Diaries of Martha and Katherine Wilmot', *Irish Slavonic Studies*, 23 (2011), 25–34.

[63] Pamela Buck, 'From Russia with Love: Souvenirs and Political Alliance in Martha Wilmot's The Russian Journals', in *Eighteenth-Century Thing Theory in a Global Context: From Consumerism to Celebrity Culture*, ed. Ileana Baird and Christina Ionescu (Farnham, 2013); Pamela Buck, 'Collecting an Empire: The Napoleonic Louvre and the Cabinet of Curiosities in Catherine Wilmot's Irish Peer on the Continent', *Prose Studies*, 33:3 (2011), 188–199. These noteworthy and important articles primarily rely on the printed twentieth-century editions of the Wilmots' writing noted above. Buck's forthcoming book will also include a chapter on the Wilmots in relation to women's use of 'souvenir collecting to circulate revolutionary ideas and engage in masculine realm of political debate'. See *Objects of Liberty: British Women Writers and Revolutionary Souvenirs* (Newark, 2024).

[64] Gleadhill, *Taking Travel Home*; like Buck, Gleadhill relies on the heavily edited editions of the Wilmots' life writing as source material.

[65] Deborah Kennedy, *Helen Maria Williams and the Age of Revolution* (Lewisburg, 2002); Gary Kelly, *Women, Writing and Revolution, 1790–1827* (Oxford, 1994).

[66] Katrina O'Loughlin, *Women, Writing and Travel in the Eighteenth Century* (Cambridge, 2018), p. 9.

Transnational Women Writers in the Wilmot Coterie, 1798–1840: Beyond Borders and Boundaries contributes to on-going feminist-literary efforts to reveal how non-canonical women's writing was in fact central to the transnational circulation of ideas in the late eighteenth and early nineteenth centuries. The book is arranged as five thematic chapters, which also trace chronologically the sisters' travels and networks while examining their main literary interests and outputs associated with each time period.

Chapter 1 begins by exploring how expatriate salons and publishing communities in Napoleonic Paris enabled women writers to compose, circulate and publish first-hand commentary on French Revolutionary politics. I discuss a previously unknown archive of eighteenth-century Irish women's life writing, which includes a new manuscript version of Katherine's narrative of her journey to France written during the Peace of Amiens (1801–03). The manuscript reveals the surprising representational strategies of upper and little-known middle-class women writers negotiating national affinities against a backdrop of cross-channel political upheaval, as they were compelled to respond to controversial revolutionary ideologies. This chapter considers closely the writing style of women's diaries and life-writing documents, as well as variant versions of manuscripts written for both private use or wider circulation. Throughout, I highlight the risks facing women travel writers in the period, such as issues surrounding the stigma of print for women authors, as well as the threat of sedition due to the historical-political constraints of British sentiment during the Peace of Amiens.

Chapter 2 turns to look at the systems of social manuscript authorship that enabled the exchange of women's writing between provincial and transnational constellations within the Wilmots' coterie and wider circle. It does so through a dual focus on writing and reading practices in Ireland and Russia, beginning with the Wilmots sisters' work as scribes, translators, and editors while resident in Russia (1803–08) as guests of Russian noblewoman and Enlightenment thinker, Princess Ekaterina Dashkova. The sisters worked for a period of two years to assist Dashkova in composing her personal and political memoirs and copied an abundance of state and scientific documents in her private collection with a view towards editing her life story posthumously. In Russia, the Wilmots also wrote large volumes of manuscript travel writing in the form of letters, which they sent back home to Ireland to be preserved, shared and enjoyed by their family's wide sociable circle. I examine the collaborative practices of writing, transcription, translation, illustration and language acquisition engaged in by the Wilmot women, whether they travelled abroad or remained at home in Ireland. The emotional dimension of literary and material sociability is examined, exploring how communities of women writers collaborated to create, sustain and communicate a shared sense of legacy through the use of commonplace books, epistolary travelogues, journal writing and bodies of correspondence. Throughout, I explore how travel was a shared act for families and literary circles in the eighteenth-century, allowing for vicarious learning and literary sociability through transcription and preservation.

Eighteenth-century women travellers made significant contributions to antiquarianism and early forms of ethnography, despite their exclusion from formal institutions. Chapter 3 analyses a cache of antiquarian and ethnographic records created by the Wilmot sisters during their time in Russia, which are linked with national and cosmopolitan discourse across eighteenth-century Europe. The diverse manuscripts investigated include Martha's travel writing on the Jews of Poland and Katherine's observation and documentation of peasant rituals in Russia. Efforts to collect and translate Russian folk songs are read in the context of emergent trends towards gathering and classifying national identities through popular song and folk tradition in the eighteenth century. The chapter examines the Wilmots' role as foreign observers carrying out antiquarian and ethnographic pursuits in Russia from a middle-ranking, British-Irish perspective, particularly within a colonial context as guests of Dashkova, a feudal landowner. Women's involvement in and contribution to these emerging knowledge genres is considered, particularly in relation to the formation of the Royal Irish Academy's institutional practices surrounding antiquarianism and ethnography, disciplines from which women were excluded. Women's ethnographic and antiquarian manuscripts are interpreted as travel artefacts that both facilitate coterie practice and further institutionalised forms of Enlightenment knowledge.

Chapter 4 examines the transformation of the Wilmot sisters' long-standing manuscript practices into print through the 1840 publication of *Memoirs of Princess Daschkaw*. The publication is examined in several contexts, including the Wilmot sisters' efforts to translate Dashkova's manuscripts; editorial attempts to posthumously correct Dashkova's maligned public persona; and the collective imprinting of the coterie, which links the Wilmot sisters' textual work and relationships to those of Dashkova and Catherine II. Scholarly discourse on the manipulation of literary fame informs a reading of *Memoirs*' attempts to generate a specific legacy for both Dashkova and the Wilmots, as well as an investigation of women's collaborative translation practices across class divides. *Memoirs* is examined in the context of the rise of women-authored and women-edited female biographies in the early to mid-nineteenth century, with attention paid to how manuscript practices enabled the production of women's collective and royal biographies in eighteenth-century Europe. Changes made to Dashkova's life narrative between manuscript and text are explored in a close reading for the first time, illuminating previously overlooked editorial tactics and manipulations. In this chapter, I definitively identify the translator of Dashkova's published *Memoirs* using previously unseen archival evidence.

Women's travel narratives detailing journeys to nations broadly viewed as barbaric, uncivilised or unknown by British readers were uncommon but not unheard of in the late eighteenth century. Chapter 5 considers how such publications contributed to British interests abroad, particularly in the context of the British Empire's political conflicts, by discussing the Wilmot sisters' travel writing that was published within Dashkova's *Memoirs* in 1840. These lengthy narratives, which were printed in the back of the second volume of the text, inscribe the sisters' enduring legacy as authors and travellers by documenting their own experiences in Russia (1803–08). Through the mediation of manuscript and print, the Wilmots' travelogues enable them to embark on a new journey as participants in the republic of letters. Martha Wilmot's account of a shipwreck amidst the Anglo-Russian War forms one major case study within the chapter. Martha's representation of Russian allies as foreign and hostile stands in opposition to her sympathetic depiction of British allies, thereby positioning her travel supplement as supportive of the British Empire. The composition, content and genre of the Wilmots' narratives are read in the context of contemporary late eighteenth-century women's travel writing produced from beyond the bounds of the typical European Grand Tour, particularly by comparing Maria Graham's strategies for framing her Indian and South American narratives (1812, 1824). Throughout the chapter, I show how manuscript production, authorial self-representation and editorial intervention allowed women travellers to negotiate transnational sympathies and imperial prerogatives in the late eighteenth-century British imagination.

Finally, the conclusion argues that the Wilmot sisters' immense multilingual corpus – which remains in large part unpublished – is emblematic of widespread literary and cultural practices practised by women of their day. I argue that women's shared literary, material and non-textual practices of sociability in the late eighteenth century were facilitated by travel abroad and in turn contributed to transnational cultural formations. Study of the Wilmots' lives and letters illuminates how the coterie practices of middle-ranking women writers in the period allowed them to exert unprecedented agency over their own individual and collective authorial legacies, and influence over representations of nationhood.

The subtitle of this book, 'Beyond Borders and Boundaries', refers not only to the movement of both women travellers and manuscripts across national borders; but also to the intimacy, friendship and literary labour shared between women across class, national and familial boundaries; the 'sociable' as disrupting received notions of the 'separate spheres' of public and private; women's collecting practices beyond acknowledged institutions of knowledge; and women writers' subversions of the genre conventions of historical writing through life and travel writing, among other forms of gendered and literary boundary crossings. Drawing on the Wilmots' manuscripts and published work as a central case study, this book makes the claim that coteries of little-known and often provincially located groups of middle-ranking women writers made vital contributions to transnational cultural geographies. Throughout, I investigate how women writers navigated national and cosmopolitan contexts to write for readers in Ireland, England, France and Russia, while also exploring the role played by collective writing in the formation of female public identities.

1

Women's Views of Revolutionary Europe

In 1801, a preliminary accord, later ratified as the Treaty of Amiens, was signed between England and France, effectively ending an eleven-year period of hostilities that had left France cut off to British travellers since before the French Revolution. The tenuous peace brought a surge of tourists eager to reinstate the well-worn trajectory of the Grand Tour by traversing the Continent and visiting its key locations. British aristocrats, diplomats and intellectuals flocked to Paris in the brief years of peace from 1801–03, seeking contact with the cosmopolitan epicentre of the cultural and political sea changes that had taken place over the previous turbulent decade. As Anna Laetitia Barbauld wrote in 1801: 'now France lies like a huge loadstone on the other side of the Channel ... Those who know French are refreshing their memories – those who do not, are learning it; and every one is planning in some way or other to get a sight of the promised land [sic].'[1] James Gillray satirised this sudden disregard for hostility between the two recently warring nations in his caricature, *The First Kiss This Ten Years! – or – the Meeting of Britannia & Citizen François* (1803), which depicts a bedraggled – and titillated – French soldier seducing an overweight Britannia.[2] 'Madame, permittez me [sic], to pay my profound esteem to your engaging person! & to seal on your divine Lips my everlasting attachment!!!', the soldier exclaims, while Britannia replies, 'Monsieur, you are truly a well-bred Gentleman! – & tho' you make me blush, yet, you Kiss so delicately, that I cannot refuse you; tho' I was sure you would

---

[1] Anna Laetitia Barbauld, *Works of Anna Laetitia Barbauld. With a Memoir by Lucy Aikin*. 2 vols (1825), facsimile ed. by Caroline Franklin (London, 1996), vol. II, pp. 119–120.

[2] James Gillray, *The First Kiss This Ten Years! – or – the Meeting of Britannia & Citizen François*, BM Satires 9960, in *The Catalogue of Political and Personal Satires in the British Museum*, ed. by M. Dorothy George and others, 12 vols (London, 1870–1954), vol. 8 (1947); see BM Satires 9960: <https://www.britishmuseum.org/research/collection_online/collection_object_details.aspx?objectId=1478882&partId=1.> [accessed 3 October 2023].

Deceive me again!!!' Britannia has also let down her guard, leaving her trident and shield out of reach while Napoleon and George III preside in portraits above. Gillray's caricature underlines the sense that not all British commentators interpreted the renewed friendship as a prudent one, as well as the fact that censure could be forthcoming to members of British society who wished to align themselves with the French.

Such was the dichotomous backdrop of enthusiasm and caution at the time of Katherine Wilmot's channel crossing. Her visit to Paris during the Peace of Amiens is captured in an epistolary travelogue identified on an informal title page as 'Kitty Wilmot's Journal, 1801–1803' and contained in a medium-sized hardbound notebook with a brilliant crimson cover and gilt edges.[3] The letters within are addressed to her brother Robert, beginning on 24 November 1801 with the promise to 'send ... these sheets of paper for a beginning, and ... every now and then record the events of the day'. Katherine's manuscript travelogue provides an example of women's experiences abroad during the rapidly shifting sociopolitical period, as well as shedding light on the Mount Cashell family and the Parisian republican circle of Helen Maria Williams, through her comical prose, which is critical of the Revolutionary project. Transcription of the 'Journal' by Katherine's sister Martha in Moscow in 1805 expanded its sociable use. Multiple manuscript copies of the travelogue were read aloud for private audiences during home tours taken by Martha and her sisters through England and Ireland in 1809 and 1810.[4] Additional copies were dispersed beyond the family.[5]

---

[3] RIA MS 12 L 32, Letters of Katherine Wilmot from France-Italy, 1801–03 Copied by Martha Bradford (née Wilmot), Moscow, 1805.

[4] The original manuscript of Martha Wilmot's 1809 and 1810 Irish tour journals is not extant. A typewritten copy created in the twentieth century is present in the Blair Adam archive. See BAHC, 'Typewritten copy of a second tour in Ireland by Martha Wilmot and Her sister Alicia', Wilmot Box 1, Bundle 2, 2/8.

[5] In Bath in 1812, for instance, Lady Stanley wrote in a letter, 'I am now reading two manuscript tours, most entertaining and interesting, written by a Miss Wilmot', noting that Martha loaned the copied manuscript after the women had made a casual acquaintance; Maria Josepha Lady Stanley, *The Early Married Life of Maria Josepha Lady Stanley* (New York, 1899), p. 332; Katherine's text drew interest in the twentieth century as well. Thomas Sadleir's 1924 edition was drawn from one of several extant manuscript copies. Sadleir edited the travelogue from a manuscript held at Woodbrook, Queen's County in the 1920s, which he compared against the Royal Irish Academy copy, finding them 'almost equal in date, but differing slightly in certain passages', p. xv. An Irish Heraldic scholar, Sadleir apparently took an interest in the narrative due to its relation to the life of Lord Mount Cashell, and inappropriately titled the publication *An Irish Peer on the Continent, 1801–1803, Being a Narrative of the Tour of Stephen, 2nd Earl of Mount Cashell, as Related by Catherine Wilmot*. While Katherine did travel as a member of Lord Cashell's family party as a companion to his wife, the narrative rarely mentions the Earl. Sadleir's reconstruction of Katherine's

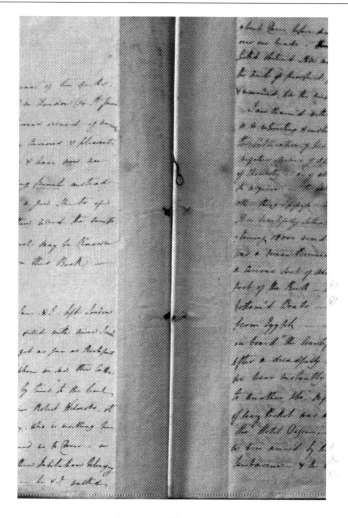

Figure 4 Blair Adam House Collection, Wilmot Box 3, 'Original journals of "Kitty" Wilmot'; binding. © Blair Adam House.

In essence, without ever seeing print during her lifetime, the manuscript copy of Katherine's epistolary 'Journal' documenting the Peace circulated through an extensive network of readers.

---

authorship stems from a gendered and classist early twentieth-century perspective. Yet his edition allowed the travelogue to serve as a reference material on the women with whom Katherine travelled and shared affective bonds, most notably in a biography of Lady Mount Cashell. See Catherine Wilmot and Thomas U. Sadleir, *An Irish Peer on the Continent, 1801–1803, Being a Narrative of the Tour of Stephen, 2nd Earl of Mount Cashell, as Related by Catherine Wilmot* (London, 1924); Edward McAleer, *The Sensitive Plant: A Life of Lady Mount Cashell* (Chapel Hill, 1958).

However, the travelogue is not, in fact, a spontaneously generated narrative, the events of Katherine's tour having been revised and adapted from an earlier fragmental diary. This earlier version provides a distinct contrast to the elegantly transcribed crimson notebook containing her travelogue.[6] The manuscript, labelled 'The Original Journals of "Kitty" Wilmot', is composed of two thick stacks of plain paper, each roughly the size of a quarto and held together with a hand-stitched seam. There is no cover on either volume, and no decorative embellishment. On the front of the first volume, which runs to forty-eight pages, Katherine has written: 'Journal – 1801.1802.1803. Travelling with Lord & Lady Mount Cashel [sic] and their family. London. Paris. Florence. Milan. Rome. Naples. &c. & c.' By way of introduction, she writes:

> I wish I had had the gumption to write a journal of the weeks which I spent with Lord & Lady Mount Cashell in London (54 St James Street) – As so many agreeable circumstances occur'd of various kinds – & we became acquainted with so many curious & pleasant People – However as I omitted doing so there – & have now an opportunity of making myself reparation – by recording *french* [sic] instead of *English* adventures – I have tack'd together a few sheets of Paper for the purpose: – & will Every now & then, record the Events of the day – so that like the snail – wherever I crawl may be known by the trail which I shall leave behind me on this Book [sic].[7]

Despite Katherine's amusing assertion that the initiation of a new writing practice will allow her 'like the snail' to be *known* by her writing, the improvised physicality of Katherine's 'Book' is reflective of its actual 'purpose': crude and informal, the pages contained in the coverless, hand-bound stack are an unadorned location for gathering anecdotes. The imagery of the snail also suggests a contrary sense of the danger of discovery, the privacy of the mollusc's shell into which its entire body can be withdrawn evocative of Katherine's hidden writings. This introduction is instantly recognisable as a draft for the introduction to the later travelogue manuscript:

---

[6] BAHC, Wilmot Box 3, 'Original journals of "Kitty" Wilmot'; RIA MS 12 L 32. For the purpose of clarity, Katherine's early journal draft, or homemade 'Book' will hereafter be referred to as her 'journal', while the later 'worked up' travelogue will be referred to as her 'travelogue'. Subsequent references to Katherine's earlier manuscript will be listed in the text as 'BAHC, 'Original', 'date'.

[7] Ibid, n.d.; Katherine frequently underlined words for emphasis. Underlined text has been italicised for clarity.

> I wish I had had the diligence to write a journal of the ten weeks which I spent in London, with Lord and Lady Mount Cashell/ 54. St James Street/ as so many agreeable circumstances occur'd of various kinds and we became acquainted with such a variety of curious, pleasant and signalized personages: however as I omitted doing so then & have now an opportunity of making reparation by recording French instead of English adventures, I send you these sheets of paper for a beginning, and I will every now and then record the events of the day, so that like a snail where ever I crawl, I may be known by the trail which I shall leave smear'd behind me in this book – [sic].[8]

Katherine's transition from her private journal to the shared format of the manuscript travelogue instigates a refinement in her vocabulary – 'gumption' becomes 'diligence'; 'people' becomes 'personages'. The intended recipient of the text changes as well: in the earlier journal, Katherine describes 'an opportunity to make *myself* reparation by recording' [my emphasis], while in the later travelogue she takes 'an opportunity of making reparation' to 'you' (her brother). Most interestingly, the anticipated format of the text, as well as its long view goals, shift: while Katherine's earlier journal modestly notes that she has 'tack'd together a few sheets of Paper' in order to occasionally record incidents, her later introduction implies a long-term correspondence with a predefined trajectory by promising: 'I send you these sheets of paper for a *beginning*, and I will every now and then record the events of the day' [my emphasis]. The consequences of these changes are significant, implying Katherine's emergent intention to share her text with a reading public.

As we shall see, her two materially and textually variant manuscripts reveal the complex strategies for representing national affinities employed by women writers responding to the shifting politics of Revolutionary Europe. Katherine's crafted narrative documenting her time in Napoleonic Paris can be linked to several sociable and literary influences. The manuscripts shed light on the literary influence of coteries of British intellectual women participating in salon sociability among radical British writers in Napoleonic Paris. A further sociable influence of particular importance to emerge from the earlier draft is a burgeoning friendship with author and salonnière Helen Maria Williams and her companion, the radical printer John Hurford Stone. Williams's salon in Paris had long been a centre for Anglophile and international republican sympathisers by the time of Katherine's arrival in Paris. While Katherine's interactions with Williams and Stone feature prominently in her earlier journal draft,

---

[8] RIA MS 12 L 32, prescript, n.d.

the relationship is considerably muted in the travelogue. An invitation to publish with William and Stone's The English Press, noted in archival marginalia, suggests that Katherine shared Williams and Stone's political sympathies, while also highlighting her preference for manuscript circulation over print.[9] Williams may have seen Katherine as a potential ally given her press struggles under Napoleon's increasingly authoritarian regime during the Peace. Williams's published travel literature influenced Katherine's later travelogue, despite Katherine's choice to distance herself from the cosmopolitan ethics and Revolutionary sympathies that the British public perceive in Williams's work.

The manuscript practices discussed in this chapter challenge how women's networks might be defined and understood in the period, particularly those that included women writers from a middle-ranking and upper-middle class background, such as Katherine, who travelled as an unpaid companion within an aristocratic family party. The eighteenth-century literary coterie has undergone substantial recuperation in recent decades as a vital locus for cultural and literary exchange, especially for women authors. Betty Schellenberg frames the coterie as 'a relatively cohesive social group whose membership may undergo shifts over time, but which is held together as a continuous identifiable whole by some combination of kinship, friendship, clientage', focusing particularly on 'at least occasional geographical proximity'.[10] Katherine's travels away from provincial Ireland seem to defy such proximity, modelling a virtual coterie bound together by writing that is sent back home while simultaneously contributing to the literary culture of Napoleonic Paris. Her manuscripts reveal the powerful influence of relationships formed abroad on the mediation and production of British women's writing, and highlight the gendered, political constraints that impacted on representational choices. In what follows, I explore how sociability underpinned women's writing in the period, considering in particular the essential influences of salon culture and manuscript circulation on transnational communities of women writers.

---

[9] The Press also operated, at times, under the moniker 'Imprimerie de la Rue de Vaugirard', thanks to the Parisian Street on which it was located between 1793–1804. Other names include 'Imprimerie de la rue de l'Echiquier', 1805, and, between 1807–12, 'Imprimerie des Droits réunis'; Madeleine B. Stern, 'The English Press in Paris and Its Successors, 1793–1852', *The Papers of the Bibliographical Society of America*, 74:4 (1980), 307–359, pp. 316–317.

[10] Betty A. Schellenberg, *Literary Coteries and the Making of Modern Print Culture* (Cambridge, 2016), p. 9.

'The events of the day': Public and Private Voices

Katherine's journal entry for her arrival in Paris on 5 December 1801 relishes the revolutionary spectacle available thanks to France's newly reopened borders:

> At about 4 o'clock we drove into Paris – with all our eyes flying out of their sockets at every thing [sic] we beheld. The streets struck me as being very narrow & the Houses, some of them seven stories high – very handsome – & built of stone. – Liberté, Égalité, Fraternité – Citoyen – Republique – &c. &c. – flitted by my eyes, on all the Publick Buildings – sign posts – &c – as we drove along.[11]

She captures several facts deemed worthy of note in this short entry: the heightened excitement of the moment, with all the party's 'eyes flying out of their sockets'; the extremely tall and handsome stone buildings, the architectural likes of which she has never seen; and, most importantly, the Republican propaganda emblazoned on the 'Publick Buildings', pronouncing the expected sentiments of 'Liberté, Égalité, Fraternité – Citoyen – Republique'. Katherine's economical three-sentence description of entering Paris is a reaction to her first encounter with the post-Revolutionary landscape as well as its manifestations in society.[12]

Nearly all of Katherine's journal entries from her days in Paris mirror the spontaneous materiality of the hand-stitched journal in which they are jotted: relatively short, they stow away moments at risk of being forgotten. The journal is composed of incomplete sentences and fragmentary commentary as Katherine rapidly lists the iconic words emblazoned on the sides of Parisian buildings, 'Fraternité – Citoyen – Republique', exclamations separated only by a dash. The entries are also embedded within the conventions of eighteenth-century typographical modes of emotional expression; namely, ruptures in punctuation.[13] Such marks could be a device for implying or expressing the inexpressible, and for suggesting an overflow of feeling or sentimental response, an interventions that can be

---

[11] BAHC, Original, 'Sat 5th Decr [1801]' [sic].
[12] This description is transposed nearly verbatim within the travelogue as part of a longer description of the travelling party's first hours seeking accommodation at l'Hôtel de l'Europe in Paris; RIA MS 12 L 32, p. 16.
[13] Dashes, ellipses, or other symbols indicating occlusions might be used as 'aposiopeses', or, in Janine Barchas's words, 'the intentional refusals to complete an idea, name or phrase so common in eighteenth-century literature': see Janine Barchas, *Graphic Design, Print Culture, and the Eighteenth-Century Novel* (Cambridge, 2003), p. 158.

traced in late eighteenth-century women's life writing. Elizabeth Craven, for instance, uses the dash to express her grief in separating from her child while journeying through Crimea, writing 'I am at this moment above a hundred miles distant from the most affectionate, the most engaging, and the most beautiful child that ever mother had – and for the first time I have ever left him.'[14] Elsewhere in the same narrative, Craven's epistolary correspondence is liberally redacted with dashes to highlight maternal agony and conceal overflows of emotion. By utilising the dash and other punctuated silences, women writers in the eighteenth century were able to take, in no small way, control of their texts.

Many British travellers to Paris, like Katherine, kept a record of their experiences in order to document intricacies of the significant historical moment. Compare the case of novelist Amelia Opie. When Opie visited the city with her husband, the painter John Opie, in August 1802, she kept a detailed journal that later appeared in *The Lady's Magazine* in 1831–32.[15] Opie also wrote of her elation over the opportunity to visit and document the infamous recent locales of revolutionary events on arriving in Paris: 'to me every other consciousness was soon absorbed in the joyful one of being at last in Paris, that city which I had so long desired to see.'[16] While Opie, on seeing revolutionary slogans of *'L'Indivisibilité de la Republique'* scrawled across buildings, reflects wryly that 'all traces of republicanism were so rapidly disappearing, that the word without the second syllable would have described it better; namely "invisibility"', Katherine on the other hand appears to reserve judgement on the Revolutionary project and withholds a specific reaction.[17] Katherine's own early impressions seem to maintain a documentary tone rather than engaging in social or political critique, perhaps due to a lack of experience, or possibly just an as yet unformed opinion on post-Revolutionary France.

The republican fervour filtering throughout Europe in the late eighteenth century had not left the Wilmot family untouched. In March 1798, the family fled Ireland for England amidst the violence surrounding the 1798 Rebellion. A palm-sized notebook, of the sort frequently used by Grand Tour travellers while *en route*, documents the family's flight. Its dark brown leather cover bears a nearly illegible title, 'Matty Wilmot Journal on

---

[14] Elizabeth Craven, *A Journey Through the Crimea to Constantinople* (London, 1789), p. 5.

[15] Amelia Opie, 'Recollections of a Visit to Paris in 1802', *The Lady's Magazine, or Mirror of the Belles-Lettres, Fine Arts, Music, Drama, Fashions, &c*, 5 (1831), 17–19, 87–89.

[16] Amelia Opie, *Memorials of the Life of Amelia Opie* (Norwich, 1854), p. 100.

[17] Ibid, p. 100.

leaving Cork at the Irish Rebellion Time.'[18] Inside, a twelve-page narrative describes the dramatic event. As Martha Wilmot wrote:

> in consequence of the alarm which my Father felt on account of the precarious state of the Kingdom he determin'd that we should quit Ireland; & with only twelve hours warning to break up our comfortable establishment at Cork, & part perhaps forever from the blessing of a home.[19]

The English-born Captain Edward Wilmot, Port Surveyor at Cork, used his naval connections to secure passage for his wife and six daughters to Brampton, where they lived for nearly a year until the violence of the Rebellion had subsided. While it is unclear whether the precaution of evacuation was a necessary step, the sense of danger perceived by the Wilmot family due to the tumult surrounding them was real enough.

When, in 1801, Lord and Lady Mount Cashell extended Katherine an unexpected invitation to join them on the Continent, the offer 'realized a dream she had cherished' to travel abroad.[20] On its surface, this offer from the Mount Cashells represented a remarkable and life-changing opportunity for an unmarried woman from a middle-ranking family to experience the Grand Tour.[21] Looking deeper, a shared political and literary affinity between the two women likely made such an invitation a natural extension of their existing friendship. The experiences of the Mount Cashell family throughout the 1790s exemplify not only the pressures and choices facing the Protestant Ascendancy in Ireland, but also the potential for literary and political engagement open to women witnessing and participating in revolutionary uprisings. Stephen, 2nd Earl Mount Cashell, was 'a patriotic if not democratic nobleman' without political ambitions.[22] A prominent landowning member of the English Ascendancy in Ireland, he had abandoned his seat in the Irish House of Commons in 1799 in favour of country

---

[18] BAHC 'Bradford/Wilmot Box 2, Item 5.d', March 1798. This notebook provides information on another previously unknown aspect of the history of Katherine and Martha Wilmot, and offers an interesting window into amateur women traveller's practices of documenting historically important moments through journal writing.
[19] BAHC, 'Rebellion', n. pag.
[20] RIA MS 12 L 32, n. pag.
[21] Mount Cashell later wrote of her life-long feeling of belonging more to the 'middle rank of life' rather than those of the 'higher sphere' into which she was born, a sentiment she attributed to Wollstonecraft's early influence. See Pforzheimer Collection, New York Public Library, S'Ana 0763, 'Holograph Autobiographical Account', p. 5; For more on the Wilmots family's class status, see Introduction, pp. 8–11.
[22] Janet Todd, *Daughters of Ireland* (New York, 2003), p. 129.

life after suffering property losses due to arson in the Irish Rebellion. Margaret Moore, Lady Mount Cashell, however, harboured different political sentiments from her husband. In childhood, she had been the pupil of Mary Wollstonecraft during her brief period as a governess in Ireland, and later attributed to Wollstonecraft 'the development of whatever virtues I possess'.[23] Despite her conventional aristocratic marriage, Mount Cashel continued to be guided by Wollstonecraft's early radical influence. In the 1790s, she had aligned herself with the revolutionary activities of the Protestant radical group, the United Irishmen. The movement was founded in 1791 in an attempt to unite Protestants and Catholics in Ireland, as well as bringing about Parliamentary reform and Catholic emancipation. Mount Cashell wrote and published anonymous broadside poetry supportive of the United Irish cause.[24] She later covertly participated in the dialogues of the Union Crisis of 1799–1800 by writing anonymous anti-Unionist pamphlets and surrounding herself with 'complaining ladies with a political agenda' of genteel classical republicanism.[25]

The Mount Cashell family's voyage to Napoleonic France took place in the very first days following the Peace, perhaps inspired by Mount Cashell's desire to witness the successful incarnation of and original inspiration for the radical principles that had so recently failed in Ireland. This inclination was undoubtedly spurred further by the French Republic's attempts to assist the United Irishmen through the disastrous French Expedition to Ireland of 1796, when a storm prevented the landing of the French Directory's fleet on Irish shores. The exchange of Republican ideology, as well as of individuals, between Ireland and France is embodied in the first few lines of Katherine's travelogue, which describes the Mount Cashell travelling party racing away from London as 'nine Irish Adventurers', 'driving full speed ... to the French Dominions'.[26] The comment underscores the particularly Irish, and possibly revolutionary, sensibility with which Mount Cashell and Katherine entered Napoleonic Paris, despite the particularly English heritage of each of their families. Given Katherine's apparent

---

[23] Oxford, Bodleian Library, Abinger Collection, MS. Abinger c. 6, fol. 44.
[24] See Alexis Wolf, 'Identity and Anonymity in Lady Mount Cashell's 1798 Rebellion Broadside', *Journal for Eighteenth-Century Studies*, 45 (2022), 259–276.
[25] Janet Todd, 'Ascendancy: Lady Mount Cashell, Lady Moira, Mary Wollstonecraft, and the Union Pamphlets', *Eighteenth-Century Ireland*, 18 (2003), 98–113, p. 105. For more on the Moira House Salon, where Mount Cashell was a regular member, see Amy Prendergast, 'The Drooping Genius of our Isle to Raise: The Moira House Salon and its Role in Gaelic Cultural Revival', *Eighteenth-Century Ireland*, 26 (2011), 95–114.
[26] RIA MS 12 L 32, 'Paris, 25 Nov. 1801'.

knowledge of Mount Cashell's covert writing, it may also imply a sentiment of mobility strongly inspired by the recent events of the Rebellion.

In Napoleonic Paris, Mount Cashell's connections quickly brought Katherine into contact with Anglocentric revolutionarily sympathetic circles, many of which Mount Cashell gained entry to through an ongoing correspondence and friendship with William Godwin, widower of her former governess. Mount Cashell and Katherine visited Godwin several times while in London in the autumn of 1801, visits that Lord Mount Cashell was likely unaware of due to his disapproval of Godwin's political sympathies and the association with his infamous late wife, Wollstonecraft.[27] Different leanings in sociable and political sympathies between the husband and wife are apparent in an incident related in a letter sent by the poet, translator and revolutionary Thomas Holcroft to Godwin in 1802.[28] Having struck up a relationship with the Holcroft family in Paris thanks to a letter of recommendation from Godwin, Mount Cashell initially offered Holcroft's daughter Fanny a position as tutor to the Mount Cashell children.[29] She later rescinded the offer, due, in Holcroft's words, to 'Lord Mount Cashell having been so repeatedly warned against me as a Democrat tried for high treason, domestic peace required her to part with my daughter'.[30] Lord Mount Cashell's protection of his family's reputation did not, however, keep his wife and her companion from making new contacts as a direct result of Godwin's other connections, which likely granted them access to the home of the English author and hostess, Helen Maria Williams.

From the early 1790s, Helen Maria Williams's multi-volume *Letters from France* celebrated the French Revolution for a British readership variably engaged with or appalled by her apparently radical affinities as she declared herself a 'citizen of the world', and her Parisian salon later embodied and advocated for what has been described as a feminised 'radicalized cosmopolitanism'.[31] Williams's early *Letters* do not shy away from embracing transformations of society and politics, documenting her shared joy during

---

[27] Godwin notes seven meetings with Lady Mount Cashell in his diary in autumn 1801, and mentions 'Miss Wilmot' specifically on three of these occasions, but does not name Lord Mount Cashell. See *The Diary of William Godwin*, ed. by Victoria Myers, David O'Shaughnessy and Mark Philp (Oxford, 2010), 'entry for Margaret King', <http://godwindiary.bodleian.ox.ac.uk/people/KIN02.html> [accessed 1 September 2023].

[28] MS. Abinger c. 7, fols. 91–92, 'Thomas Holcroft to William Godwin, 17 Feb. 1802'.

[29] BAHC, 'Original', 'Tuesday 8th Dec'r [1801]'.

[30] MS. Abinger c. 7, fol. 91r.

[31] Helen Maria Williams, *Letters Written in France, in the Summer of 1790, to a Friend in England* (Dublin, 1791), I, p. 13; Adriana Craciun, *British Women Writers and the French Revolution: Citizens of the World* (Basingstoke, 2005), p. 1.

the Fête Nationale celebrating the anniversary of the storming of the Bastille: 'Here the mind of the people took a higher tone of exultation than in the other scenes of festivity. Their mutual congratulations, their reflections on the horror of the past, their sense of present felicity, their cries of 'Vive le Nation' still ring in my ear!'.[32] Setting up permanent residence in Paris from 1791, Williams used the dual forums of her publications as well as her influential salon to express her Girondist sympathies in the early years following the French Revolution.

Salon culture had, from the mid-eighteenth century, provided sociably acceptable spaces for women to participate actively in supposedly public dialogues such as politics, as well as in the dissemination and exchange of literature and culture. The widespread establishment of 'women-headed' salon culture in Europe placed women at the centre of local and international dialogues 'despite their frequent marginality in terms of political power'.[33] While salons were frequently women-led, they were not specifically the preserve of women.[34] Indeed, Williams's salon provided a space for both sexes to debate and discuss the public events, arts, and literary cultures of the day within her domestic space. As one male attendee wrote, 'I have been three times to Helen Maria Williams's conversations. You meet here a very interesting society. Many of the literati'.[35] It was, in fact, from these intersected spaces that Williams's salon took its power by drawing on the established model of the woman-led salon space yet imbuing it with the energy of her unique and evolving ideas of a feminised, radical cosmopolitanism.[36] At the very heart of this diverse cosmopolitan meeting place was the British-born Williams's personal interest and entanglement in the shifting landscape of French republican political values, the likes of which would have given Gillray a perfect target for caricatured satirisation.

Katherine's parallel journals provide an interesting example of life-writing practices of the late eighteenth century, as they reveal how she drew on different registers, and whether these were intended to remain private or to be sociably shared. In both her journal and travelogue, Katherine clearly outlines that 'the events of the day' as well as her participation in Williams's salon in Paris are worthy of documentation. Yet her motivations

---

[32] Williams, *Letters*, 1, p. 21.
[33] Susanne Schmid, *British Literary Salons of the Late Eighteenth and Early Nineteenth Centuries* (New York, 2015), p. 7.
[34] *Readers, Writers, Salonnières: Female Networks in Europe, 1700–1900*, ed. by Hilary Brown and Gillian Dow (Bern, 2011), pp. 1–9, p. 9.
[35] Henry Sandford, *Thomas Poole and His Friends* (London, 1888), II, p. 90.
[36] Mary Favret, 'Spectatrice as Spectacle: Helen Maria Williams at Home in the Revolution', *Studies in Romanticism*, 32:2 (1993), 273–295, p. 275.

and methods for doing so are divergent between the two manuscripts. Katherine's fragmented manuscript journal is reflective of the cultural, social and historical moment, composed as it is amidst the Peace of Amiens. The earlier manuscript can be aligned with the diary or journal tradition, in which the 'self presented lacks an obvious centre and a smooth continuity'.[37] The apparatus of the personal diary has been described as an 'expanding stow', into which the diarist 'casts life's materials' in an 'attempt to hold ... experience'.[38] Yet, particularly in the study of women's diaries, acknowledging 'what is excluded is as important as what is included'.[39] This distinction, in which Katherine uses the earlier manuscript to jot down extremely personal and emotional notes while in Paris. In one such entry, she describes a lack of self-confidence following an incident that is not described, writing, 'what pass'd today has made me fathom the depths of my own weakness ... My god how very unfortunate – how wretched are the sensations which have pass'd through my heart since it has look'd into the labyrinth of its own misery'.[40] In another, Katherine writes, 'When I get up in the morning (such is the state of my nerves) – that the world appears to me a Gulft, almost as dark & fathomless as my mind [sic]'.[41] Similar entries, which describe feelings of humiliation, and perhaps even depression, are sprinkled throughout the earlier manuscript. None of these are included in the later version of the same travelogue intended for circulation, the entries in which seem to imbue Katherine's authorial voice with joviality and confidence.

Tracked through the absences and occlusions within and fragmentation of the manuscript, it is possible to identify Katherine's idea of herself as a journal writer, as well as her reservations regarding the documentation of her journey, particularly in comparison with the flowing prose of the later travelogue. As she writes shortly after her arrival:

> Here I am! Just come into a strange country! – without understanding hardly a syllable of their language. No body can conceive the vexation of such a situation! – My own language suddenly became a burthen

[37] Felicity A. Nussbaum, 'Toward Conceptualizing Diary', *Studies in Autobiography*, ed. by James Olney (Oxford, 1988), pp. 128–140, p. 132.
[38] Rachel Cottam, 'Diaries and Journals: General Survey', in *Encyclopedia of Life Writing: Autobiographical and Biographical Forms*, ed. by Margaretta Jolly, 2 vols (Chicago, 2001), I, pp. 267–268.
[39] Suzanne L. Bunkers and Cynthia A. Huff, 'Issues in Studying Women's Diaries: A Theoretical and Critical Introduction', *Inscribing the Daily: Critical Essays on Women's Diaries* (Amherst, 1996), pp. 1–20, p. 1.
[40] BAHC, 'Original', 'Febr 27th, Saturday [1802]'.
[41] Ibid, '11 Ventose, Mardi, March 2nd [1802]'.

– & my thumb eloquence, the melancholy substitute, for elucidating my mutilated ideas! – I don't know, whether the misfortune does not overbalance, the pleasure of coming abroad.[42]

Katherine highlights her previously conceived notions of her journey: to experience pleasure, and absorb and exchange 'ideas'. The Grand Tour offered British women travellers a platform to 'display their linguistic and social skills in spaces devoted to conversation, such as French and Italian salons'.[43] Yet for Katherine, these opportunities for intellectual improvement and sociable exchange produce anguish. While Katherine's original journal contains several entries detailing her struggles with French amidst the dinners, salons and intellectual events she frequents in Paris, no mention of her low French linguistic ability appears in the later travelogue, the concerns outlined in private having been expunged from public representation. In a subsequent entry, Katherine continues to focus on the intellectual and social barriers presented by her inability to speak the language: 'It is for me alone – to know the irritation of filling my mind on the Chaff of words – at an age when I ought to store it with ideas'.[44] As she writes in December 1801:

> Now that I am in a country full of Novelty – where Libraries – Philosophical Lectures – Museums – Sensible Conversations – & c. *may* by attainable – I am oblige'd to go thro' the intolerable drudgery of slaving over a language – which gives me no ideas – & stupefies my very existence![45]

Here, the dash becomes a substitute for that which Katherine literally cannot say. Her inability to speak and understand French is an obstacle to the fulfilment of her main ambitions while abroad. This entry highlights the importance of speaking French for understanding the living history unfolding around her; without the ability to absorb and internalise the rapidly shifting political debates, Katherine could not capture those experiences into her travelogue.[46]

---

[42] Ibid, '29th Novr [1801]'.
[43] Marianna D'Ezio, 'Literary and Cultural Intersections Between British and Italian Women Writers and Salonnières During the Eighteenth Century', *Readers, Writers, Salonnières: Female Networks in Europe, 1700–1900*, ed. by Gillian Dow and Hillary Brown (Bern, 2011), pp. 11–29, p. 11.
[44] BAHC, 'Original', 'Thurs 17th Decr [1801]'.
[45] BAHC, 'Wednesday Dec'r 16th [1801]'.
[46] See Marcus Tomalin, *The French Language and British Literature, 1756–1830* (London, 2016).

Difficulty with French leaves Katherine feeling initially cut off in sociable settings in Paris. Yet this impediment also brings her into closer proximity with authentic French society and human embodiments of Revolutionary principles through her decision to take up residence as a lodger with a French family in Versailles. As she writes to her father to explain her motivation, the removal to Versailles is 'occasioned by the conflict of two contending tides in my nervous system, the one impetuously compelling the attainment of french [sic]; the other resisting its operation from the dearth of opportunity'.[47] 'Monsr & Mdm de Pescholoche', the hosts with whom she lodges in Versailles, not only offer her the expected linguistically immersive experience, but also give an intimate window onto French citizens who 'thru the adversity of the Revolution have changed for the superfluity of wealth, all the stamina of wisdom, with all the beauty of its moderation [sic]'. This cultural and linguistic arrangement leads Katherine to conclude that 'My star certainly peep'd from beneath its cloud when I was conducted to their protection'.

Katherine's letter to her father from Versailles attempts to allay concerns that the family may have on hearing both of her separation from the Mount Cashells as well as her decision to take up residence with an unknown French family. Katherine focuses on the ability of the Pescholoches to offer adequate 'protection', as well as Katherine's self-professed need for looking after as a young woman traveller. The letter indirectly underlines her familial role even as she journeys across unchartered areas of a foreign landscape. Separate from the solitary experience of writing she is practising in her journal, the individual letters sent by Katherine to her family from France embody a particularly framed version of her lived experience that she desires them to receive, and that she assumes will be recounted among their extended family and friends. For women of the long eighteenth century, 'letter writing was not simply a form of recreation or a second-best alternative to public writing; it was a crucial step in developing a consciousness of themselves as gendered subjects in the modern world'.[48] Katherine plays with the experimental capacity of the letter in Versailles, using the form to fashion gendered burlesque of her foreign experiences for the delight of Martha, whom she refers to by the alternative code names of 'Oliveria' and 'Oliver'. Satirically responding to 'sundry inquisitional queries relative to my personal decorations! My moral

---

[47] RIA MS 12 M 18, '23rd Floriel 18th, Near Versailles [1801]', n.d.
[48] Dena Goodman, *Becoming a Woman in the Age of Letters* (Ithaca, 2009), p. 4.

conduct!', Katherine's letter 'commence[s] with the mysteries of the toilet'.[49] Katherine writes that attempts to make her fashionable have resulted in a 'waist … shorten'd to nothing', yet nevertheless she has 'again' … 'upset fate I am as great a savage as ever'. The letter spans several pages and is written in a tight hand eager to stage as many scenes from her specifically female experiences in France as possible for the consumption of her curious sister.

Katherine's choice to undergo a period of language immersion while abroad would prove fortunate in a number of future contexts. A stronger French-language ability enabled her contribution to collaborative, transnational coterie work on Dashkova's *Memoirs* while resident in Russia later in the decade. In the shorter term, her continuing efforts to speak French facilitated integration among cosmopolitan radical sociable circles through regular attendance at Williams's bilingual French and English salon gatherings.

Networked Expression in Napoleonic Paris

In May 1802 Katherine writes in her journal that she has received a letter from her brother Robert 'exhort[ing]' her to 'keep a journal'; he:

> talks of the methodising effect it wd have upon my life – which otherwise naturally tends to diffuse itself in vacancy like a bankless stream – Here is my Journal! – & a pretty narrative it is! – I wonder Bob can talk to me with such gravity of the possibility of my working up materials into any form fit for Human kind! – save my own poor blind optick. – god knows how powerless I am – But I suppose I deceive him, as I do every one else – with the notion of vivacity &c. – I resemble nothing more than a Brown pot of Mustard – which in itself is odious – But which lends a zest to others of which it is unconscious. – & heaven knows how unconscious I am of affording pleasure to human Being! [*sic*].[50]

Katherine's description of herself as 'nothing more than a Brown pot of Mustard – which in itself is odious', and her own expressive abilities as only capable of 'lend[ing] zest to others of which it is unconscious' is not only revelatory in terms of its self-deprecating and comical nature. This assertion also reveals the depth and purpose of her journal writing practice

---

[49] RIA 12 M 18, '4 Floréal An 10/ 25th April [1802]/ Saturday Paris Hotel à Rome, Rue St Dominique'.
[50] BAHC, 'Original', 'Sunday 16 May – 26 Floréal [1802]'.

to date, one that she never intended to be 'fit for Human kind!' Robert's request appears from the pages of the hand-stitched and informal journal as a type of turning point: an interjection to her intermittent and privately orientated writing practice, which causes Katherine to reassess her methods, goals and audience. The request to work up her journal also presents a substantial predicament: to select a definitive opinion of France, and its young Republic, that can be put in writing as authoritative. Any record of her journey sent to Robert would undoubtedly be read by others, given that eighteenth-century letters functioned as public documents often 'composed in company, voluntarily circulated beyond the addressee and frequently found their way into print'.[51]

Katherine's journal entries spanning 1802 indicate a continual proximity to Williams's salon and a growing friendship with the hostess as well as her long-time companion, John Hurford Stone. As Katherine notes on 27 January 1802, 'Spent a most delightful evening with Miss Williams ... Mr Stone and I had a metaphysical duel'.[52] Stone was an influential participant at Williams's weekly gatherings and an important figure to the literary culture of Napoleonic Paris. He was already married when he first met Williams in Paris, though from the time of his divorce in 1794 he shared a residence with Williams, an arrangement the two maintained until his death in 1818. Their intertwined lives included mutual investment in Stone's printing press, a venture begun shortly after his arrival in Paris in 1793. Williams was active in the managing the press's affairs: in 1803 she was described as a 'femme Libraire'.[53] In 1806, she became co-owner by contributing 40,000 livres.[54]

From the time of her first mention of the pair until her departure from Paris later that year, Katherine records twenty-one encounters with either Williams or Stone in her journal, and it is possible that they met on further undocumented occasions. This new connection, clearly an important component of Katherine's formative Parisian experience in her private journal, is subdued in the travelogue written later with her family in mind. Katherine relates meeting Williams, whose manners she admires, and notes that the Mount Cashell party has 'a general permission to frequent these societies twice every week'.[55] Later references to Williams and Stone are depersonalised; the anecdotes transform the seemingly impactful relationship that Katherine shares with the pair into an ambiguous series of encounters. The

---

[51] Clare Brant, *Eighteenth-Century Letters and British Culture* (Basingstoke, 2006), p. 5.
[52] BAHC, 'Original', 'Wed 7th Pluviose 27th Jan [1802]'.
[53] Stern, p. 316.
[54] Paris, France, Archives de Paris, 'Acte de Société', D31U3 carton 3, #4371.
[55] RIA MS 12 L 32, p. 67.

journal entries, however, reveal that Katherine's relationship with Williams and Stone extends beyond the bounds of the regular visits to Williams's salon noted in the travelogue. Katherine writes of 'walking on the Boulevard' and drinking tea with Williams and Stone, also noting the presence of Joel Barlow.[56] The numerous visits are related in the fragmentary and brief style typical of the journal, often only comprising one incomplete sentence: 'in the even'g Mr. Stone, Miss Williams & I walk'd from 7 till 11.'[57] Where these events are not occluded completely from the later travelogue, details of the persons present are carefully revised; for instance, Katherine records accompanying Williams to the home of the son to the Prince of Condé, 'where the famous Le Brun (the French Pindar) recited his own poems'.[58] When writing of this visit in her later travelogue, Katherine fails to mention Williams's presence, implying that Mount Cashell alone joined her.[59] Similarly, Katherine notes in her journal that she has travelled '2 leagues west of Paris' with Williams, Stone and Barlow to see the ruins of Chateau Meudon; just after a passing storm she and Stone 'ventured to explore our way through the Courts in the Square Pavements which the tufts of grass burst rude & neglected'.[60] One week later she writes in her journal of returning to Meudon with Lord and Lady Mount Cashell, Williams, Stone and Amelia Opie.[61] Yet in the travelogue entry describing the earlier visit, the members of the party are not named. Instead, Katherine elaborately describes the chateau with details not included in the journal, praising 'the mouldering Turrets and old Iron Gates', which were 'lit with a thousand colours by the quick fork'd flashes of Lightning' of the storm on her first visit while excising the presence of her actual companions.[62]

The journal also reveals the extent to which Williams's published writing may hold an influence on and provide a model for responding to Katherine's brother's request. Two months later, in July 1802, she writes in the journal that she has recently 'read Miss Williams' tour thro Switznd [sic]'.[63] This is the only direct allusion Katherine makes to an awareness of her new friend's extensive body of publications. However, given Williams's

---

[56] BAHC, 'Original', 'Wednesday 9 June [1802]'.
[57] Ibid, 'Sunday 19th June [1802]'.
[58] Ibid, 'Monday 1st Feby (12 Pluviose Lundi) [1802]'; Katherine is referring to Louis Joseph Ecouchard, Prince of Condé (1736–1818) and French lyric poet Ponce Denis Écouchard Lebrun (1729–1807).
[59] RIA MW 12 L 32, p. 73–74.
[60] BAHC, 'Original', 'Sat 10 Fructidor: 28th Aug [1802]'.
[61] Ibid, '17 Fructidor Sat: 4 Sep [1802]'.
[62] RIA MS 12 L 32, p. 117.
[63] BAHC, 'Original', '17 Messidor 12 July [1802]'.

prolific and infamous status as an English author reporting on the events in France, this documented reading experience is quite unlikely to have been Katherine's first encounter with Williams's books. The eight-volume *Letters From France*, published between 1791–96, had made Williams 'perhaps the best-known contemporary author to magazine readers of her generation'.[64] The fact that Katherine does not feel the need to introduce Williams to her audience in the travelogue affirms her status as a household name.[65]

Amidst the landscape of the woman-led salons of Napoleonic Paris, the potential influence of Williams's book on Katherine's nascent writerly ambitions and later style stand out as significant. If Williams's ability to embody the spotlight through both publication and politically minded social engagement proves an inspiration to Katherine during this period, it is equally possible that the repercussions Williams encountered for these activities provided a cautionary counterbalance for her self-representations in text. The revolutionary sympathies that Williams had expressed in *Letters from France* had provoked public outcry and backlash: she was accused of treacherous disloyalty in Britain in the 1790s, the criticism predominantly juxtaposing her transgressive cosmopolitan political affinities with her womanhood.[66] Horace Walpole, for example, famously denounced Williams as a 'scribbling trollope [*sic*]'.[67] In 1793, Laetitia-Matilda Hawkins published the inflammatory *Letters on the Female Mind, Its Powers and Pursuits. Addressed to Miss H. M. Williams, with particular reference to Her Letters from France*, which directed a sustained two-volume assault not only on Williams's lack of 'loyalty' to Britain, but also her choice to enter public political discourse in the first place.[68] Hawkins's attack on Williams is extreme for the period – the *Analytical Review* dismissed it as a 'rant ... written with much ill temper' – yet the example makes explicit the risks faced by women writers who dared to publish controversial public opinions.[69] While Williams consistently gathered a cosmopolitan mix of politicians and the literati at her salon, her negative reputation at times

---

[64] Robert D. Mayo, *The English Novel in the Magazines, 1740–1815* (Evanston, 1962), p. 259.
[65] RIA 12 L 32, p. 66.
[66] Steven Blakemore, 'Revolution and the French Disease: Laetitia Matilda Hawkins's Letters to Helen Maria Williams', *Studies in English Literature, 1500–1900*, 36:3 (1996), 673–691, p. 676.
[67] Earl Leslie Griggs, *Wordsworth and Coleridge* (New York, 1962), p. 114.
[68] Laetitia-Matilda Hawkins, *Letters on the Female Mind, Its Powers and Pursuits. Addressed to Miss H. M. Williams, with particular reference to Her Letters from France*, 2 vols (London, 1793) I, p. 110.
[69] *Analytical Review, or History of Literature, Domestic and Foreign*, 15 (London, 1793), p. 527.

held her back from social acceptance. As Maria Edgeworth wrote in Paris in 1802, 'Miss Williams we did not chuse [sic] to go to see, though many English do'.[70] Edgeworth's unwillingness to attend the salon may be equally attributed to Williams's republicanism as to her long-time companionship with Stone, the man with whom Katherine engaged in 'metaphysical' duels in Williams's home.[71]

The nature of Katherine's discussions with Stone is elaborated in a marginal postscript on the travelogue manuscript's back cover by her sister Martha in 1870, four-and-a-half decades after Katherine's death. Martha recounts an interaction between Katherine and 'the celebrated Mr. Stone'. Stone attempts to commiserate with Katherine over her inability to speak French by pretending himself to be unfamiliar with the language as well. Though intended as a harmless ruse, Katherine is 'indignant of having been so duped'; nonetheless:

> her new acquaintance had found her conversation so delightful, that he singled her out in every society where they met, & would fain have induced her to write him some papers for a work he was then preparing for publication, declaring the originality of her remarks, their naiveté, & brilliancy w.d [sic] so embellish his book, as to entitle her to share its fame and its profits.[72]

Judging from Katherine's travelogue, it is, at first, difficult to understand why Williams and Stone might have wished to publish her writing, let alone admit her to their inner circle. The travelogue gleefully dismisses the ongoing Republican project as a false idol. 'Republicanism' she writes, reminds one of the 'Classical Duck who laid a golden egg every morning. While I was in England a Republican Egg was laid every day. But now that I am in the vitals of the Bird, I find no egg at all'.[73] While such comments are likely the result of a redrafted representation amenable to her intended recipients, they also may reflect the increasingly disillusioned political sentiments of the Anglophile and international community frequenting Williams's salon during the Peace, particularly with regard to Republican ideals under Napoleon.

Literary scholarship has tended to associate Williams solely with the early political sentiments of her salon as a moderate Girondin republican

---

[70] Maria Edgeworth, *Maria Edgeworth in France and Switzerland: Selections for the Edgeworth Family Letters*, ed. by Christina Colvin (Oxford, 1979), p. 53.
[71] RIA MS 12 L 32, n. pag.
[72] RIA MS 12 L 32, n. pag.
[73] RIA MS 12 L 32, p. 51.

space, rather than examining the ensuing transformations of her political sentiments. Craciun takes a more nuanced approach by noting that the salon later acted as springboard for Williams to 'plunge' much deeper 'into the revolutionary fray' by continually navigating 'the shifting tides of French revolutionary politics'.[74] She often found herself at the centre of controversy long after the Girondists had fallen, most notably with Napoleon. At the outset of Napoleon's rise to power, Williams's outlook was decidedly optimistic about his desire to carry the core tenants of the Revolutionary project forward, referring to the new century as becoming 'the age of rights'.[75] However, she grew rapidly disenchanted with his foreign policies as well as his increasingly totalitarian methods of governing French society as First Consul, including rampant censorship of the press and theatres, and the reinstatement of slavery in the Colonies. Other previously enthusiastic British authors, including Coleridge, Southey and Wordsworth, shared Williams's disillusionment.[76] When, in November 1801, Williams published her 'Ode to Peace' in the *Morning Chronicle*, she 'deliberately omitted any reference to Bonaparte, in order to test his vanity'.[77] Bonaparte took direct offence, eventually having her papers searched by the police and her mother imprisoned for twenty-four hours. Government surveillance was routinely conducted on her gatherings, creating palpable tension. As a visitor wrote of Williams's salon in February 1802, at the height of Katherine's own participation: 'we are told the government keep an exact watch over all who frequent it', while another described it as 'chiefly composed of liberal republicans and anti-Bonapartists'.[78]

The absence of a written record in which Katherine professes herself to be aligned with the 'anti-Bonapartists' poses obstacles for teasing out her affinities; however, the manuscript evidence in this case illuminates her feelings. The anecdote capturing an invitation to publish suggests that Katherine's opinions are, at the very least, inoffensive to the climate of government criticism prevalent in Williams's household. In the 1870 postscript, Martha notes that she 'steadily refused' to publish with Stone, a decision attributed to the fact that her sister 'thru' life undervalued her own superior talents'.[79]

---

[74] Craciun, pp. 131, 132.
[75] Helen Maria Williams, *Sketches of the State of Manners and Opinions in the French Republic* (London, 1801) II, p. 216.
[76] Simon Bainbridge, *Napoleon and English Romanticism* (Cambridge, 2005), p. 17.
[77] Deborah Kennedy, *Helen Maria Williams and the Age of Revolution* (Lewisburg, 2002), p. 178.
[78] Kennedy, p. 176.
[79] RIA MS 12 L 32, n. pag.

However, Katherine may well have had practical concerns for her own safety, autonomy and reputation should she choose to print with The English Press. As Madeleine Stern noted, 'The publication of so-called treasonable pamphlets [in the 1790s in England] led directly to trials for sedition.'[80] Stone published his own inflammatory *A Letter from John Hurford Stone to Dr Priestley* in 1796, addressed to the scientist-theologian who had exiled himself to avoid seditious charges under Pitt's government. In *A Letter*, Stone argued for the enduring validity of the French Revolution: 'Resistance to tyranny … [is] the first of moral and civil obligations, and no one deserves freedom who is not prepared to sacrifice his life in its defence.'[81] Stone habitually published authors who had previously been charged with sedition, or who were at the very least embroiled at the centre of controversy in Britain. For instance, in 1795 The English Press published Thomas Paine's *Dissertation on the First-Principles of a Government*.[82] Katherine's personal introduction to 'Tom Payne', who repeated 'the most elegant' poetry she 'ever heard' in his Paris home in March 1802 may have kept the links between sedition and creative practice alive in her mind, while the French government's similarly menacing behaviour towards Williams, as well as to the wider press, echoed the British sedition witch-hunts against radicals of the 1790s.[83] Williams had ceased to write about events unfolding in France following the fracas with Napoleon in 1801. Under new constraints of censorship, it is possible to see how the conversational quick wit and satirical opinions of Katherine, a sympathetic British woman traveller, might have appealed to the silenced Williams and Stone as an extension of the work Williams was being forced to lay aside.

If the decision not to associate herself with The English Press had anything to do with fear of sedition or imprisonment, Katherine was perhaps wise not to do so during the brief window of the Peace. Williams and Stone soon found themselves under renewed government pressure with the 1803 publication of *Political and Confidential Correspondence of Louis XVI*, papers that Williams had purchased purporting to be written by Louis XVI.[84] Choosing to work with historical documents as editor, Williams

---

[80] Stern, p. 307.
[81] 'I Fructidor An IV [18 August 1796]', *A Letter from John Hurford Stone to Dr Priestley* (Paris: The English press, IV year of the Republic [1796]).
[82] Thomas Paine, *Dissertation on the First-Principles of a Government* (Paris, 1795); Stern suggests that Stone may also have been anonymously involved with Paine's Age of Reason by assisting Joel Barlow in using his press for the purpose (p. 325).
[83] RIA MS 12 L 32, pp. 89–90.
[84] Correspondance Politique et Confidentielle Inédite de Louis XVI … Avec des Observations par H. M. Williams, 2vols (Paris, 1803).

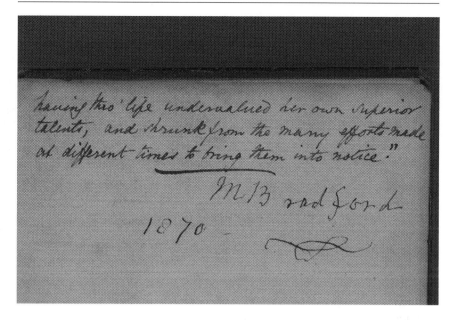

Figure 5   Royal Irish Academy MS 12 L 32, 'Letters of Katherine Wilmot from France-Italy 1801–03', Moscow, 1805; endpaper detail, n.d. © Royal Irish Academy.

believed that she could portray the French Revolution in a more positive light, shifting public opinion away from a renewed interest in the monarchy. The papers, however, were forged, and her efforts infuriated the government. The police seized the expensive print run and opened a case against Stone, Williams and their associate James Smith.[85] This frightening experience led Williams to abstain from publishing further until after the battle of Waterloo ten years later, realising, perhaps, that 'Napoleon was too formidable an antagonist'.[86] Three years after the censorship proceedings of 1803–04, Stone attempted to realign his press in Napoleon's favour, promising that 'The government could count on his sentiments'.[87] Temporarily renaming the press 'Imprimerie de J. H. Stone', perhaps to disassociate it from the recent frictions, he gained a lucrative contract to print 'Droits Réunis', and benefited from state compensation and support.

At the time of Katherine's association with Williams and Stone, no such reconciliation between The English Press and the government appeared to be on the horizon, and it is not difficult to imagine that Katherine wished

[85] Stern, pp. 340–341.
[86] Kennedy, p. 181.
[87] Archives Nationales, MS Stone 70, F18, #2371; 'Le gouvernement peut compter sur ses sentiments'; [my translation].

to avoid drawing any notice at all from either the French or the British authorities by such a connection. Ironically, given her refusal to print an authentic version of her own opinions with The English Press, Katherine's manuscript travelogue is frequently cited as a source on Williams's salon and movements, though these references do not necessarily reflect the depth of her integration within William and Stone's circle. The 1870 postscript to Katherine's manuscript travelogue suggests that she 'shrunk from the many efforts made' to bring her writing 'into notice' by choosing not to print with The English Press, nor to pursue print publication opportunities for her writing thereafter. However, Katherine's refusal of Stone's offer was not a decision to hide her writing away, as evidenced by the subsequent circulation of her manuscript. Katherine's manuscript travelogue may be interpreted in two contexts: first, in light of the assumed values of her anticipated readers in Britain; and second, through the influence of Williams' own politically inflected travel writing.

Shaping Revolutionary Encounters

Women-authored travel literature was on the rise in the years prior to Katherine's journey, if quite modestly, with 'around twenty travelogues by women' published in Britain between 1770 and 1800, a rise linked to the consumption of travel and geographical texts as a common educational method for young women.[88] In *Mental Improvement* (1793), Sarah Green recommends that young women on the verge of entering society 'divide one morning in the week between the study of geography, and the reading of voyages and travels', as 'the one will naturally lead you to like the other, and make your memory retentive of both'.[89] Travelogues were viewed as straightforward and rewarding in terms of composition. As *The Critical Review* remarked at the end of the eighteenth century, 'Travels are a species of writing which, besides being particularly easy in point of composition, prove highly gratifying to curiosity'.[90] Katherine makes use of this popular framework to 'work up' her writing, transforming it from a fragmentary

---

[88] Katherine Turner, *British Travel Writers in Europe, 1750–1800: Authorship, Gender and National Identity* (Aldershot, 2001), p. 3.
[89] Sarah Green, *Mental Improvement for a Young Lady, on her Entrance into the World* (London, 1793), p. 91.
[90] *Critical Review; or, Annals of Literature, Extended and Improved*, 5, ed. by Tobias George Smollett (London, 1792), p. 294.

form to a continuous narrative.[91] Archival evidence suggests that Katherine's travelogue continued to be read aloud for a number of years. Far from being created for merely private familial enjoyment, her narrative and manuscripts like it were treated as literary objects worthy of circulation and central to sociability.[92]

Aspects of Katherine's revised travelogue take cues from Williams's oeuvre of travel literature. Reiteration of events for her familial readers employs the epistolary travelogue model also taken up by Williams, an eighteenth-century genre that evolved as a response to the political upheavals of the Romantic period by documenting foreign experience.[93] Williams translates her foreign experience into something exportable and comprehensible through the intimacy of the epistolary form, a tactic that creates a sense of understanding and camaraderie: 'You, my dear friend.'[94] Katherine stages a similar frame of intimacy in addressing her journal to her brother, whom she periodically addresses as 'you', and 'my dear Brother'.[95] Williams's ability to capture unfolding moments of history, interpreting and manufacturing events for an audience through the apparatus of her journalistic epistolary style offers Katherine a model for interpreting the Republican sentiments she encounters in Paris. For women readers with an interest in political affairs in the eighteenth century the act of reading 'straddle[s] the public-private divide' in its inherent potential to move from an internalised act to a more political action.[96] The act of reading one of Williams's recent books, published four years earlier in 1798, may

---

[91] As Turner has written, '[v]irtually all eighteenth-century travelogues took the form of letters or a journal, and could therefore be "worked up" for publication with minimal effort, especially since the genre's evolving conventions came to associate apparent artlessness with authenticity', p. 3.

[92] Assertion of a wider readership for Katherine's travelogue in no way undermines the importance of the text's reception among the Wilmot family's immediate community of readers. The practice of reading familial letters aloud was a common and intrinsic one throughout the eighteenth century, whether as a method of collective education, or as an aid to conversational sociability. See Leonore Davidoff and Catherine Hall, *Family Fortunes: Men and Women of the English Middle Class, 1780–1850* (London, 1987), p. 162.

[93] Kelly notes that 'Williams feminizes the Revolution formally and rhetorically as well as thematically, mainly through use of the familiar letter, well established as a predominately feminine discourse, conventionally seen as informal'; Gary Kelly, *Women, Writing and Revolution, 1790–1827* (Oxford, 1994), pp. 38–39.

[94] Williams, *Letters*, I, p. 109.

[95] RIA MW 12 L 32, p. 32.

[96] Charlotte Sussman, 'Women's private reading and political action, 1649–1838', in *Radicalism in British Literary Culture, 1650–1830: From Revolution to Revolution*, ed. by Timothy Morton and Nigel Smith (Cambridge, 2002), pp. 133–151, p. 135.

hold added meaning given Katherine's personal contact with the author by providing a tangible blueprint for constructing her own narrative. The practice of reading familial letters aloud was a common one throughout the eighteenth century, whether as a method of collective education, or as an aid to conversational sociability.

Similarities between Katherine's manuscript travelogue and Williams's published writing can also be found in a mutual gendered representation of both form and political spectatorship. As Williams pointed out in *Letters Written in France*, 'While you observe from a distance the great drama which is acting in France, I am a spectator of the representation'.[97] Williams's *Letters Written in France* allows her to generate 'a spectacle of her own spectatorship', as she brings the reader along for every stage of her revolutionary encounter, moving closer towards revolutionary sympathy by presenting the immediacy of key sites and events.[98] Williams's account of her first visit to the Bastille, for instance, re-enacts the horrors faced by those imprisoned there:

> Before I suffered my friends at Paris to conduct me through the usual routine of convents, churches, and palaces, I requested to visit the Bastille; feeling a much stronger desire to contemplate the ruins of that building than the most perfect edifices of Paris ... We drove under that porch which so many wretches have entered never to repass, and alighting from the carriage descended with difficulty into the dungeons.[99]

By insisting that she visit the Bastille immediately after arriving in Paris, Williams underlines the importance of recently historicised locations to her British readers. A popular spot for tourists in the years following the Revolution, Williams nonetheless gives a sense of intimacy and personal experience through the device of a murky, stooped and candlelit tromp through the dungeons. Williams draws on devices popularised by the Gothic genre not only to animate her experience, but to invoke a sense of sympathy with victims who had been tortured by the tyrannical former government. Williams exclaims 'Good God!' to indicate the emotional outpouring she feels at personally witnessing the Bastille's 'regions of horror', asserting that only those with 'a strong spirit of curiosity' would be compelled to visit there.[100] She tries to emotionally stimulate her readers by

---

[97] Williams, *Letters*, I, p. 3.
[98] Favret, p. 280.
[99] Williams, *Letters*, I, pp. 23–24.
[100] Williams, *Letters*, I, p. 23.

referencing the immediacy of the recent revolution; the juxtaposition of bravery in the face of terror infuses her narrative.

Katherine similarly creates a theatre of sentiment relative to unfolding political history through the selection of specific sites of revolutionary action in her travelogue, often using locations or anecdotes either never noted in her private journal or detailed in a vastly different way. Two different accounts of a visit to the Cathedral of Amiens while *en route* to Paris provide an example of the transitions that occur between the journal and the travelogue, as well as the potential influence of Williams's published writing. The incident is recorded in Katherine's journal in passing as follows:

> We saw the beautiful Cathedral reckon'd I believe one of the finest in France. – I was surpris'd to find it so little injur'd – when those in all the Towns we pass'd thro' before – lay in mouldering desolation about the streets – with scarcely two stones together. – Many of the Convents exhibited the same melancholy appearance! I don't think I ever saw so fine a building as this Cathedral, by resigning all the silver & riches at the time of the Revolution the People of Amiens, contrived to preserve almost uninjur'd their lovely Cathedral – for the first time, I saw Canoniz'd noses & fingers – the Original head of John the Baptiste – relics & c & c. The Alter is a sort of composition – which gives the appearance of floating, fleecy clouds – thro' which Angels are seen & c. On the Alter piece, is the Paschal lamb [*sic*].[101]

This first version of her visit to the cathedral is characterised by touristic fascination as well as an appreciation for the local worshippers and their religious customs. Katherine is pleased to find the building 'so little injur'd [*sic*]' despite the revolutionary desecration she has already witnessed elsewhere. She emphasises that the 'People of Amiens' acted shrewdly by 'resigning all the silver riches at the time of the Revolution', thereby shielding the cathedral from damage. Thanks to their efforts she is able to enjoy, 'for the first time' the 'Canoniz'd [*sic*]' Catholic relics in person, noting eagerly that these include 'the Original head of John the Baptiste'.[102] By contrast, Katherine's travelogue account of the same visit is extended significantly and the tone altered. The second account stresses that the building is a 'Gothic Cathedral', and positions her experience as a scene of heightened revolutionary tension in the space following her earlier description:

---

[101] BAHC, 'Original', 'Thursday 3d Decr [1801]'.
[102] Ibid, 'Thursday 3d Decr [1801]'.

> On the Altar piece is the Paschal Lamb. I must tell you I never got into such a fright in my life, as on seeing the massy Gates of the Cathedral close upon me. For a moment the high vaulted Aisles, and the grandeur of the columns absorb'd my attention so thoroughly that till I heard a hundred echoes through the Church reverberating the loud shutting of the Iron Gates (which considerably diminished the light), I never observ'd eight or nine men at our heels, gigantic and scowling, and obviously of the very lowest class of the people. All the beauty of the Cathedral was obliterated and nothing but the Murders of the Revolution danc'd before my imagination … I walk'd up to the Pascal Lamb upon the Altar like a guilty Victim, whose impending slaughter was about to appease the Vengeance of the angry Gods.[103]

Here, Katherine's previous admiration for the cathedral's relics is substituted with 'fright' as she distances herself from appreciation of Catholic customs. She draws on Gothic convention to position herself as 'a guilty Victim, whose impending slaughter was about to appease the Vengeance of the angry Gods'. Her earlier appreciation of the actions of the 'People of Amiens' is replaced by a fanciful episode that temporarily demonises them. The revised text invents 'eight or nine men' who approach uncomfortably close. She depicts the men as 'gigantic and scowling', thereby disparaging the space of the cathedral itself by indicating that common worshippers are 'obviously of the very lowest class of people'. Unlike Williams, who paints the victims of the Bastille as the object of pity, Katherine depicts the lowly French residents of Amiens as potential agitators – and places herself in the role of the victim. Realising the errors of her own imagination, Katherine acquits the lower class 'Executioners' as 'poor innocent fellows' and pokes fun at her own 'triumphant flow of Spirits'. Yet both women draw on Gothic apparatuses of darkness, ancient buildings, violence and horror to communicate crucial revolutionary sites to their readerships, historicising and glorifying their own personal experiences as intertwined with the spaces they describe.

Katherine also echoes Williams's humble protestation to her readers. In the *Letters*, Williams writes: 'I am well aware how imperfectly I shall be able to describe the images which press upon my mind … I shall be able to give you a faint sketch, to which your own imagination must add colouring and spirit.'[104] Katherine begins her travelogue with a diffident prefatory letter that states "tis by your exhortation I have attempted to keep a journal", and

---

[103] RIA MS 12 L 32, p. 13.
[104] Williams, *Letters*, I, p. 2.

claiming to 'abhor the act of journalising!'[105] She continues to pepper her writing with regrets throughout the early pages of the travelogue; an engaging description of the history of the treasures of the Louvre is prefaced by a promise not to 'bore' with her comments, as 'besides not having the skill, or the eye of an artist, I am not qualified to do anything more than admire.'[106] Yet both she and Williams intermingle their contrition with the resolute right to offer unique first-hand experiences and analyses. Prefacing her *Tour in Switzerland*, Williams states that she must 'clear' herself 'from the charge of presumption', writing that 'it is the present moral situation of Switzerland that justifies the appearance of these volumes'.[107] Despite her own repentance regarding her ability to 'journalise', Katherine is well placed for observing and animating the political moment of the Peace, and she leverages her unique circumstances to claim space on the page. Empowered by first-hand experience, she is able to offer her readers scenes unique to the setting and moment. For example, on first seeing Napoleon from a window in the 'Thuilleries [*sic*]', an event not noted in the earlier journal, Katherine writes in her travelogue:

> But we must talk of Bonaparte who we saw ... reviewing his troops just under our eyes, surrounded with his beautiful aides de camps ... Bonaparte rode on a white charger ... He look'd as pale as ashes, & the expression of his countenance was stern severity ... I was more gratified than I ever was by a warlike pageant in all my life.[108]

This representation allows her British readers to palpably engage in the moment of first gazing on their recent rival and share in her sense of awe. Such anecdotes of fleeting historical urgency validate her eyewitness experience and choice to document it.

However, Katherine's use of eyewitness experience is radically different from Williams's in that she utilises proximity to revolutionary events to offer critique rather than cosmopolitan sympathy. Aligning herself with the sentiments of her domestic reading community, Katherine exploits republicanism as a prop to highlight foreignness rather than as a sentiment she may identify with. Waking for the first time in France, in Calais, she experiences 'a moment of such unfeign'd extacy [*sic*]', and 'imagin'd some metamorphosis was taking place', jokingly conjecturing that her nightcap

---

[105] RIA MS 12 L 32, p. 2.
[106] RIA MS 12 L 32, p. 28.
[107] Williams, *Tour*, n. pag.
[108] RIA MS 12 L 32, pp. 63, 64.

has been transformed into a 'cap of liberty'.[109] While this assertion is meant to entertain her brother, the professed recipient, along with other potential readers, it also suggests the unique authorial position of participant and spectator granted to her by being abroad. The travelogue's initial representation of republicanism as an entertaining subject for light mockery swiftly shifts into scepticism and commentary on the moral situation of the French. "Tis nonsense to talk of the french being republicans' writes Katherine, 'I don't think a spark exists amongst them – they are excessively fond of rank, honours, and every etiquette that can distinguish them from the multitude'.[110] Yet her eyewitness experience also details some of the benefits of the aftermath of the Revolution and the peoples' general remorse for the bloodiness of the Terror:

> there is a great independence in the lower ranks of People, that I hear is a blessing of the Revolution. I have never met with any creature who did not speak with regret of the past and horror of the events wch [sic] were the consequence of political subversion; but remember I have but three weeks experience to quote![111]

This careful construction of reserved sympathy shows Katherine's desire to make her familial readers aware of a broader narrative of republicanism, all while delicately positioning her own opinions by inserting them between pointed critique and authorial disclaimer.

Katherine's later travelogue frequently mutes encounters with known revolutionary sympathisers. Writing in the travelogue, for example, of repeated visits with Thomas Holcroft in Paris, she hints at her curiosity about his philosophies, while also adding in a healthy dose of critique:

> I feel as if I shou'd like to say a hundred bitter things of Holcroft, but I have such a trick of not penetrating into people's characters that I don't like to trust myself – He has been here several times, & has entered fully into conversation wch he seems very fond of – a long enquiry into the nature of Truth into wch he enter'd eloquently struck me as very good; but I begin to smoke a little of the visionary on the Godwinean System of living beyond the term of Man.[112]

Katherine's professed uncertainty at her own ability to judge Holcroft's character is correlated to her desire to perform her gender appropriately

---

[109] RIA MS 12 L 32, p. 10.
[110] RIA MS 12 L 32, p. 48.
[111] RIA MS 12 L 32, p. 49.
[112] RIA MS 12 L 32, pp. 25–26.

in the text. At the same time, she uses criticism to align her representation with the non-republican political affinities of her readership. She derides Holcroft as overly 'fond' of 'conversation' yet provides a caveat that she found his subject matter interesting. Before her readers believe that she has been carried away by radical philosophical sympathies, Katherine satirises her own susceptibility to the 'Godwinean System of living beyond the term of Man'. The mocking tone relating to William Godwin is particularly interesting, given that she and Mount Cashell socialised with him and his family repeatedly while in London.[113] By contrast, Katherine's earlier journal correspondingly refers to several enjoyable social engagements with the Holcrofts, who, appreciating her intelligence, heaped 'undeserv'd praise' upon her until she 'felt [her] mind crush'd to nothing'.[114] She strategically excises details pertaining to these social connections, which would have, in reality, occupied a considerable amount of the women's attention in Paris, while also omitting her personal associations with Godwin.

Such revisionism illustrates how Katherine's actual experiences are rehearsed, tested, and revised until a coherent narrative acceptable to her readers emerges. While Katherine's travelogue does not advocate for the same cosmopolitan radicalism espoused in Williams's earlier writing, it draws cues from Williams's representational tactics: her interactions with Williams's salon and writing as well as an awareness of her political struggles and personal reputation impact Katherine's choices in her text through a seeming reversal of affinities towards a Francophobia that protects her from the censure heaped on Williams by British readers. In the same way, the exclusion of her participation in the sociable circles of radical British intellectuals and writers including Williams, Stone, Godwin and Holcroft safeguards her from public affiliation with their viewpoints. Katherine also protects herself from the attention of the French government through her refusal to submit her travel writing for publication with The English Press. The occlusions and repurposed incidents between Katherine's two manuscripts therefore represent a series of carefully calculated choices. These transformations shed light on the gendered, social and political constraints facing British women travel writers in the Revolutionary period as they grappled with communicating their complicated affinities, experiences and associations.

---

[113] *The Diary of William Godwin*, entry for 'Margaret King'; Abinger Collection, MS. Abinger c. 7, fols. 56–57, 'Lady Margaret Mountcashell [Margaret Mason] to William Godwin, 6 Aug. [1801]': Lady Mount Cashell wrote to Godwin, the widower of her former governess, exchanging methodologies of childhood education, and arranging an upcoming visit to Godwin's home in London.

[114] BAHC, 'Original', 'Wednesday Dec'r 16th [1801]'.

'The idea that I have not liv'd in vain': Communal Forms of Writing

In seeking to recover the variations between Katherine's two manuscripts, this chapter has contended with the shifting political and nationalistic sentiments facing eighteenth-century women writing between home and abroad. As we have seen, the travelogue develops due to Katherine's participation in a dynamic network linking Ireland and France, its final shape the result of multiple communal models of representation and dissemination. The coterie's polyvocal and transnational influence is embodied in the transformation of a journal entry written by Katherine at the conclusion of her time in Paris. In her original journal, Katherine states:

> I feel myself after this residence here – as having pass'd thro' an existance ... I feel as if I had a stronger hold in Life, than I had the Day I entered this charming town! ... Altogether Paris has been a school – which has taught me the powers of Equality – not indeed in the political sense – but socially speaking in the means of moving all the world by the same spring. – I have been twitch'd myself I suppose in the same way. – mais 'que voulez vous'.[115]

Katherine attributes her own personal growth, or 'stronger hold in Life', to the social movement and 'powers of Equality' that she met with in Paris, feelings that have 'twitch'd' her into a sense of futurity and progress. She also notes having formed 'the sincerest friendship'. Given their repeated and frequent interaction, this is likely to refer to time spent with Williams and Stone. This representation of egalitarian and intellectual bliss is far from the ambivalent message that is represented to her readers in the travelogue entry covering the same period:

> I bid adieu to this charming town with the sensation of having pass'd thro' a little existence, & please myself with the idea that I have not liv'd in vain – I reflect on the variety of novel circumstances which have kept all my character in exercise.[116]

The above entry, which was later copied into the manuscript travelogue by Martha for circulation purposes, was tepid enough to make Paris seem merely a helpful place for moral and intellectual improvement. Yet further comments in the same entry were apparently deemed too overtly

---

[115] Ibid, 'Thursday 29 Fructidor 16 Sepr: [1802]'.
[116] RIA MS 12 L 32, p. 120.

Francophobic to be included in the copied text, and are therefore excised through Martha's transcription:

> If in some instances I appear to estimate the state of Society and manners here too highly, I hope you will have the candour to attribute it to the effect of novelty and of that seductive influence which marks the manners of the French. I know your antipathy to this nation, and when contrasted with the sounder morals of the English I do not wonder at your dislike.[117]

These interventions illustrate how one member of an eighteenth-century literary coterie might see her text significantly moulded and repurposed by others. As the following chapter will show, the creation of eighteenth-century women's travel writing was commonly a collective and transnational endeavour. By engaging in the production of writing sent back from abroad, women who stayed at home participated in a virtual coterie, gaining a stake in the foreign experiences and literary outputs of those who travelled. The resulting manuscript corpus showcases the connections between provincial literary sociability and transnational travel in the late eighteenth century, as well as the ways in which women's networks shared and shaped writings and legacies over time and across borders.

---

[117] Wilmot, *An Irish Peer*, p. 85. This version was printed in the 1921 edition of Katherine's journals edited by Thomas U. Sadleir, which was edited from a manuscript in a private collection.

2
Literary and Material Sociability at Home and Abroad

When Martha Wilmot arrived in Russia in 1803 to stay as a guest of the Russian noblewoman Princess Ekaterina Dashkova, she came with a strong awareness of her host's illustrious status. Martha's aunt, Catherine Hamilton, a lifelong friend and correspondent of the Princess, had regaled the young traveller with stories of the noblewoman's international renown as an intellectual and political figure, as well as recommending her generous and kind character. Dashkova was a prominent woman amongst a European Enlightenment landscape populated by great men, many of whom she corresponded with or knew personally, and she was among the first women in Europe to hold public office.[1] Martha's interest in Dashkova's achievements is apparent in a journal entry written shortly after her arrival at Troitskoe in late September 1803:

> in the Eveg the Princess talk'd a little of the Wonderful scenes of the revolution in wch she acted so wonderful a part at the age of 18 – the Empress Katherine was 16 years older than her, tis a curious circumstance that Peter 3rd was Godfather to Princess Dashkoff who as she says herself, 'I dethroned' [sic].[2]

By October, Martha writes, 'the Princess conversed so openly upon her own feelings on the subject of her family, as really to touch me most sensibly'.[3] In early November, she adds: 'at dinner she conversed for a long time about the Empress Katherine, who certainly did not treat her with

---

[1] Dashkova's modern biographer, A. Woronzoff-Dashkoff, notes her contemporary reputation as 'a prominent woman of letters publishing translations of Helvétius, Hume, and Voltaire, and articles on education, agriculture, travel', as well as being 'the first modern stateswoman in Russia'; A. Woronzoff-Dashkoff, *Dashkova: A Life of Influence and Exile* (Philadelphia, 2008), p. xxvi.
[2] RIA MS 12 L 17, 'Sep 23rd 1803', p. 125.
[3] RIA MS 12 L 17, 'Friday, 14th [October 1803]', p. 138.

all the gratitude – if I may use the expression – that her conduct merited.'[4] The sympathetic and intimate audience that Dashkova found in Martha inspired the elder woman to reassess, in Martha's words, her own 'constant refusal to commit to paper the events of a life so varied, & singular as hers as been [sic]'. By February of 1804, the pair's frequent discussions had revitalised Dashkova's enthusiasm for her own life story. As Martha records in her journal: 'the Princess has begun to write her life, her motive for so doing is friendship to me, as she says she will give me the manuscript, & liberty to publish it. It will probably be a most interesting work.'[5]

Martha recognises the project as historically important, writing in her journal that 'it would have been a million sins, if she had continued to withhold from the public, the events of a life so interesting as hers, or the sentiments of a heart so little known & so often misrepresented.'[6] Dashkova's composition process engages Martha's focus and attention from the outset. She describes their shared practices in April 1804: 'I am very much engaged in writing, copying the Memoirs of the Princesses life, as she writes them [sic]'.[7] Teasing apart this sentence offers a view into the actual terms of the textual labour taking place. Martha notes *copying* the text as an act of *writing*, done simultaneously as Dashkova *writes*. Martha's use of the same verb indicates a process of mirroring, imitation and identification. There is evidence elsewhere of the sociable nature that accompanied the collective composition and scribal efforts. For instance, Martha writes of copying only one page of the manuscript per day during certain periods, due to the distraction of 'the Gentillesses [sic] of Life, such as chit chat.'[8] At times, Martha expresses anxiety in her journal about the slow speed at which Dashkova composes the text: 'the Princess is writing her History very diligently at present, but tis [sic] really astonishing to see with how little trouble it gets forward.'[9] Though instigated in the intimate and remote setting of Dashkova's Russian estate, the public future of the text is an inevitable reality, making the project feel less like a pleasant pastime for Martha and more of a serious responsibility. As Martha writes at the time of the dedication in 1805, 'may it be long before, either dedication, or book of memories retrace to the public the scenes of life which must be closed before they are publish'd.'[10]

---

[4] RIA MS 12 L 17, 'Tuesday 1st November 1803', p. 143.
[5] RIA MS 12 L 18, 'Sat: 10th [February 1804]', p. 56.
[6] RIA MS 12 L 18, 'Sunday 25th [August 1804], p. 211.
[7] RIA MS 12 L 18, 'Monday 9th [April 1804], p. 104.
[8] RIA MS 12 L 20, 'Tuesday 6th [May 1806]', p. 102.
[9] RIA MS 12 L 18, 'Sunday 25th [August 1804]', p. 211.
[10] RIA MS 12 L 19, 'Saturday 8th [Nov 1805]', p. 119.

Martha's participation in the writing of Dashkova's memoirs as assistant, copyist and confidante would have life-changing implications for the young Irish woman, aged twenty-five at the time of her arrival, as well as for the legacy of Dashkova, a Russian noblewoman in her early sixties. The extensive body of manuscript materials collectively produced by the pair, as well as by Martha's sister Katherine Wilmot following her own arrival in Russia in 1805, would go on to provide the basis for the posthumous *Memoirs of Princess Daschkaw, Lady of Honour to Catherine II* (1840). Literary labour surrounding Dashkova's memoir and manuscript materials associated with it resituated Martha from a passive student of history to a guardian responsible for its care, first through acting as Dashkova's scribe, and, later, through editing the work for publication. Katherine's shared role in identifying and preserving Dashkova's legacy, along with her translation work added to the collaborative project. At the same time, the sisters wrote a significant body of letters describing their experiences in Russia, which were sent back to the family home in Ireland. Collected, copied and circulated by their female relatives, their correspondence acted as a bridge between Russia and Britain that extended the bounds of their literary community between 1803–08. This chapter considers the scribal publication and collaborative manuscript practices of the two geographically separate branches of the coterie. It addresses the relationship of literary mentoring shared between Dashkova, Martha and Katherine during the sisters' residence in Russia and the production of the noblewoman's memoir. The simultaneous activities of sister Alicia and mother Mary Wilmot in Ireland are examined in relation to the gathering, copying and disseminating of the sisters' travel writing.

These parallel manuscript practices, seen here between Ireland and Russia, signal the impact of women's transnational connections. Forged by either friendship or familial connection, women's coterie bonds were capable of shaping literature and culture in the late eighteenth century across national borders and generational boundaries. The manuscript texts created by the provincial, middle-ranking Wilmot women survive today in large part thanks to their association with Dashkova's illustrious history. Yet the strategies and practices taken up by them indicate the prominence of such literary activities by provincial women more generally. Margaret Ezell, in her influential work on women's manuscript cultures of the centuries prior to the Wilmots' own active period, calls on scholars to look beyond metropolitan publication records as sole proof of literary activity. 'Who was writing and who was reading as opposed to who was printing and who was purchasing?' Ezell asks. 'If one was ... a young woman living almost anywhere outside London, what did it mean to be an "author"?'[11] In what follows, I draw on a voluminous body of life-writing manuscripts – whether formal memoirs, 'private' journals, or socially minded letters and travel writing – to consider wider practices of women's authorship, literary production, and circulation in the period. As we shall see, these documents shed light on an exciting and vibrant manuscript culture well beyond the borders of the Wilmot coterie, and reveal the transnational horizons of provincial culture open to groups of literary women in the late eighteenth and early nineteenth centuries.

Writing Public and Private Histories at Troitskoe

By the time of the Wilmots' arrival in Russia in the early 1800s, Princess Ekaterina Dashkova had grown accustomed to her distance from public life. Her first period of banishment in the 1770s and 1780s was undertaken willingly following a gradual falling out of political favour with Catherine II in the mid-1770s, to whom she had seen herself as a loyal advisor and servant. During this time Dashkova travelled and lived in Europe, mainly in France and Scotland. Following an eventual return to Russia, she re-established ties with the Empress and was subsequently appointed the first head of the St Petersburg Academy of Arts and Sciences in 1794. The staging of a politically controversial tragedy at the Academy incited a renewed estrangement between Dashkova and the Empress. Dashkova was stripped of her duties and accused of revolutionary complicity. Following the death of the Empress in 1796 and the subsequent accession of the Emperor Paul I, Dashkova was censured publicly for her previous involvement in the Coup d'État of 1762, which had originally raised Catherine II to the position of Empress. Seeking revenge for his father's murder in the coup, Paul I exiled Dashkova to the remote Novgorod province to ruminate on her role in the events of the 1760s. The banishment was soon rescinded thanks to pressure applied by Dashkova's allies in the court. The noblewoman was allowed to retire to her own estate in the years immediately preceding Martha's arrival. Gossip continued to be directed at Dashkova, and reached Martha's ears *en route* to Troitskoe in 1803. As she later wrote:

> She was represented to me as a most cruel and vindictive person, violent in temper, and destructive of the happiness of every creature who was unfortunate enough to approach her. I was told she lived in

[11] Margaret J. M. Ezell, *Social Authorship and the Advent of Print* (Baltimore, 2003), p. 2.

a castle situated in a dreary solitude, far removed from the society of any civilized beings, where she was all-powerful, and so devoid of principle that she would invariably break open and read the letters which came to me ... taking care to suppress any that might be displeasing to her.[12]

Martha soon formed her own opinions on Dashkova, finding her to be 'a being of so superior an order' rather than the monstrous embodiment of tyranny which had been described to her.[13]

Dashkova's public identity as a strong female figure in Russia throughout the second half of the eighteenth century, and her ability to manage and command her own large estate, having been widowed in 1764, likely provoked its own measure of disapproval from outsiders.[14] Serving as the head of the household was, for Dashkova, a mere extension of the roles of authority that her station and experiences in life had provided her. As Katherine Wilmot described Dashkova in 1805:

> For my part, I think she would be most in her element at the Helm of the State, or General of Army [sic], or Farmer General of the Empire. In fact she was born for Business, on a large scale which is not irreconcilable with the Life of a Woman who at 17 headed a Revolution & who for 12 years afterwards govern'd an Academy of Arts & Sciences.[15]

Katherine appears fascinated by the various roles that Dashkova assumes in the control of the estate, writing of the humble and compassionate approach by which she exercises her power locally:

> In the midst of this immense Establishment and in the centre of riches and honours I wish you were here to see the Princess go out to take a walk, or rather to look over her subjects – ... she shells the corn, she talks out loud in Church, & corrects the Priest if he is not devout, ... she is a Doctor, an Apothecary, a Surgeon, a Farrier, a Carpenter, a Magistrate, a Lawyer.[16]

---

[12] *Memoirs*, II, pp. 224–225.
[13] *Memoirs*, I, p. xxi.
[14] Woronzoff-Dashkoff attributes disparate sentiments regarding the noblewoman's character to the extreme gender 'biases of the age', noting how 'her achievements were both highly praised as well as roundly condemned': Woronzoff-Dashkoff, p. xxiv.
[15] RIA, MS 12 L 30, 'Ms in English, 1805–07, Copies of Katherine Wilmot's letters from Russia', Monday, December 8th 1805, K. Wilmot to sister Alicia, p. 68.
[16] RIA MS 12 L 30, 'Oct 1 1805', K. Wilmot to Anna Chetwood, p. 44.

Katherine describes Dashkova as a landowner who not only examines the *'subjects'* on her estate but also joins them in their daily labours, attributing to her the skills of masculine professions across the class spectrum. The participatory, capable and honourable command that Dashkova wields over her estate and its inhabitants provides an interesting contradiction with the tyrannical public perception encountered by Martha on entering Russia. This inconsistency is telling if the extensive correspondence and private journals of the Wilmot sisters are to be believed. The divergence between public and private opinion of Dashkova at the time exposes the noblewoman's paucity of allies, as well as a vulnerable point of entry for those who may wish to support or deride her. Such discrepancies set the stage for the major acts of legacy recuperation through life writing that take place at Troitskoe during the Wilmot sisters' stay, in addition to the intimacy and trust on which those acts of writing are founded.

Dashkova's guardianship in Russia provides a welcome safety net for Martha, a young woman travelling alone to a country beyond the traditional boundaries of the European Grand Tour. British views of Russia shifted somewhat throughout the eighteenth century, due in part to the enlightened programmes of national refinement implemented by Peter the Great and Catherine II. Yet, as Beatrice Teisseir notes, Russia was also often portrayed 'as a land of despotic and arbitrary rules, corrupt nobles and governors, and ignorant, brutal and drunken people and clergy'.[17] Given Martha's vulnerable status, Dashkova is implicitly responsible as the protector of her young guest. In one of her earliest letters from Russia, written in August 1803, Martha reports to her parents that Dashkova 'bids me assure you she will study my happiness as if I were her own child'.[18] Dashkova's guardianship, however, extends to an affective language of surrogacy. She asks the younger woman to refer to her as her 'Russian Mother', addressing the latter frequently as 'my Angel Child'. Dashkova's notions of chosen family were not unusual in the late eighteenth century, the word 'family' being defined in Johnson's *Dictionary* (1755) merely as 'those who live in the same house'.[19] Martha's presence as a member of Dashkova's family unit may have also compensated for a lack of intimacy that Dashkova felt with her own adult children, who lived far from the family estate and who, despite a lengthy process of international education, failed to develop the enlightened sensibility cherished by their mother. Dashkova's own daughter,

---

[17] Beatrice Teissier, *Russian Frontiers: Eighteenth-Century British Travellers in the Caspian, Caucasus and Central Asia* (Oxford, 2011), p. 4.
[18] RIA MS 12 L 24, 'Aug 25th, 1803', p. 102.
[19] Samuel Johnson, *A Dictionary of the English Language* (London, 1755), s.v. 'family'.

Anastasia Shcherbinina, had married against her mother's wishes and rarely visited Troitskoe. By contrast, Dashkova's niece, Anna Petranova, a charming, loyal and well-educated young woman of a similar age to Martha, also lived at Troitskoe. Anna Petranova was an essential member of the household social circle, yet her continued presence did not seem to provoke an emotional attachment in Dashkova similar to that enjoyed by Martha. An explanation for the imbalance in warmth between Dashkova's resident blood relatives and Martha can be traced to a comment recorded by Katherine Wilmot, who wrote of Dashkova's vocal affection for Martha:

> Sometimes she exclaims with devotion when she looks at Matty: 'Dere is de mark of Heaven's best love to me. My darling Child sought me out on de credit of my name & came by herself from a distant Country on de faith of my Character! Now do tell me Sister Kaightty what shall I ever do to prove my love and gratitude to her?' Regularly every 3 or 4 days I am told the Story over & over again with renew'd energy.[20]

Overlooking Katherine's caricature of Dashkova's English-language ability, the comment offers insight on the bonds of loyalty between the two women, and the extent to which Martha's outsider status is intrinsically linked to Dashkova's affection. Dashkova views Martha's devotion to her as not only a sacrifice of the younger woman's own native land, but also, it seems, as a long-term commitment to serve as her companion in Russia, a role that may include the permanent eschewal of other prospects afforded by home, such as marriage.[21]

The intimate friendship formed between Martha and Dashkova is linked, at least in part, to the younger women's ability and willingness to act as a worthy intellectual apprentice and literary collaborator. The circumstances of Martha's educational upbringing within a middle-ranking Protestant

---

[20] RIA MS 12 L 30, 'Dec 8 1805', pp. 67–68.
[21] Dashkova may have expected Martha to remain her companion until the time of her death. However, by 1808 Martha's limited prospects for marriage would inspire her to return to Ireland, a factor that ran parallel to concerns for the safety of the British in Russia at the outset of the Anglo-Russian War. Martha's desire to return to her actual family was also a powerful force: in 1806, motivated by the support of her sister Katherine during her own visit to Russia, Martha would propose to Dashkova that she temporarily return to Ireland, as she wrote, 'even for one year', but the idea 'was to produce anguish, which I know not how to combat [sic]'. The younger friend could not imagine remaining permanently removed from her actual kin, despite the pain it caused Dashkova, as she documented in her journal, 'everlasting separation like what this implys, is dreadful, & must not be'. See RIA MS 12 L 20, 'Tues'y 22nd [July 1806]', pp. 125–126.

Irish family, particularly one that appears to have cherished culture and literature in the home, differs significantly from those of the Russian women in Dashkova's immediate circle, despite their elevated class status. Martha compares the education of the women she meets with that which she experienced in her own upbringing in her journal. Writing of one of the Dashkova's close female relatives, who lives in an apartment in the grounds of Troitskoe: 'She does not know how to write, which circumstance proves the backwardness of education here, as she was born to a good fortune, & is of a first rate family.'[22] Though Martha's observation is, in this case, based on a woman of 'good fortune', the woman's educational experience reflects that of the vast majority of women in Russia, as illiteracy ranged far and wide across social classes throughout the nineteenth century. According to one estimate, women's literacy rates in Russia only reached 14 per cent by as late as 1890, whereas Britain achieved a 40 per cent women's literacy rate by 1790.[23] Dashkova's respect for the Wilmots is surely also furthered by her own long held appreciation for the British, as well as their educational systems, having accompanied her son to Britain in order that he could complete his studies at Edinburgh University in the 1770s.[24] If Dashkova's appraisal of Martha's worth was due in part to her Britishness, she was not alone in valuing collaboration between the two nations in the eighteenth century. As Anthony Brough wrote in a pamphlet in 1798:

> There is no nation on the records of history that has so rapidly risen from a state of darkness and barbarism, to a great height of splendour and civilization, as the Russians have done during this century. The causes of this rapid and wonderful change have been many; but I would venture to affirm, that her intercourse with Great-Britain has been the greatest.[25]

Dashkova's invitation to Martha to form a pseudo-parent/child relationship, based on Martha's regard for the elder woman as a 'superior being', can also be contextualised through political and familial hierarchies. Martha's respect for Dashkova as both a royal and intellectual being simultaneously elevates her 'reverence' for the elder woman as a parental figure in a

---

[22] RIA MS 12 L 18, 'Saturday 14th [January 1804]', pp. 34–35.
[23] Linda Clark, *Women and Achievement in Nineteenth-Century Europe* (Cambridge, 2008), p. 40.
[24] Woronzoff-Dashkoff, pp. 128–130; Dashkova was resident in Britain throughout her son's seven-year period of study.
[25] Anthony Brough, *View of the Importance of the Trade between Great Britain and Russia* (London, 1789), p. 45.

classic embodiment of the long-standing structures of filial and noble dominance.[26] Dashkova's obvious role model for navigating an unequal power dynamic within the bounds of an intimate mentorship would have been based on her own foundational relationship with Catherine II, particularly in light of her early marriage and subsequent youthful widowhood. In her memoir, Dashkova wrote of the influence of Catherine II as a mentor and role model, indicating that their connection was reciprocally beneficial, despite the skewed balance of hierarchical power. As she described one conversation on the subject of their relationship shortly after Catherine II's rise to power in 1762:

> The empress, in her own peculiar tone of kindness, turned to me, and said, 'What can I ever do to testify the sense I have of your services?' 'Enough', said I, 'to make me the happiest of mortals; to be a mother to my country, and let me still live in your friendship.' 'All that', said she, 'is merely my duty; but I want to diminish this weight of gratitude which I feel.' 'I was in hopes', replied I, 'that offices of friendship could never be felt as a burden.' 'Well, well', said she, embracing me, 'you may tax me with what you please, but I shall never be at rest till you tell me, and I must this very instant know, what I can do to give you pleasure.'[27]

The recorded memory of this conversation indicates a great deal about the way Dashkova perceived both mentorship and friendship. While Catherine II attached an economic language of repayment, taxation and exchange to their relationship, Dashkova maintained an idealised notion of surrogate role modelling. This fidelity is given in turn back to Dashkova as a mentee, creating a circular pattern of affection. Catherine II later discarded Dashkova – yet despite this sudden fall from favour and the more powerful woman's seeming change of heart, Dashkova remained devoted to her. Dashkova's formative connection to Catherine II provides the backdrop for her burgeoning relationship with Martha, which is similarly imbued with emotional, literary and political undertones. The elder woman, however, clearly offers a more affectionate and supportive form of mentorship than that which she had experienced in her own youth.

Katherine notes that Dashkova's stately house is adorned with images of the former leader:

---

[26] See Lynn Hunt, *The Family Romance of the French Revolution* (Berkeley, 1992), p. 3; and Naomi Tadmor, 'The Concept of the Household-Family in Eighteenth-Century England', *Past & Present*, 151 (1996), 111–140, p. 112.
[27] *Memoirs*, II, p. 99.

the principle reception room at Troitska is ornamented with an immense picture of Catherine on Horseback in Uniform taken the very day of her husband's destruction, & the Pss says a perfect resemblance. Besides this, there are Portraits of her in Every room [sic].[28]

The many images of Catherine II that cover the walls allow Dashkova to stay close to her memories of intimacy with the Empress, and often lead her to nostalgic recollections of their personal relationship, as Katherine recounts: 'her mind wanders so naturally back to the Court & Study & Toilet & Boudoir of Catherine that I am beginning to fancy I recollect her habits of life & conversation.'[29] Textual remnants prove central to awakening Dashkova's intensely sentimental remembrances. Katherine describes returning to Troitskoe one evening to find Dashkova sitting with a 'great paper parcel ... the successive Correspondence that pass'd between her & Catherine 2d from the time she was 18 years of age till she resign'd the Academy.'[30] The reading aloud of these letters causes 'a painful sort of agitated animation to her Countenance', a result, Katherine perceives, 'of ripping up a life almost past.'[31] These performances of friendship with Catherine II are deeply embedded within a material form of written correspondence, highlighting the significant value of Dashkova's significant collection of manuscripts, which she amassed throughout the course of her life.

The Wilmots' recognition of the historically important narratives and documents to which they are exposed at Troitskoe is certainly related to the growing role that women were playing throughout the eighteenth century as both readers – and writers – of history. Most likely beginning their historical education as girls within their childhood home, both Martha and Katherine would be aware of the sanctioned status of history as a genre through which women could, cautiously, engage with the world. While women generally did not have a long list of reasons to travel far from home, an understanding of the world through the reading of ancient and modern history was encouraged. The reading of history represented a 'substitute for experience, standing in for those parts of the world that "ladies" should not see'.[32] History was a developing mode of enquiry and engagement for girls in the late eighteenth century, as evidenced by the proliferation of educational publications such as *Mentoria: or, The Young Ladies Instructor*,

---

[28] RIA MS 12 L 30, 'KW to Anna Chetwood, 1st Oct 1805', p. 45.
[29] Ibid, p. 45.
[30] RIA MS 12 L 30, 'KW to sister Alicia, Dec 2nd 1805', p. 61.
[31] RIA MS 12 L 30, 'KW to sister Alicia, Dec 2nd 1805', p. 61.
[32] Devoney Looser, *British Women Writers and the Writing of History, 1670–1820* (Baltimore, 2000), p. 18.

in *Familiar Conversations*, first published in 1776 and later revised in 1791. Its author, Ann Murry, extols the benefits of making history a young lady's 'peculiar study', and lists the most beneficial topics of history for ladies as 'sacred history, biography, natural history and ancient history'.[33] The focus placed onto history as an indispensable discipline in girls' education led to more women engaging with history as a form of literary production. Murry, for instance, engaged in the writing of ancient and sacred history herself, composing a multi-volume work in 1783 entitled *The Concise History of the Kingdoms of Israel and Judah; Connected with the History or Chief Events of the Neighbouring States and Succeeding Empires to the Time of Christ.*[34] History's illustrious status as an immortal and essential discipline, yet one that was deemed relatively appropriate for the consumption of women, appealed to women who wished to contribute to the general improvement of knowledge within society.[35]

Martha's biographical writing at Troitskoe – seen in her letters, diaries and through her copyist practices as Dashkova's amanuensis – responds to a perceived climate of misinformation surrounding both Dashkova and Catherine II's historical legacies. In April 1804, for instance, Dashkova encourages Martha to participate in the manufacture of public statements that she is writing in relation to Catherine II. Martha notes helping Dashkova to prepare correspondence for the press: 'today she has requested me to copy some notes, in which she wrote on the margins of a French author entitled "vie de Catherine 2d of Russia" where he asserts so many falsehoods that she could not resist refuting those'.[36] After Martha performs the requested task to a suitable order, Dashkova apparently allows or requests her to transform the notes into a refutation: 'begun to write the observations of the french Mans, Life of Kath: 2d this morng [sic]'.[37] Participation in publicly orientated literary work lays the foundation for Martha's later work as editor of Dashkova's *Memoirs* following the elder friend's death.

Dashkova's drive to correct her own defamed reputation, as well as her desire to pay homage to Catherine as a friend and sovereign are among the

---

[33] Ann Murry, *Mentoria: or, The Young Ladies Instructor, in Familiar Conversations on Moral and Entertaining Subjects* (London, 1791), p. 119.

[34] Ann Murry, *The Concise History of the Kingdoms of Israel and Judah; Connected with the History or Chief Events of the Neighbouring States and Succeeding Empires to the Time of Christ* (London, 1783).

[35] For more on this, see Chapter 4, pp. 139–142.

[36] RIA MS 12 L 18, 'Monday 9th [April 1804]', p. 105; for the biography of Catherine II noted here, see Jean Henri Castera, *Vie de Catherine II, Imperatrice de Russie*, 2 vols (Paris, 1797).

[37] RIA MS 12 L 18, 'Tues.y 10th [April 1804], p. 106.

central motives for the memoir project. For A. Woronzoff-Dashkoff, Dashkova's 'decision to write an autobiography was primarily a response to the inaccurate manner in which others had inscribed her life with Catherine [II]'.[38] However, Martha's motivating presence cannot be underestimated. In their study of women's poetry in the period, Paula Backscheider and Catherine Ingrassia write that to understand eighteenth-century 'women's social interaction, literary bonds, and ultimately, poetic production', one must consider the ways in which female friendship 'profoundly shaped their conception of a personal and poetic self'.[39] It is Martha's intimate bond with Dashkova, as well as the substantial labours of herself and Katherine as literary assistants, which not only encourages the work's production but also ensures its survival and eventual publication.

Sociability and Fair-Copy Publication in Ireland

Martha's exceptional position as Dashkova's guest is not lost on her family remaining in Ireland. International travel would be a matter of note for any young English or Irish woman; yet Martha's journey to Russia is unusual for going so far beyond the boundaries of the conventional European Grand Tour, and particularly as the guest of a noblewoman with close ties to Catherine II. Martha proves to be a prolific correspondent from the early days of her journey. The letters she sends home to family and friends in Glanmire, near Cork, are animated by the exotic foreign scenes of her journey to and residence in Russia. Katherine's journey to Russia in 1805 furthers the remarkable set of circumstances that the Wilmot family can claim. Steps to collect the written records of the sisters' journeys are soon commenced in earnest by their female relatives.

Mary Wilmot, their mother, undertakes the task of collecting, collating and transcribing Martha's extensive body of letters. The inscription on the inside cover of the journal which now contains her gathered correspondence reads 'Martha Wilmot's Letters from Russia (Copied by her Mother), from Ap. 1803 – to Oc: 1806 [*sic*]'.[40] Today, the collection sits within a bound marbled notebook. The binding appears to have been added to the sheaf of papers at a later date, suggesting that Mary's recognition of the

---

[38] Woronzoff-Dashkoff, p. 269.
[39] Paula Backscheider and Catherine E. Ingrassia, *British Women Poets of the Long Eighteenth Century: An Anthology* (Baltimore, 2009), p. 303.
[40] RIA MS 12 L 24, Martha Bradford née Wilmot letters from Russia, p. 1; original punctuation maintained.

narrative capacity of the letters as a set may have emerged over time.[41] Following the departure of Katherine to Russia in 1805, younger sister Alicia repeats the same process of collection, beginning a fresh notebook to hold Katherine's travel letters. This book contains the inscription, 'Alicia Wilmot, Cork, September 31st, 1805 – Begun to transcribe K. W's letters from Russia.'[42] Alicia records an index of the letters on the first page of notebook, a list that she adds to with each new arrival to come into her hands, some of which are copied into the volume out of order. Katherine gives a sense of how the letters are creating a complete work – which can be read as a *book*: writing to another sister, Harriet, in August 1805, she refuses to recount the recent days of her journey, having followed the exact same route as Martha: 'for when that book of M.'s lies before you, a description of either persons or places would be absolutely a work of supererogation.'[43] The two manuscripts likely take a cue from Katherine's earlier epistolary manuscript travelogue of 1801–03, which by this time was already circulating among family, friends and other readers. Mary and Alicia's copy work involves the wait for the letters to arrive, the collection of letters sent to various family and friends outside the family home, the task of writing fair copies, as well as the letters' eventual return to their rightful recipients. The writing accumulated by their labour transforms Martha and Katherine's loose correspondence into epistolary narratives that may be preserved and shared as cohesive texts.

From the family home in Ireland, Alicia and Mary Wilmot are central to the scribal practices of the Wilmot coterie. Alicia never, it seems, went abroad on her own Tour, though she was a favourite correspondent for both Martha and Katherine.[44] This may have been due to her ill health, which Martha records from time to time, such as when leaving Ireland for Russia in 1803, wherein she also mentions her mother's fragile health when writing of the difficulty of separation:

> My Mother far from being well, tho' much recover'd of the nervous attack which the influenza brought on, I wonder how I found courage to go thro' the scene, & can only account for it by the uncertainty I was

---

[41] Ibid.
[42] RIA MS 12 L 30, Katherine Wilmot letters from Russia, p. 1.
[43] *Memoirs*, II, p. 318.
[44] Martha Wilmot's 1798 Irish Rebellion journal notes that Alicia was among the party fleeing Ireland in fear of an uprising. The family remained temporarily in Brompton, England, until the threat of violence subsided. As previously noted, this journal is held in the Blair Adam House Collection.

kept in, to the last house, of Alicia's being well enough to accompany me to Dublin, or not.[45]

If the prospect of a trip to Dublin from Cork was potentially too damaging to Alicia's health to be risked, it is possible to imagine the importance the younger sister might affix to Martha's letters sent home from abroad, as well as her own recognition of her role in the transcription process.[46] Clare Brant describes the ability of travel letters to transport readers as 'a suspension of self', noting that 'the intersubjectivity of letters gave travels an extra cultural charge and one that resists turning solely on difference'.[47] What can be understood as a transformational experience for the reader here proves even truer for the transcriber, who intimately engages with the material textuality of the journey.

The fair-copy texts produced by the Wilmot women were each created for distinctive purposes and can be understood within active networks of manuscript circulation. As Harold Love writes in his seminal work on scribal publication, 'when we speak today of an unpublished manuscript we mean an unprinted manuscript', cautioning that when assessing historic manuscripts it is vital to 'consider how handwritten texts are to be classed as published or unpublished within a culture in which scribal transmission might be chosen without any sense of its being inferior or incomplete'.[48] Love's distinctions characterise seventeenth-century manuscript production rather than late eighteenth-century epistolary production. In his view, the rise of print effectively abolished the need for manuscripts by the late eighteenth and early nineteenth centuries.[49] However, Love's timeline has been disproven by subsequent scholarship on manuscript culture the late

---

[45] RIA MS 12 L 17, '12th of April 1803', pp. 1–2.
[46] Alicia's constitution was a recurring theme: in August 1809, Martha accompanied her to Bantry for sea-bathing to improve her health. See Beinecke OSB MSS 54, Box 3 f.151, 'Bantry, 10th August 1809', 1r.
[47] Clare Brant, *Eighteenth-Century Letters and British Culture* (Basingstoke, 2006), p. 244.
[48] Harold Love, *Scribal Publication in Seventeenth-Century England* (Oxford, 1993), p. 35.
[49] Nicolas Barker revises Love's end point, suggesting that the birth of manuscript culture must be defined in relation to the rise of the printing press in the sixteenth century, a historical moment in which manuscripts circulated as a concurrent form of communication 'linking writers with readers through a system of diffusion, that all its participants cultivated'; See Nicolas Barker, 'In Praise of Manuscripts', in *Form and Meaning in the History of the Book: Selected Essays* (London, 2003), p. 27.

eighteenth century and Romantic period.[50] Important recent studies of manuscript culture in the late eighteenth century have repositioned the creation of manuscript texts and their circulation as a vital and on-going practice that spurred literary exchange and developed new genres.[51] Such revaluations of manuscript circulation reframe the practices of the Wilmots and their networks as acts central rather than peripheral to cultural production.

The hand-copied epistolary narratives assembled by the Wilmot women who remain in Ireland raise significant questions about collaborative practices of scribal publication among groups of lesser-known women writers. These include those who transcribed for one another from within the parameters of the family, from a middle or upper-middle class status, or from the provincial fringes. As Ezell has written, 'When we come to look at social or provincial writers, we do so only through a previously determined set of expectations; the analysis we do of them tends to isolate and fragment the literary culture in which they participate.'[52] Melanie Bigold pushes against the narrative that the print marketplace represented a lesser accomplishment for women in the eighteenth century, suggesting instead that we might approach the 'period from a more holistic point of view – one that recognises that there was a form of social authorship wider than the print market … not only were women not silent, but that they were much more prolific and involved than is generally assumed.'[53] Such nuanced historical suppositions work to dispel persistent notions of a stigma of print for women in the period, which have long suggested that women merely didn't publish due to the taint of exposure. What role might the compilation of manuscripts play in the Wilmot women's collective sense of themselves as literary agents, engaging not only with their own sociable circle, but also with the transnational subject matter they laboured on?

The Wilmot family's literary activities run parallel to emerging and established systems of reading and communication available to women in

---

[50] See, for example, *Women's Writing and the Circulation of Ideas: Manuscript Publication in England, 1550–1800*, ed. by George L. Justice and Nathan Tinker (Cambridge, 2002); Michelle Levy, *Family Authorship and Romantic Print Culture* (Basingstoke, 2008); Michelle Levy, *Literary Manuscript Culture in Romantic Britain* (Edinburgh, 2021).

[51] See Rachael Scarborough King, *After Print: Eighteenth-Century Manuscript Cultures* (Charlottesville, 2020).

[52] Ezell, p. 4.

[53] Melanie Bigold, *Women of Letters, Manuscript Circulation, and Print Afterlives in the Eighteenth Century: Elizabeth Rowe, Catherine Cockburn, and Elizabeth Carter* (Basingstoke, 2013), p. 7.

Ireland in the period. Though women's debating societies sprung up as official forums in London from the 1770s–1790s, provincial examples of book collecting clubs and reading societies can be located throughout the eighteenth century.[54] The difficulty in attaining books in Ireland as late as the early nineteenth century in provincial Ireland left readers feeling 'starved of literature' due to the 'high price of books and newspapers' and the fact that there was 'almost nowhere to buy them' outside of Dublin.[55] The lack of available literature led to endeavours to secure books for local communities through the collective formation of subscription libraries. There is evidence of the trend as popular among women in Ireland, with one group of women in Cork attempting to establish a circulating library in 1794, advertising for members in the local newspaper.[56] Circulation libraries, historically established and organised in order to propagate the circulation of more rarefied texts that would form an enduring resource for the reading community, may or may not have been exclusionary to women readers.[57] In all likelihood the audience to which the sisters' letters are exposed in their absence is formed by the Wilmot women's extended familial and social circle, rather than a formal intellectual or debating society. The practice of reading letters and books aloud was common among the middle and upper-middle classes, whether as a method of collective education or as an aid to conversational sociability.[58] The collection of the Wilmot letters from recipients and subsequent hand-copying ensures the letters will be preserved for future enjoyment by the transcriber, in this case the Wilmot family. It also ensures that the letters can be safely circulated as a whole to an extended circle, included as fixtures of social interactions for collective enjoyment with a lowered risk of loss or damage to the originals. The regularity of the letters, pieced together, creates a developing

---

[54] For more, see Amanda Vickery, *The Gentleman's Daughter: Women's Lives in Georgian England* (New Haven, 1998), pp. 10, 257.

[55] Marie-Louise Legg, 'The Kilkenny Circulating-Library Society and the Growth of Reading Rooms in Nineteenth-Century Ireland', in *The Experience of Reading: Irish Historical Perspectives*, ed. by Bernadette Cunningham and Máire Kennedy (Dublin, 1999), p. 109.

[56] According to Máire Kennedy, 'Surviving membership lists and rules of societies show that women played a very small role in them: in some they were not allowed membership, in others they had no deciding power'; see Máire Kennedy, 'Women and Reading in Eighteenth-Century Ireland', in *The Experience of Reading: Irish Historical Perspectives*, ed. by Bernadette Cunningham and Máire Kennedy (Dublin, 1999), p. 83.

[57] Kennedy, p. 83.

[58] See Abigail Williams, *The Social Life of Books: Reading Together in the Eighteenth-Century Home* (New Haven, 2017).

travelogue, and a fascinating view of the foreign land into which Martha and Katherine are integrating, providing useful entertainment and educational value for the reader or, as the Wilmot women apparently intend, for the listener.

The sociable sharing of original writing was held as a valuable form of entertainment and education.[59] Though no direct allusions are made in writing to Martha's and Katherine's letters being read aloud during their absence, assumptions about the reading of their fair-copied travelogues can be made by viewing Martha's later behaviour with the same bound notebooks following her return from Russia in 1808, using them for sociable purposes. As Martha's early biographers write:

> If the interest of a party ever showed any signs of flagging, a Russian song and dance skilfully executed by Martha or a few selections from Catherine's diary of her adventures of the Continent, read by one of the members of the party, invariably commanded the attention and applause of the others.[60]

The Wilmot sisters' tendency to share their manuscript travelogues within an extended circle of readers, whether through performances as they travelled or visited friends and relations in Ireland and abroad, or in circulation as fair copies, also provided another mode of sharing their literary efforts. In Bath in 1812, for instance, several years after the Wilmot sisters return from Russia, Lady Stanley wrote in a letter 'I am now reading two manuscript tours, most entertaining and interesting, written by a Miss Wilmot', noting that Martha has loaned her the copied manuscript 'tours on condition of keeping the secret'.[61] Yet this anecdote, along with countless other instances of the Wilmots' circulation of the texts authored and scribally published within the family, indicates a sophisticated network of transmission rather than one of secrecy or limitation. Far from being created for merely private family enjoyment, these examples display the benefits of elevated sociable and literary status that the Wilmot sisters, and

---

[59] As Davidoff and Hall note, 'writing, whether in journal, diaries, letters, memoirs, poetry or prose, was a favoured occupation for large numbers of women and men ... the vast majority of whom wrote for their own pleasure and edification and that of their family and friends'; see Leonore Davidoff and Catherine Hall, *Family Fortunes: Men and Women of the English Middle Class 1780–1850* (London, 1992), p. 162.

[60] H. N. Hyde and the Marchioness of Londonderry, 'Introduction', in Martha Wilmot and Catherine Wilmot, *The Russian Journals of Martha and Catherine Wilmot* (London, 1935), pp. xx–xxi.

[61] Maria Josepha Lady Stanley, *The Early Married Life of Maria Josepha Lady Stanley* (New York, 1899), p. 332.

by extension, their family, enjoyed as a result of the writing they collectively composed and collated through scribal publication.

Though the scribal copies produced by the Wilmot women in Ireland are not initially planned for publication in the print marketplace, their efforts tending towards what Love classifies as 'soft publication' of a social variety, the dual collections of travelogue-like letters fit in with the growing standards of similar works in the genre which had seen proper publication, thus making it easily transferrable for social introduction. Zoë Kinsley, in her study of the British women's home tour, has outlined how manuscript publication could enable rather than 'stifle' creativity.[62] For Susan Whyman, 'one of the ways in which travelogues developed was in private letters and journals'.[63] Letters, especially travel letters, were held to a different standard of quality than other forms of writing. Given the widespread appeal of travel literature throughout the eighteenth century, travel letters were as one genre in which experience itself could often adequately denote qualification, regardless of formal training or previous authorship. Lived experience and miles travelled bolstered the authority of Martha and Katherine, who lacked literary credentials but whose letters describe foreign scenes, especially given that 'by the 1770s ... public authorship had become openly accepted for women of lesser abilities'.[64] Travel literature was, in fact, an increasingly viable arena for women authors in the late eighteenth century. According to Katherine Turner, 'the years between 1770 and 1800 see the publication of around twenty travelogues by women, including several voyage narratives'.[65] The statistic, however, is likely nowhere near the total number of manuscript tours written and circulated by women in the late eighteenth century, whether epistolary or otherwise.

Although scribal practices were no longer specifically a physical or economic necessity by the late eighteenth century, they answered the needs of the Wilmots' familial and social circle, defined by associations of gender, class and geographical proximity. Allowing the homemade texts to 'define communities of the like-minded' through the parameters of circulation, the fair-copy publication method chosen by the Wilmot women who remained in Ireland could not only be easily shared, but also reasonably well controlled, while still achieving a sociable persona founded on agency and authorship.[66] This choice to limit readership is the point at which a distinction can be

---

[62] Zoë Kinsley, *Women Writing the Home Tour, 1682–1812* (Aldershot, 2008), p. 54.
[63] Susan E. Whyman, *The Pen and the People: English Letters Writers 1660–1800* (Oxford, 2009), p. 195.
[64] Whyman, p. 189.
[65] Turner, p. 125.
[66] Love, p. 33.

drawn between the scribal publication practices Alicia and Mary Wilmot perform in Ireland and the transcription work begun by Martha and Katherine in Russia on Dashkova's memoirs, correspondence with Catherine II and other manuscript papers around the same period. As the next section shows, the historical importance of Dashkova's memoirs and presumed interest of a wider readership imbues the Wilmot sisters' own scribal publication practices with markedly different pressures and meanings.

Transnational Collaboration and Literary Apprenticeship

The dynamic of literary mentoring intended to enable entrance to the public literary marketplace was a common feature of coteries in the period. Julia M. Wright, in her work on the Sheridan-Lefanu circle, notes how 'intergenerational mentorships' function 'in the interstices between public and private spheres through a fortuitous confluence'.[67] In these tasks, Dashkova offers guidance to the sisters, knowing that the outcome of these efforts will not only secure her legacy, but that it may also give the younger women a foothold in the republic of letters. Martha's description of the co-writing process at Troitskoe highlights how text and friendship are interwoven. In Dashkova's cabinet, they work side by side, the elder woman writing as the younger woman copies. As Martha records in a pen portrait of an average day at Troitskoe:

> wrote for half an hour in the P.'s cabinet, and have finish'd copying the 1st vol: of her history – and a little Russ – Dress'd, dined, after Dinner read a newspaper for P. D. – who took a *Sciesto* [sic] [rest] – wrote a few lines in her history not to break the regular rule – then read Voltaire.[68]

Frequently, Dashkova would 'take the pen out of my hand and write a line or two herself'.[69] Chirographic examples of these moments of shared scribal duties are evident in Martha's copy of the manuscript. Distinctions between the women's writing can be made by the difference in their penmanship: Martha's forward-leaning scrawl is tidy and more easily legible, with thin, angular lettering and a softer tone of brown ink, while Dashkova's

---

[67] Julia M. Wright, '"All the Fire-Side Circle": Irish Women Writers and the Sheridan Lefanu Coterie', *Keats-Shelley Journal*, 55 (2004), 63–72, pp. 65, 72.
[68] RIA MS 12 L 19, 'Friday 28th [June 1805]', p. 85; author's own translation.
[69] BL Add MS 31911, p. 1; examples of Dashkova writing several lines herself can be found throughout the manuscript, see, for instance, p. 48.

thick applications of dark brown ink have a messy and rounded fullness to them.[70] Dashkova's handwriting typically begins near the end of a page, as if temporarily alleviating Martha's copying duties, often continuing through several subsequent leaves.[71] These two writing styles are distinguishable from Martha's editorial changes made at a later date, when full sentences are carefully crossed out, with a revision written above in a smaller version of the same handwriting, often made in pencil or black ink. Dashkova also seemingly interrupts her assistant's work to make additions throughout the copying work, squeezing further sentences above or below an existing anecdote copied by Martha.[72] These revisions would have been fairly immediate, as Martha claims to have copied the materials almost simultaneously.

The air of collaboration and intimate friendship grants Martha a growing agency, leading her to commence transcription projects on other texts previously written by Dashkova, with the work in progress or end results circulated within Dashkova's sociable circle in Moscow. An example of this can be read in Martha's transcription and circulation of a tour of the Scottish Highlands, which she apparently finds among Dashkova's private papers in either 1803 or 1804.[73] The travelogue was originally composed between August and September 1777 during Dashkova's temporary residence in Scotland, while her son was enrolled at university in Edinburgh. Dashkova's travelogue may have been inspired by Samuel Johnson's own tour of the Highlands a few years earlier.[74] The journey took her to a region that, according to Anthony Cross, was 'not known to have been visited by any other Russia visitors in the eighteenth ... or nineteenth centuries'.[75] Martha's practised hand at transcription work, as well as her own interest in retaining a copy of the tour for her future use, compels her to create a fair copy from the original manuscript, which was written in French. Martha records the first mention of this project in her diary in March 1805, noting the afterlife of the transcribed text as a sociable tool. Having previously

---

[70] A list of places where Dashkova's handwriting appears is bound in with the title page of the manuscript. Martha's daughter created this list at the time of the manuscript's insertion into the British Museum in 1882. The list was intended to bolster the provenance of the manuscript and prove the veracity of Martha's version of events leading up to its creation. See BL Add MS 31911, f. 002v.
[71] For an example, see BL Add MS 31911, pp. 63–64.
[72] See BL Add MS 31911, p. 42r for an added anecdote on the royal habit of keeping one's money in one's pocket during gambling at the Imperial Palace.
[73] For a print version of this tour, see H. Montgomery Hyde, *The Empress Catherine and Princess Dashkov* (London, 1935).
[74] Samuel Johnson, *A Journey to the Western Islands of Scotland* (London, 1775).
[75] Anthony Cross, 'Poezdka kniagni E. R. Dashkovoi (1776–1780)', trans. by I. D. Levin, *XVIII*, 19 (1995), 223–260, p. 230.

circulated the text, Martha is delighted to find that Salvatore Tonci, an Italian painter of historical portraiture who had recently painted a retrospective portrait of Dashkova in exile, has added illustrations to her new version of the manuscript:

> Tonce [sic] also ... shew'd me a little manuscript book, cover'd with Marble paper, which I have lent him, as he wish'd to read Princess Daschkaw's Tour thro the Highlands of Scotland, that I had copied into it, this book he has so transmogrified by drawing groups of the most extravagant figures, moreover his ever ready imagination caught an idea in the caprices of the marble cover, that he has made it quite an amusement, & an everlasting monument.[76]

The 'little manuscript book' is unfortunately not among the extant archival materials that Martha collected and created in Russia; however, Martha produced a further copy of Dashkova's highland tour, dated 1804, though it is sadly not illustrated.[77] Nonetheless, the above description gives insight into the different types of collaboration in which she engages with other members of Dashkova's cultural circle. Perhaps not viewing her own scribal work of the Scottish tour as remarkable in the first instance, here it is her ability to pair the notebook with Tonci's handiwork that transforms the object into 'an everlasting monument'. Such successes provide motivation to take on further literary transcription projects, as well as to continue to draw on the special manuscript material and social contacts within her reach in Russia.

Following her own arrival in Russia in September 1805, Katherine Wilmot quickly becomes an active participant in the on-going literary work at Troitskoe. Dashkova reads aloud from her correspondence with Catherine II as a way of introducing the new arrival to her relationship with the Empress. As Martha writes shortly after Katherine's arrival, 'Tonight I again heard the Empress Katherines letters to the Princess D who read them for Kitty – & again I admired her spirited, charming style of writing [sic]'.[78] Martha writes in her diary of the letters that 'Many of them were written while [Catherine] was Ld Dutchess, & those letters, are in the most peaceful easy style of friend correspondence'; a tone that is contrasted with the one used by Catherine II '[a]fter she became Empress, her style changed into more measured phrases, & greater formality'.[79] Katherine creates scribal

[76] RIA MS 12 L 19, 'Saturday 12th [March 1805]', p. 50.
[77] BAHC, 'Contents of the Letter File of Princess Dashkoff'.
[78] RIA MS 12 L 19, 'Sunday 30th [November 1805]', p. 126.
[79] RIA MS 12 L 18, 'Tuesday 7th [May 1804]', pp. 124–125.

copies of the Catherine II correspondence while resident at Troitskoe, later taking the copies out of the country with her.[80] Martha documents in her diary that she and Katherine spend their evenings at Troitskoe, 'reading out the Copy of the Princesses History & comparing it with the original, which is a very disagreeable way of reading it, but necessary'.[81] The Wilmot sisters clearly see the letters as valuable proof of Dashkova's special relationship with Catherine II, understanding that their inclusion in any future publication will validate Dashkova's claims while also enhancing the overall appeal of the memoir due to its association with the Empress. Their efforts to compile materials from Dashkova's archives preconfigure the structure of *Memoirs*, where the letters, translated into English, will be reproduced in print.

Scribal practices at Troitskoe required a high level of language acquisition due to the fact that the majority of the manuscripts in Dashkova's possession were written originally in French or Russian. Despite an imperfect mastery of French, Martha intends to create a full translation of the manuscript herself. She is initially confident about her French translation skill set, declaring in March 1804 'I have begun to translate into English the dear Princess's history, as she writes it in french [sic]'.[82] She later revises her language in her journal, writing: 'I am very much engaged in writing, copying the Memoirs of the Princesses life, as she writes them, & then trying to translate them into English [sic]', modifying the earlier claim of 'translat[ing]' to 'trying to translate'.[83] Martha soon passes the task of translation to her sister, whose knowledge of French is somewhat more advanced. As Martha notes in her journal in the spring of 1806, 'I write (I should say I copy) the Princesses History, every day – Kitty translates it and that occupies both our mornings [sic]', and 'K is continually employ'd when alone, in translating P's history [sic]'.[84]

The self-conscious attempts of both sisters to operate in French during their time in Russia nearly equal the considerable difficulties and demands for use of the language that Katherine had encountered during 1801–03 in France. As Martha recalled years later in her travelogue supplement to *Memoirs*, Dashkova placed an immediate priority on being able to speak French from the time of Martha's arrival. Martha noted the instructions

---

[80] BL Add MS 31911, f. 214: 'Letters of the Empress Catherine II. to the Princess, circ. 1762–1794; Transcripts by Miss Kitty Wilmot'.
[81] RIA NS 12 L 19, p. 114.
[82] RIA MS 12 L 18, '29 March 1804', p. 99.
[83] Ibid, p. 104
[84] RIA MS 12 L 20, 'Tuesday 19th [April 1806]', p. 99; 'Tuesday 6th [May 1806]', p. 103.

that Dashkova gave her, and also the role that the elder woman took on in facilitating her protégée's linguistic education:

> As French would be the language I should hear in all companies, I ought to accustom myself to the familiar sound and use of it, and that she would be my instructress. For this purpose she desired me to write her a note every morning, as an exercise, which she would correct and send back to me. We continued this practice for several months, and I preserved the exercises, with her comments upon them, as memorials of her affection and goodness to me.[85]

The status of French as an Enlightenment export had long influenced the Russian court as well as the intellectual elite, permeating Russian society. 'French was a powerful means of negotiation, exchange and transfer in European space', note Gesine Argent, Derek Offord and Vladislav Rjéoutski. 'It pervaded the spheres of diplomacy, science, learning, art, literature, and other forms of culture.'[86] The use of French as a sociable and diplomatic language ensured that a channel of exchange remained open between Russia and Western Europe. Russia was not alone in adopting French as a language for Enlightenment networks, though the country's geographical location on the fringe of European society meant that 'Russia was affected strongly – or even to an exceptional degree, some would argue – by this cultural and linguistic influence.'[87] Katherine's commentary on the French-speaking Muscovites at the Russian court details the awkward atmosphere invoked by the artificial import of French language and culture as a societal mode of operation:

> though a sort of French exterior is universal, and the French language the language of society, the dress the same, and the youngers educated by French mademoiselles and French abbés, yet they are for the most part ... obviously imitators, and, as such, overacting the externals, without have the slightest pretention to that soothing suavity of manner so generally prevalent and pleasing in France.[88]

Despite this judgemental description of the false French environment dominant in Russia, both Katherine and Martha go to great lengths to

---

[85] *Memoirs*, II, p. 229.
[86] Gesine Argent, Derek Offord and Vladislav Rjéoutski, 'French Language Acquisition in Imperial Russia', in *Вивлioѳика: E-Journal of Eighteenth-Century Russian Studies*, 1 (2013), 1–4, p. 1.
[87] Argent, Offord and Rjéoutski, p. 1.
[88] *Memoirs*, II, p. 362.

successfully integrate themselves within it. For the Wilmots, French-language skills are essential not only for solidifying relational bonds and mentorship with Dashkova, but also for successfully carrying out their literary practices.

Katherine's Russian journal documents the progression of her translation work relevant to the memoir. One month after she has begun, she writes: 'My translation will be finish'd in 6 weeks – having work'd (at 2 pages a day) 3 weeks at the 2.d Vol [sic]'.[89] She continues to document steady progress throughout November, writing 'these last Nine days I have gone on at my translation. I have only 50 pages to finish it [sic]'.[90] In December, she notes 'I finish'd the translation completely in the Evenging [sic]'.[91] The steady flow of pages implies a lack of intervention, with the focus placed on producing a quick copy. Following Katherine's completion of the translation project, her journal suddenly switches from English to French without any commentary as to why, and she continues to write in French until the journal's completion. This switch perhaps symbolises Katherine's sense of accomplishment in having finished the translation project, as well as underlining her daily use of French. It is important to note, however, that her French is far from elegant. Her sentence structures appear to be translated from English somewhat perfunctorily, rather than achieving fluidity, writing for example: 'nous avons souffert beaucoup dernièrement à cause du Silence de nos Parents en Ireland [sic]' ('we have suffered much recently due to the silence of our parents in Ireland)'.[92]

It is notable that no copy of Katherine's English translation of the memoir remains in the archives, particularly given her questionable level of French fluency. Martha refers to duplicating the translation in her journal in November 1806, writing 'begun yesterday to copy out Kitty's translation of the Princesses History, after having finish'd copying the same thing in French, & since that, all the Empress Katherines Letters to Princess Daschkaw [sic]'.[93] While the French translation and the copies of Catherine II's letters have been preserved, Katherine's translation or any of the multiple copies made of it are conspicuously absent.[94] Martha may have destroyed the translation following her realisation that its quality was not fit for publication. In doing so, Martha would have shielded Katherine's literary reputation for posterity. While the actual destruction of Katherine's

---

[89] RIA MS 12 L 31, 'Oct 26 1806', p. 1.
[90] Ibid, p. 1.
[91] Ibid, p. 3.
[92] RIA MS 12 L 31, 'Lundi le 30me [sic] de Mai', p. 50; my translation.
[93] RIA MS 12 L 20, 'Monday 9th Novr 1806', pp. 186–187.
[94] BL Add MS 31911.

English manuscript translation is impossible to prove, its missing presence among the surviving material matches other patterns of manipulation in the Wilmots' archives. As the next section shows, Martha's scribal practices created legacy through a proliferation of text, but the act of transcription could also be used as a corrective tool capable of censorship and revision.

Editing Scribally, Curating Legacy

The manuscripts created by the Wilmot sisters and their networks embody the collective textual practices of authors, copyists and many subsequent readers. These interventions span several decades and incorporate corrective measures to frame specific written legacies for individuals as well as the group at large. Viewed from the distance of history, non-print texts, such as manuscript compilations and miscellanies, can 'baffle our print-based habits of reading', as they 'resist our attempts at classification and interpretation'; yet amalgamated, script-based texts can also grant understanding of 'an earlier world of reading and producing the literary'.[95] Delving into the Wilmots' surviving papers offers just such an opportunity to reconnect with the literary practices that guided their sociability and travels.

A variety of manipulations are evident across the manuscripts, using several different techniques and to multiple ends. Minor changes were habitually made to fair copy manuscripts as they were produced. For example, Mary Wilmot frequently omitted details from Martha's letters as she copies them using a system of dashes. Such editorial snipping can be seen in many redacted passages in the bound book, such as in one letter addressed from Martha to her father.[96] These absent details may have been seen as too personal, or perhaps too trivial, to be included in the volume given its sociably orientated purpose, which included circulation and performative readings to the wider circle. Other modifications to the Wilmot family manuscripts appear to have been made for the purpose of continuing legibility. For instance, an underlying layer of ink or pencil frequently shadows darker lines. This can be seen throughout the manuscripts compiled by Mary and Alicia, the retracing done at a later date to prevent disappearance of the important texts due to age and wear.

More aggressive modes of censorship are also apparent in the scribal volumes of Martha and Katherine's travel letters from Russia. These changes

---

[95] Betty A. Schellenberg, *Literary Coteries and the Making of Modern Print Culture* (Cambridge, 2016), p. 206.
[96] RIA MS 12 L 24, p. 8.

Figure 6 Royal Irish Academy MS 12 L 24 'Ms in English, 1821–22, Martha Bradford (née Wilmot): Letters from Russia, April 1803–October 1806 (Copied by her mother)', p. 123. © Royal Irish Academy.

may have been made by Martha herself following her return to Ireland. Prominent dark black lines cut through the pages sporadically, inking out passages beyond recovery. These black lines often function in tandem with the dashed omissions originally embedded in the text by Martha's mother as she copied, giving a sense of the multigenerational and long-term editorial labour exacted on the fair copy volumes. Elsewhere, sections of the text appear to be rubbed away. In these sections, the paper is rough and crinkled, leaving a light but unreadable trace of obscured words, paragraphs and sentences. While some of these scoured down lines indicate a name or a private detail omitted, other lengthy blank spaces introduce mysterious gaps in the travel letters, which seem impossible to recover. One such example details a gift from Dashkova to Martha of £3,000 in cash.[97] The erasure of other lines surrounding the sum suggests that further gifts were given, and possibly of a higher value. Martha likely scours out these lines to circumvent future accusations of greed or impropriety, charges that may suggest financial motivations.

Other heavy-handed acts of censorship are evident in the manuscripts. This can be seen, for instance, in the scribal volume of Katherine's letters

[97] RIA MS 12 L 30, p. 40.

copied out by Alicia Wilmot. Writing to a friend on the eve of her departure from Russia, Katherine emphasises her low appraisal of the literary quality of Dashkova's manuscript, and comments negatively on the hierarchical circumstances under which it was produced:

> I don't think I am bringing home anything [rare or surprising] As for [word omitted] I will bring it about my own person – … has been finished these several weeks, but you need not expect to find it intelligible, 'till it has undergone a complete dislocation from begining [sic] to End – the Princess is perfectly content with it, because it is according to her own desire, … but in my opinion, it is not fit to read.[98]

Katherine's statement that she is not bringing home anything of value has been altered, the words 'rare and surprising' written over a patch of paper rubbed out, likely replacing a more derogatory comment thought to demean the quality of the manuscript. An entire section of the passage appears to have been previously hidden by another sheet of paper glued over the top, now removed. The covering paper was affixed over Katherine's most inflammatory comments: that the work itself was unintelligible, that it required a complete 'dislocation' to make it fit for reading, and, importantly, that despite its inherent deficiencies and lack of fluidity, Dashkova was nonetheless 'perfectly content with it'. This revision emphasises the terrain crossed by the Wilmots in their transition from Dashkova's mentees to editors responsible for the future of her text: an agency has been gained through textual apprenticeship that allows room for pointed criticism. The reason for this omission is clear, given that Katherine's bold statements might damage the manuscript's possibilities for publication while also reflecting negatively on Dashkova as an author, as well as the scribal and collaborative efforts of the Wilmots by proxy.

Subtler editorial strategies can be detected by comparing multiple scribal volumes of Katherine's letters from Russia. For Martha, the creation of new volumes of the sisters' writing, through scribal practices, also offers a revised narrative through textual alterations made during the transcription process. Martha begins a further transcription of Katherine's travel writing while touring through Ireland with Alicia in 1809, writing, 'I am copying Kitty's letters from Russian into a book, I write a page or two every morning before breakfast'.[99] Martha's transcription of the new book full of Russian letters is inspired by the success of recent readings of Katherine's

[98] RIA MS 12 L 30, 'To Anna Chetwood, Moscow, Feb.ry the 2d 1807', p. 148.
[99] BAHC Wilmot Box 1 Bundle 2, 2/8 'Typewritten copy of a second tour in Ireland by Martha Wilmot and her sister Alicia', 'Sunday 15th [October 1809]'.

French travelogue manuscript. A journal entry from ten days earlier while staying with friends in County Tipperary reads: 'in the evening I read out *Kitty's Journal*, thro' France, Italy, etc. etc. the poor dear old Major enjoys it more than *all* the rest of the Family.'[100] The benefits of the new book are soon proven, as Martha writes of its sociable debut on November 22nd, 'the greater part of the society assembled in the drawing-room and work'd while one read out Kitty's Letters from Russia. Mrs Galway's enjoyment of them is beyond all expression, indeed everyone seem'd charm'd, and Mrs Gough was in extacys [sic].'[101] Later, in December, Alicia and Martha arrive at a 'hospitable, gentlemanlike mansion'; after loaning the manuscript volume containing Katherine's letters to the lady of the house, they are read 'out to in full assembly'. Martha writes of growing 'so nervous that I quitted the room, and left Kate's fame to their mercy'.[102]

This convivial yet pressurised sharing of the fair-copy volumes gives the travel writing created by the Wilmots an attentive audience, a reception which apparently inspires Martha to make greater changes and omissions. Parallel versions of Katherine's letter written on the eve of her departure from Russia display an example of the way that the text is altered through copying. In the earlier version, Katherine notes that her luggage has been sent ahead to Ireland, 'so that you see I shall go to you literally naked as I was born.'[103] Martha revises this line to read 'so that you see I shall go to you as bare as a Thrush!', perhaps striving for elegance of style and general propriety.[104] More telling, though, are the changes made to the text describing the state of Dashkova's manuscript. In place of Katherine's damning comments that the memoir is not 'intelligible', requires 'a complete dislocation', and is not 'fit to be read', Martha's later scribal version merely reads: 'As for – – if it ever is to be published, it is to be illustrated with portraits of the Princess' (p. 85). Whereas the original comments were formerly censored with glue and paper, Katherine's unsavoury thoughts are here entirely redacted.

Martha's editorial censorship of the manuscripts can be seen as a function of criticism within the coterie, a fluid entity whose tasks, according to Betty A. Schellenberg, include practices of 'composition, circulation, and collaborative criticism of literary materials of its own.'[105] Martha's work

---

[100] BAHC, 2/8, 'Wednesday 4th [October 1809]'; the collection she copies is RIA MS 12 L 33.
[101] BAHC 2/8, 'Wednesday 22nd [November 1809]'.
[102] BAHC 2/8, 'Saturday evening 2nd December [1809]'; 'Monday 18th December [1809]'.
[103] RIA MS 12 L 30, p. 148.
[104] RIA MS 12 L 33, p. 85.
[105] Schellenberg, p. 210.

frequently revises unfavourable representations of Dashkova's personality, accomplishments and legacy, as well as the parameters of her relationship with the noblewoman, particularly when questions of authorship arise. Beyond the editing of the epistolary manuscript tours, which have a clear audience in their limited sociable circulation, Martha's interventions include reframing the Wilmot sisters' life writing from Troitskoe, even within the realm of their 'private' journals. Such changes most likely occurred both in the years leading up to and proceeding from the publication of Dashkova's *Memoirs*, as Martha became aware of the ways in which her own Russian journals could be connected with the Princess by posthumous readers and historians. For instance, a journal entry from January 1804 is notably censored to sanitise Martha's own misgivings about the intensity of her friendship with Dashkova, and her fears about remaining in Russia long-term:

> her affection & consideration for me, have a tenderness in them, that at times goes to my very heart – it makes me too, fear to look forward – gratitude is a strong chain & my feelings acknowledge its force, [*sic*] affection, too, is not I hope less sincere than the Princesses – yet, alone, separated from every relation, with new circumstances, people, dispositions to deal with, there are moments when I feel deeply my own insufficiency.[106]

Following this admission, a line of the journal has apparently been erased, the paper worn down to exclude the remark that follows. Martha's later editorial manipulation of her own manuscript omits this moment of brutal honesty. The safeguarding of Martha's perceived importance as Dashkova's intimate friend and literary collaborator is in turn essential to the overall importance of the Wilmots' literary networks, validating the collective scribal work of Katherine, Mary, and Alicia by association. The significant manipulations made to the fair-copy texts produced by the Wilmot women raise questions about what shape, size and significance the extant archives might have encompassed had they not been revised and corrected over several decades. At the same time, the editorial prowess that functions to create and manage their collective legacy is dually responsible for the survival of any of the material at all.

---

[106] RIA MS 12 L 18, 'Friday 30th March 1804', p. 100.

Exploring 'Foreign Climes'

In the pages of a commonplace book dating from 1782–1816 sits a lengthy poem addressed 'To Miss Wilmot, now Bradford, on her arrival from Russia.'[107] Written by its author 'when 12 years old', the poem breathlessly reflects on Martha Wilmot's epic six-year excursion to Russia, where she had stayed as a guest of the Russian noblewoman Princess Ekaterina Dashkova between 1803–08. 'Ye vagrant muses!', it begins, questioning Martha's choice to face such a difficult journey: 'Why tempt old Ocean's sullen, ceaseless, roar / A long seclusion from your native shore.'[108] The poet frames Martha as 'The sweet Matilda' exploring 'foreign climes', brandishing a shield of 'Innocence' and an armour of 'Truth'. Continuing across three pages, Martha braves tempests and chases 'from her soul nocturnal fears away'. Finally, she arrives back home, 'Blest in her talents, in her temper blest', with her 'cultured mind a blooming garden' – the fruits of her difficulty and the danger of her journey all justified in the learning and growth brought about by her experience.

The commonplace book was apparently used to collect and share poems by members of the Wilmot-Chetwood family's extended circle over a period of four decades. It was owned by Elizabeth Wilmot, Katherine and Martha's sister-in-law through their brother Robert.[109] The author of the poem in question is named only as 'F.S.I.' While her identity is not explicitly given, those in the family's extended circle who might read from or contribute to the commonplace book would have been able to put a name to the poem through other entries that serve as clues elsewhere in the bound volume. On the second page, for instance, a poem by 'Eyles Irwin, Esq'r' is titled 'Sonnet, on reading some of his daughter's poetry'. Irwin was an Indian-born Irish writer who had spent time in China in service to the East India Company, as well as being a member of the Royal Irish Academy. His daughter, Frances Sally Irwin – the F.S.I. whose prolific verses pepper the commonplace book – was born in 1795.[110] The other entries copied into

---

[107] Senate House Library, University of London, MS 704, ['Commonplace book, written in the early 19th century, containing copies of poems by various authors, including Mrs. R. Wilmot, the Reverend John Chetwood, and Edward Wilmot'].
[108] Ibid, p. 135.
[109] The sisters' literary relationship with their sister-in-law is evident in the many letter they sent to her on their travels. Her husband and their brother, Robert Wilmot, was the declared recipient of Katherine's manuscript epistolary travelogue written during the Peace of Amiens (see Chapter 1, pp. 44–45).
[110] Eyles Irwin's sonnet is dated 1809, which coincides perfectly with Martha's return from Russia, but not as well with Frances Sally's age: she would have been closer to

the volume include further poems by Frances Sally, such as one addressed 'To her father' on the page immediately following her commemoration of Martha. Frances Sally would go on to publish her own writing later in life, including plays written in verse.[111] The frequency of entries by both the elder and younger Irwin imply that they probably spent considerable time with the extended Wilmot-Chetwood family. Frances Sally's entries, in particular, reveal a lively culture of manuscript sociability designed not only to encourage but also to include young writers in collective literary pursuits.[112] The presence of her poems in the shared manuscript album demonstrates a continuation of the modes of apprenticeship discussed earlier in this chapter, with multiple women across generations sharing in sociable literary exchange. As this chapter and indeed the example of this commonplace book have shown, Martha Wilmot's inspiring example as a member of the circle returning from abroad with a trove of travel writing and biographical manuscripts to share is clearly an important part of this sociability – one that transformed an otherwise provincial and inter-familial Protestant Irish coterie into a site of transnational networking for young women with writerly aspirations.

---

thirteen or fourteen years old rather than '12', as stated in the heading to her poem.

[111] *The Innocents. A Sacred Drama. Ocean, and the Earthquake at Aleppo: Poems [By Mrs. Edwin Toby Caulfeild.]* (Bath, 1824); Frances Sally Caulfeild, *The Deluge: A Poem* (London, 1837).

[112] Entries in the commonplace book were also written by the young Edward Wilmot, son of Elizabeth Wilmot, owner and apparent compiler of the book.

3
Women's Networks of Knowledge

In 1807, Katherine Wilmot sent a letter home to Ireland describing a bathhouse ritual performed by Russian peasant women on the occasion of a marriage. She had been in the country since 1805, when she had arrived to join her sister, Martha, as Princess Ekaterina Dashkova's guest. Katherine's letter offers a glimpse of the unique spectacles to which the Wilmots were frequently witness in Russia:

> perhaps 'tis the *most* amusing circumstance arising from a *Russian* tour, to witness *in the Peasantry* of the present day, a living picture of the utmost ages! ... the *Vapour Bath* (that universal panacea in this country) remains to *illustrate itself*, in the present instance of *Sophia's marriage*.[1]

Katherine notes that the sisters have become regular observers of the customs of the peasants, and that both have 'attended several weddings in Church'. This anecdote, however, records a new experience, as she never before 'had the courage to suffocate myself in the cause of seeing things with my own Eyes'. Katherine focuses on the great effort she has put into collecting information abroad, writing that she 'resolved not to quit the country without doing so'. She describes the actions of the women bathers in preparing the bride:

> They then took their own clothes [off], & after scouring her to their hearts content, danced round about, (in all their national dances) clapping their hands, & drinking wine, which was dispensed by another Eve, who sat with a bottle in one hand, & a glass in the other, her long tresses falling down about her shoulders, which, like all the others, was the only shadow of covering they cou'd boast. They then let up a universal song.[2]

---

[1] RIA MS 12 L 30, p. 132; emphasis original.
[2] RIA MS 12 L 30, p. 134.

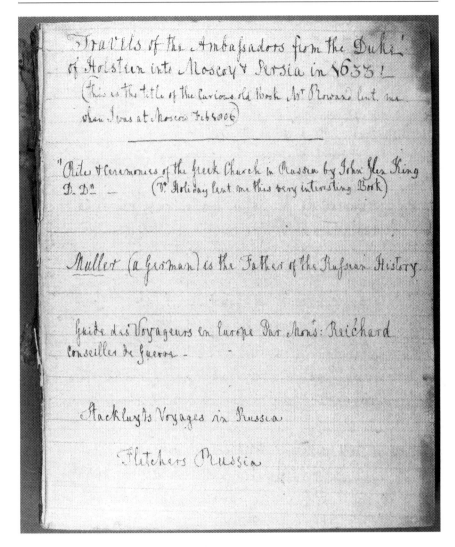

Figure 7   Royal Irish Academy MS 12 L 34, 'Note-book of Katherine Wilmot, Moscow, 1806', p. 1. © Royal Irish Academy.

The detailed account of the ritual, related from 'beginning to end', reveals the observational methodology the Wilmot sisters gleaned from emerging trends of popular antiquarianism in the late eighteenth century. While the anecdote was originally circulated to a relatively small circle, its ultimate readership and impact proved much wider. The description was copied by another sister, Alicia, into a manuscript collection of the sisters' correspondence from Russia. It was subsequently edited by Martha for inclusion in the Wilmots' substantial travel writing supplements within *Memoirs of Princess Daschkaw* (1840).[3] The bathhouse ritual and countless similar sketches would later be assimilated as significant parts of institutional archival collections, scholarly bodies of Enlightened knowledge from which women travellers and antiquarians were excluded in the late eighteenth century.

The origins of and inspiration for the bathhouse ritual can be traced to Katherine's 1806 commonplace book.[4] The now-brittle blue pages of the notebook contain an array of information reflective of its purpose as a daily compendium for accruing knowledge. The commonplace book incorporates transcribed fragments of published correspondence, lines of text encountered in Dashkova's library and pages of unattributed poetry. The prefatory pages of the notebook, in particular, highlight the intellectual and cultural improvement that could be gained by upper-middle-class women travelling abroad in the period.[5] Spanning seven pages and detailing more than three-dozen texts, the reading list records how the Wilmots engaged with Enlightenment dialogues both from within and beyond the borders of eighteenth-century Russia. Katherine's interests as a reader are reflected in intermittent commentaries. Some titles on the list receive high praise: '*Muller* (a German)', writes Katherine, 'is the Father of the Russian History', referring to the work of historian Gerhard Friedrich Müller (1705–83), a founding member of the Academy of Russian Sciences. The list gathers several works of travel writing and history centred on Russia and the Near East, including 'William Coxes travels through Poland, Russia, & Sweden in 1784'.[6] These cosmopolitan texts hold immediate relevance for the Wilmots as British travellers in Russia immersed in transnational connections and experiences. A small number of texts on the list concerned with the region are women-authored: Madame de Cottin's fictional *Élisabeth ou Les Exilés de Siberie* shares space with 'Madames Guthries Letters from the Crimea [sic]', which is appended by 'Lady Cravens ditto [sic]'.[7] A further Russian historical text translated by a woman, Isabelle de Montolieu, concludes

---

[3] The original letter has not survived; the fair copy version can be found in RIA 12 L 30, pp. 132–134; for the published version; see *Memoirs*, II, pp. 410–413.
[4] RIA MS 12 L 34, Note-book of Katherine Wilmot, Moscow, 1806.
[5] RIA MS 12 L 34, pp. 1–5.
[6] William Coxe, *Travels into Poland, Russia, Sweden, and Denmark* (London, 1784).
[7] RIA MS 12 L 34, p. 5; Sophie Cottin, *Élisabeth ou Les Exilés de Siberie* (Paris, 1806); Maria Guthrie and Matthew Guthrie, *A Tour, Performed in the Years 1795–6, through the Taurida, or Crimea* (London, 1802); Elizabeth Craven, *A Journey Through the Crimea to Constantinople* (London, 1789).

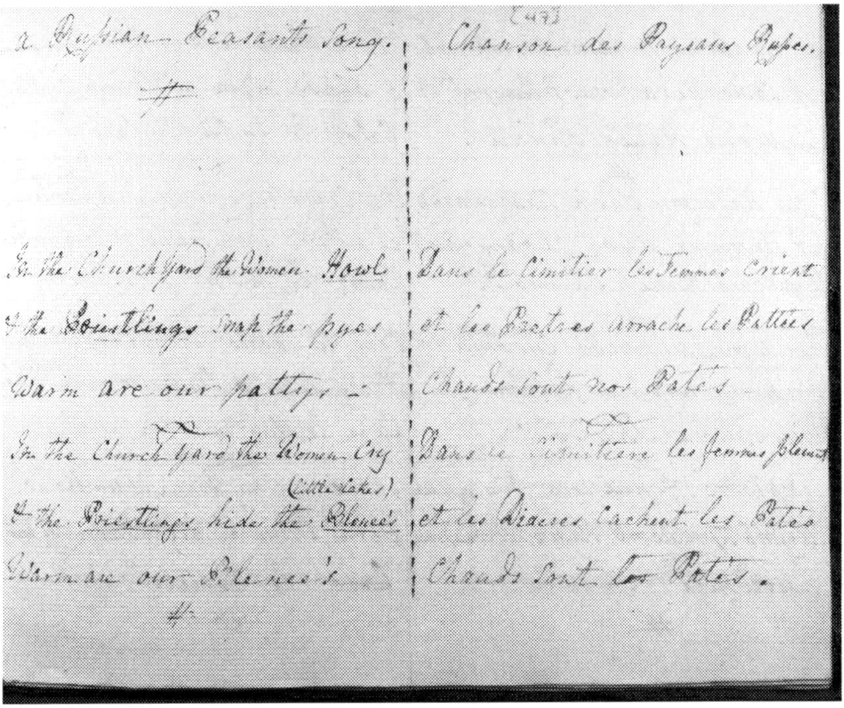
A Russian Peasants Song. | Chanson des Paysans Russes.
In the Churchyard the Women Howl | Dans le Cimitier les Femmes Crient
& the Priestlings snap the pyes | et les Prêtres arrache les Pattées
Warm are our patty's – | Chauds sont nos Patés
In the Church Yard the Women Cry | Dans le Cimitière les femmes pleurent
(Little cakes)
& the Priestlings hide the Blenees | et les Diacres Cachent les Patés
Warm are our Blenee's | Chauds sont les Patés.

Figure 8 Royal Irish Academy MS 12 L 20, 'Ms in English, 1803–08, Martha Bradford (née Wilmot): Journal of stay in Russia', p. iii: 'A Perisloff Merchants Wife [*sic*]'. © Royal Irish Academy.

the brief section.[8] While the low proportion of women-authored titles on the list is hardly surprising, the grouping together of the texts on the final page, the texts' specific focus on Russia, as well as their relatively recent publication dates, raises interesting questions. Positioned at the end of the list, these women-authored texts are simultaneously intertwined with and removed from the male-authored texts that dominate the majority of the reading list. The grouping of these texts raises questions about how the Wilmots' reading practices shape and inform their own Russian writings, as well as the ways in which emerging eighteenth-century discourse such as antiquarianism and ethnography influence their mediation of foreign experiences. The 1806 notebook offers an ideal window into the relationship between reading and observation, showing the impact that contemporary

8 August Lafontaine; *Isabelle de Montolieu, Marie Menzikoff et Fedor Dolgorouki: Histoire Russe en Forme de Lettres. Traduit de l'Allemand d'Auguste Lafontaine, par Mme Isabelle de Montolieu* (Paris, 1804).

scholarship had on the Wilmot sisters' analysis and writing. For instance, a lengthy article on the 'Religion of the Slavic people' was carefully transcribed into the notebook, taken directly from Pierre Charles Levesque's *Histoire de Russie* (1800).[9] This article on Slavonic mythology and ceremonies occupies thirty-two pages of Katherine's notebook, perhaps due to its capacity to inform and guide the Wilmots' observations and interpretations of the rituals and customs they habitually sought out in Russia.

The Wilmots appreciated their privileged position as observers in Russia. As Martha wrote in her journal in November 1807 of witnessing a particular ritual for the first time, 'I have been above 4 years in the Country, & anxious to see all the Ceremonys [sic]' of the Russian peasants. The Wilmots' dynamic attempts to understand and interpret the peasant culture they encountered by drawing on and incorporating existing knowledge are apparent in both extant texts and images. For example, a set of four amateur drawings of Russian national costume pasted by Martha into the prefatory pages of one of her Russian journals emulate the lush coloured plates of *Description de toutes les nations de l'Empire de Russie* (1776–80), a three-volume ethnographic text gifted to the Wilmot sisters by Dashkova as a tool for recognising the various peoples they might encounter.[10] Dashkova's past as Director to the Russian Academy of Arts and Sciences under Catherine II provides the Wilmots with an important role model of female institutional affiliation and achievement.[11] Thanks to her patronage, they gained access to a wide institutional archive as well as contemporary writings. As British-Irish travellers and guests of Dashkova, a feudal landowner to 3,000 peasants at Troitskoe and a further 5,000 on her estate in Poland, the Wilmot sisters had ample opportunities to explore and document the customs of the peasant class at a time when such observations were often used to construct narratives of national identity. Considering

---

[9] RIA MS 12 L 34, pp. 8–32; Pierre-Charles Levesque, *Histoire de Russie, Nouvelle Édition, Corrigée et Augmentée par l'Auteur, et Conduite Jusqu'à la Mort de l'Impératrice Catherine II* (Hamburg, 1800), I, pp. 22–43; 'Religion des Slaves'; my translation.

[10] Johann Gottlieb Georgi, *Description de Toutes les Nations de l'Empire de Russie*, 3vols (St Petersbourg, 1776–80). For Martha's drawing, see RIA MS 12 L 20, 'Ms in English, 1803–08, Martha Bradford (née Wilmot): Journal of stay in Russia', p. iii: 'A Perisloff Merchants Wife [sic]'.

[11] One example of this can be seen in a printed Russian notice and a corresponding handwritten version in French, both of which are bound up in the BL manuscript of Dashkova's memoirs. This documents her gift of her 'Cabinet of Natural Curiosities' to the University of Moscow in 1803. The collection consisted of 15,430 items, including minerals and fossils, gathered by her over a period of more than thirty years. It is likely that Martha would have been present for the voluminous collection's preparation and accounting prior to donation. See BL Add MS 31911, 205r–208v.

their own class-status as unmarried women of a middle-ranking and provincial background, the connections, power and access to learning brought by Dashkova's position was immense. The Wilmots' observations and collection practices can also be read within the context of an increasingly globalised eighteenth century, one in which encounters between peoples take on new meaning and produce generative moments of cultural exchange, particularly through the lens of their participation in an Enlightened and transnational Republic of Letters.

Comparison between the two surviving transcriptions of Katherine's bathhouse ritual, noted above, reveals the work of analysis, interpretation and censorship intervening between the first and second version. However, both records of the ritual bear strong similarity with a text on Katherine's reading list, *Dissertations sur les antiquités de Russie* (1795), by Scottish physician and mineralogist Matthew Guthrie (1743–1807). Under the reading list entry, Katherine writes 'this is the most peculiarly interesting little Vol I have ever read of the kind'. *Dissertations* is a little-known study of Russian peasant folk song and custom printed in 1785 under the patronage of Catherine II, and dedicated to the Society of Antiquaries of Scotland. Katherine's intertextual borrowing of Guthrie's own description of Russian marital bathhouse rituals illustrates how mediation and authorship mingled in women traveller's antiquarian and ethnographic collection practices. The translation raises questions about the reliability of Katherine's first-hand observation, as well as the ways in which writing of eighteenth-century women travellers was moulded by their reading practices.

International networks of women travellers played a significant role in developing and disseminating antiquarian and early ethnographic practice within and across national contexts. This chapter explores how several texts created or collected by the Wilmots in Russia function not only in active dialogue with texts from the reading list, but also as an extension of prominent discourses of the day to which they were exposed through travel. These include Martha's 1804 journal and correspondence, which engages in extensive observation of Jewish peasant culture and religious custom in Poland in a manner evocative of Müller's institutional ethnographic writing; both sisters' correspondence documenting premarital Russian women's bathing rituals, which engage with Guthrie's *Dissertations* and echo Mary Wortley Montagu's Turkish travel writings, later published in part as a supplement to Dashkova's *Memoirs* (1840); a soft-bound notebook containing dozens of Russian folk songs collected and translated by Martha, with accompanying paratextual commentary, which speaks to the developing discipline of antiquarian song collection as a national project pioneered by, among others, Thomas Percy in Britain and Charlotte Brooke in Ireland; and a

1796 illuminated Russian manuscript, previously owned by Catherine II and interleaved with Martha's own translation, which illustrates her desire to participate in collection and mediation practices as an independent woman practitioner working outside the bounds of conventional institutional practice.[12] The sisters engaged in a wide range of practices in order to interpret, mediate and translate foreign experience. In what follows, I argue that these writings and collection practices resonate with contemporary trends in the disciplines of antiquarianism, as seen in their efforts to collect specimens of the ancient past through both living rituals and rare manuscripts, as well as early ethnographic practices in their efforts to observe and describe peoples. As we shall see, such activities underscore the adaptability of these disciplines for the purposes of networks of women travellers, who were pointedly excluded from their institutional practice both at home and abroad.

Observing 'Manners & Customs' Abroad

> We enter'd poor conquer'd Poland ... The first little Town we pass'd thro', mark'd it in one respect in the number of *Jewish* establishments, for that sect abound in Poland, and there I saw for the first time the *Israelitish habit* [sic].[13]

In the summer of 1804, Dashkova and Martha travelled from Troitskoe to a remote area of Poland, staying for a period of two months in order to survey and maintain Dashkova's assets there. Catherine II had granted the estate of Krouglo to Dashkova during a broader effort to place the provincial lands of 'White Russia' under 'the control and administration of Russian nobles' in the mid-1770s.[14] Dashkova had initially expressed trepidation about the 'management of people half Polish and half Jews', while being 'ignorant both of their manners and their language' (I, p. 278). She feared the distant location of the estate would prevent her from 'improving

---

[12] RIA MS 12 L 18, 'Journal of Martha Wilmot', pp. 125–210; RIA MS 12 L 30, pp. 132–134; *Memoirs*, II, pp. 410–413; RIA MS 12 L 29; the Royal Irish Academy catalogue lists 'Letters of Martha Bradford (née Wilmot) and Katherine Wilmot, n.d. Include Russian poems and verses with translations into English, French and Italian, c.1806–08'; the specific manuscript in question is labelled RIA MS 12 L 29.1; RIA MS 12 L 16 'Ms in Russian, 1796, An account of the wedding celebration of Tsar Mikhail Fyodorovich copied from earlier manuscript. Illustrated, with descriptive text in Russian and translation in English, at end of volume by Alexei Molinofsky, 1796. 67 ff'.
[13] RIA MS 12 L 24, 'Krugla July 5th [1804]', p. 223; emphasis original.
[14] *Memoirs*, I, p. 279.

their condition', the result being that 'I should lose half the pleasure of the possession' of the estate (I, p. 279). Dashkova eventually accepted control of Krouglo, a burgh with 2,500 inhabitants spread out in villages within the forest.[15] While Catherine II originally promised that Krouglo would be a profitable estate, it consistently failed to pay for itself and ran into 'deficiencies' due to a bifurcation of valuable land caused by the First Partition of Poland.[16] Throughout the 1780s and 1790s, Dashkova visited Krouglo periodically in an effort to improve the estate and maintain a relationship with the area's inhabitants. 'My peasants', she later wrote in her memoirs, became 'less miserable and less idle' under her management, 'esteeming themselves much happier than they were formerly, either as living under the Polish government, or belonging to the crown of Russia' (I, p. 343). While Dashkova treated the positive management of the estate as a duty, she also viewed the burgh's Jewish inhabitants and their culture as a curiosity worthy of tourism, bringing Elizabeth Hamilton, the Wilmots' aunt, to visit in 1783 (I, p. 337).

For Martha, the visit to Krouglo clearly offered an early opportunity to test her capacity for observing and describing foreign customs in her travel writing. Letters sent to her family from this period, along with her journal entries, graphically detail the religious rituals, clothing and customs of the Jews of Krouglo with a pseudo-scientific voyeurism. As she writes to her mother in early July, having just arrived, 'I shall soon introduce you to a Jews Synagogue and several of the *fraternity*, for the village of Krugla has several familys resident in it [*sic*] ... no doubt I shall see plenty of Jews'.[17] She subsequently includes further details of her subjects' exotic and unusual clothing, writing that the women 'dress'd in a sort of winker'd cap of *pearls* which shades the face very becomingly; above this border is a turban [*sic*]' (p. 223; emphasis original). She describes that their 'earings, necklaces, and rings, sparkle in every direction, while a sort of waistcoat of one colour, and petticoat of another, finish their attire [*sic*]' (p. 223). Their 'rich Cloathes [*sic*]' are all the more remarkable for the low class within society of these

---

[15] Modern day Krugloe, or Kruhlaye, is located in Belarus in the Mogilev region, which was annexed during the First Partition of Poland in 1772 and incorporated as part of Belorussia. Dashkova's *Memoirs* and Martha's journals both give the burgh's name as 'Krouglo', which has been used here for continuity with the source material.

[16] *Memoirs*, I, p. 310, p. 279; The First Partition of Poland of 1772 ended the Polish-Lithuanian Commonwealth and forcefully divided Poland's lands between the Austrian, Russian and Prussian Empires. See 'The Commonwealth of the Two Nations', in Jerzy Lukowski and Herbert Zawadazki, *A Concise History of Poland* (Cambridge, 2001).

[17] RIA MS 12 L 24, 'Krugla July 5th [1804]', pp. 226, 227.

women who, she writes to her mother, are 'very few degrees about *Nelly your Milk Woman*' (pp. 233, 223). Martha illustrates the pearls worn by the Jews in her letter, drawing a diagram of two separate sizes (p. 226). The image brings the fashion and lifestyles of the Jewish women to the eyes of her family circle in Ireland, encouraging an evaluation of social structures.

Martha's writing on the Jews of Krouglo can be tied to emergent trends in the ethnographic observation of rural customs and peasant life in Russia, as well as across wider Europe, as a means of forging and configuring national identity. Anatoly M. Kuznetsov traces the roots of ethnographic enquiry in Russia to Peter the Great's 1714 foundation of the country's first museum, *Kunstkamera*, which included ethnographic materials by the middle of the eighteenth century.[18] While the formation of the modern discipline of ethnography is rooted primarily in the proliferation of professional Victorian-era efforts at delineating anthropological disciplines, particularly in Britain, scholars such as Christie McDonald locate a collective 'ethnographic imagination' as an essential component of eighteenth-century travel literature.[19] The rise of the study of peasant customs in eighteenth-century Russia has been linked by Slavonic anthropologists and historians with Emperor Peter the Great's attempts to establish and consecrate a national history. Attempts to construct a Western-leaning national identity revolved around a thorough review of Russia's history, a programme of study rooted in Peter's 1724 decree for the formation of The Saint Petersburg Academy of Sciences (Akademia Nauk).[20]

The inclusion on Katherine's commonplace book reading list of a French translation of Gerhard Friedrich Müller's great historical travelogue, *Voyages et découvertes faites par les Russes le long des côtes de la mer glaciale,*

---

[18] Anatoly M. Kuznetsov, 'Russian Anthropology: Old Traditions and New Tendencies', in *Other People's Anthropologies: Ethnographic Practice on the Margins*, ed. by

[19] Christie McDonald, 'On the Ethnographic Imagination in the Eighteenth Century', in *French Global: A New Approach to Literary History*, ed. by Christie McDonald and Susan Rubin Suleiman (New York, 2010), pp. 223–239. For the origins of ethnography as an Anglo-America discipline, see Clifford and Marcus; James Buzard and Joseph Childers, 'Introduction: Victorian Ethnographies', *Victorian Studies*, 41:3 (1998), 351–353; George Stocking, *Victorian Anthropology* (New York, 1991). James Chandler has questioned 'how might one produce the history not only of disciplines, but of the changing concepts of disciplinarity?', suggesting that disciplines 'should be articulated' as 'a network of autonomous practices in asymmetrical relation to each other'; James Chandler, 'Critical Disciplinarity', *Critical Inquiry*, 30 (2004), 355–360, pp. 359, 360.

[20] The Saint Petersburg Academy of Sciences would come to be known as The Imperial Academy of Arts and Sciences (1747–1803) during Dashkova's association with it as Director, beginning in 1782.

signals the sisters' awareness of eighteenth-century Russian interest in the exploration of its vast empire and the study and documentation of the remote indigenous peoples found on its fringes.[21] Müller's study of Siberian indigenous populations contributed to the widening Russian investment in the 'description of peoples', a national project which continued into the reign of Catherine II.[22] Müller was a founding academic of the Academy in St Petersburg, arriving at the age of twenty in 1725. He participated in the building of the academy's university library, and instigated the *Sammlung Russischer Geschichte* (1732–37, 1758–64), a German-language publication that gave Western Europeans easier access to Russian historical materials.[23] Müller later joined the Second Kamchatka Expedition, which set out to chart the supposed passage between America and Asia. During the decade-long expedition, Müller focused his extensive research on Siberian indigenous cultures and history.[24] He returned to the Imperial Academy after travelling, publishing his histories of Siberia and Russia. Müller became the imperial historiographer in 1748 and enjoyed the patronage of Catherine II following her rise to power. His reputation as the leading eighteenth-century authority on Russian history was well established, as seen in Katherine's description of him as 'the Father' of the discipline. It is possible that Müller's role as an important founding member of the Imperial Academy of Arts and Sciences may have also played a part in Katherine's high appraisal, given Dashkova's later connection to the Academy as Director.

Much of Müller's descriptive work on Siberian peoples remained in manuscript form, and has only been published in recent decades.[25] Nonetheless, palpable traces of Müller's endeavours to integrate cultural observation as an essential aspect of historical and scientific research emerge in his contemporary published works, and the potential influence of his *Voyages et découvertes* on the Wilmot sisters' own practices of observation and accumulation is apparent in the French translation of the text read by

---

[21] Gerhard Friedrich Müller, *Voyages et Découvertes Faites par les Russes le Long des Côtes de la Mer Glaciale* (Amsterdam, 1766).

[22] Han F. Vermeulen, *Before Boas: The Genesis of Ethnography and Ethnology in the German Enlightenment* (Lincoln, 2015), p. 131.

[23] Gerhard Friedrich Müller, *Sammlung Russischer Geschichte*, 9vols (St Petersburg, 1732–64).

[24] See Joseph Lawrence Black, *G.F. Müller and the Imperial Russian Academy of Sciences, 1725–1783: First Steps in the Development of the Historical Sciences in Russia* (Kingston-Montréal, 1986).

[25] Gerhard Friedrich Müller, *Ethnographische Schriften I*, ed. by Wieland Hintzsche and Aleksandr Christianovich Elert unter Mitarbeit von Heike Heklau. Quellen zur Geschichte Sibiriens und Alaskas aus russischen Archiven VIII (Halle, 2010).

the Wilmots. Writing of his participation in the Second Kamchatka Expedition, Müller outlines his own contribution:

> knowing of its commencement at the beginning of 1733, I also offered my services, to write the civil history of Siberia, the antiquities, manners and customs of the people, and the very history of the journey we were to undertake.[26]

The documentation of 'manners and customs of the people' presents a social branch of enquiry, opening up a wide range of possibilities for travellers to document their experiences. Müller's firm declaration that the Second Kamchatka expedition 'surpasses in its importance all of the others which had come before it', despite not having achieved its primary goal of discovering the elusive Northwest Passage, adds value to descriptive practice.[27]

Martha's writing on the customs of the Jews of Krouglo is also concerned with capturing the description of peoples. This can be drawn out in her frequent attendance at and documentation of the local synagogue as well as religious rites. 'Yesterday Evening they were sinners in the Wilderness, sorrowing for their transgressions', she writes in a letter of 17 July 1804, describing a Jewish procession through the village towards the house of prayer.[28] 'After *sunset*, all pearls, diamonds, rich Cloaths & c were laid aside, and the worst of every sort Collected – the metamorphas might almost be call'd *Sack Cloath and Ashes* [sic]' (p. 233). In the synagogue, she notes, 'the Men and Women [were] separated by a high partition', and 'most of the congregation had books, and read and wept for themselves, one in particular sob'd aloud' (p. 233). Her journal entry for 19 September 1804 notes that she has 'just return'd from the Jews synagogue [*sic*]', to witness 'the ceremony of the bullrush rods' for the autumnal festival of Sukkot.[29] 'This was a day of rejoicing and they wore their best robes, & *veils* like so many *blankets* which they once or twice even threw over their heads' (p. 229, emphasis original). In a letter to Anna Chetwood, she carefully describes the ritual customs surrounding observance of the Sabbath, in that no woman delivering a baby may be attended by a surgeon and no one in the community may fall ill, adding, 'What I tell you comes from Jews themselves who practice

---

[26] Müller, pp. 176–177; 'savoir au commencement de 1733, j'offris aussi mes services, pour écrire l'histoire civile de la Sibérie, les antiquités, les moeurs & les usages des peuples, & l'histoire même du voyage qu'on alloit entreprendre'; my translation.
[27] Müller, p. 174; 'les meours & les usages des peuples'; 'surpasse par son importance tout ce qui avoit été fait auparavant'; my translation.
[28] RIA MS 12 L 24, 'Krugla, To Mrs R. Wilmot, 15th/17th July 1804', pp. 232–233.
[29] RIA MS 12 L 18, 'Thurs. 19th [September 1804]', p. 229.

all I say and a great deal more'.[30] She hints that future information about the religious rites among the Jews will soon follow by writing that 'I am to see a Wedding in a few weeks, as yet I know nothing of their Burial service' (p. 244). Martha writes in her journal of attending 'a Jews Christening – the ceremony of circumsicion [sic]', though 'the preparation turn'd me so sick I could not look at the ceremony'.[31] Careful description of the procedure ('the Rabine [sic] spit a little blood which he drew from the infant'), illustrates the priority Martha places on witnessing as many specifically Jewish rituals as possible, despite unpleasant personal reactions (p. 189).

Eighteenth-century discourse interpreted the Jews as a specific – and problematic – ethnic group embedded within yet consistently separated from national identities and political formations. Yaacov Deutsch writes that, given the voluminous range of literature devoted to Jewish life and customs in early modern Europe, 'ethnographic accounts about the Jews … may be associated with the ethnographic writing about other cultures – a genre whose popularity steadily grew from the end of the fifteenth century' through the eighteenth.[32] Descriptive texts focused on the Jews 'were part of a broader genre that essentially contrasted and rejected anything that fell under the heading of "other"' (p. 251). Ronald Schechter asserts that, given the voluminous literature devoted to them in the period, European 'contemporaries were indeed interested in Jews', and that, among the French in particular, both individual eighteenth-century authors and their assumed readerships displayed 'an unusual interest' in the lives of European Jews.[33] The isolation of the Jews was a particular problem for efforts towards urbanisation and unification of nations in Europe in the period, with commentators arguing that 'Jews could be "useful" citizens without converting to Christianity if they made some changes to their way of life, such as abandoning traditional Jewish clothes … languages (Yiddish and Hebrew in everyday speech and written contracts), and occupations'.[34] Frequent commentary on the Jews' separation from society led to inevitable hostility in discourse, in part due to the religion's association 'with a cluster of the most problematic issues in Enlightenment thought – the nature of myth,

---

[30] RIA MS 12 L 24, 'To Anna Chetwood, Kruglo [sic], 7th of August, 1804', p. 243.
[31] RIA MS 12 L 18, '29th [July 1804]', p. 189.
[32] Yaacov Deutsch, *Judaism in Christian Eyes: Ethnographic Descriptions of Jews and Judaism in Early Modern Europe* (Oxford, 2012), p. 4.
[33] Ronald Schechter, 'The Jewish Question in Eighteenth-Century France', *Eighteenth-Century Studies*, 32:1 (1998), 84–91, p. 85.
[34] Daniel Stone, 'Jews and the Urban Question in Late Eighteenth Century Poland', *Slavic Review*, 50:3 (1991), 531–541, p. 533.

the problem of origins, and the question of group identity'.[35] Paradoxically, the same tensions that limited mutual understanding, or created open hostility, often invited the most capacious commentary. Voltaire notoriously dismissed the Jews as 'vile people, superstitious, ignorant, deprived of science, deprived of commerce', yet he also 'wrote voluminously on the subject [of the Jews], sometimes denouncing persecution of Jews, sometimes lambasting the Jewish religion itself'.[36]

Martha's travel journal about the Jews of Krouglo is, at times, punctuated with opinions that are as likely to have been shaped by widespread eighteenth-century antisemitism as by her own first-hand experiences. The wealthiest woman in the village, a Mrs Hoanen, referred to as 'Our rich Jewess', is painted as a hypocrite for her willingness to let Martha play with her children on the Sabbath while not allowing her to hold the house keys: she 'could consign her child to a Christian but could not entrust her Keys underneath whose influence were untold treasures'.[37] Martha details Mrs Hoanen's supposed duplicity, yet she, Dashkova, and Dashkova's niece, Anna Petrovna spend a considerable amount of time socialising with Mrs Hoanen both in her own home, and at Dashkova's feudal seat in Krouglo. Elsewhere, Martha reiterates common stereotypes of the Jews' greed. In a letter to Anna Chetwood she writes:

> They wou'd not eat with Christians for *any bribe*; and Money is, you know, the grand touchstone with them more than any other people, the love of it is literally implanted, and the Effects visible in Brats of less than 2 years of Age.[38]

Describing the synagogue's 'Altar in which the Commandments are kept' in a separate entry, Martha notes that it has been 'more ornamented than usual' for the holiday, yet 'still their [the Jews'] dirt is intolerable'.[39] Martha's journal entries frequently fail to demonstrate a nuanced understanding of the Jewish religion and expose her prejudice against the Jews, despite careful observation. For instance, Martha includes an extended account of a 'ceremony of humiliation' performed in the 'Jews Synagogue' in July 1804,

---

[35] Adam Sutcliffe, 'Myth, Origins, Identity: Voltaire, the Jews and the Enlightenment Notion of Toleration', *The Eighteenth Century*, 39:2 (1998), 107–126, p. 111.
[36] Voltaire, *Oeuvres Complètes de Voltaire* (Sautelet, 1827), p. 784; Schechter, p. 85; 'ce vil peuple, superstitieux, ignorant, privé de science, privé de commerce'; my translation.
[37] RIA MS 12 L 24, 'To Mrs R Wilmot, Krugla, 15/17th July 1804', p. 235.
[38] RIA MS 12 L 24, 'To Anna Chetwood, Kruglo [sic], 7th of August, 1804', p. 244.
[39] RIA MS 12 L 18, 'Thurs 19th [September 1804]', p. 229.

noting that for the holiday in question the Jews 'dress in the worst they have' and 'must not sleep in their Houses, but on the *bare Earth* [sic]' (pp. 172–173; emphasis original). The concluding comment seems particularly obtuse given that the holiday she describes, Tisha B'Av, represents a day of mourning on which Jewish law prohibits bathing, laundering clothing and certain acts of personal grooming.

Similarly, Martha's descriptions understate the Jews' oppression, instead focusing on their separation from Christian society at large, and a refusal to bend religious laws: 'such is their strictness that cannot taste the wine made by a Christian', she writes, '& as tis difficult for Jews to obtain a licence for making it', 'the Jews pay dear for bad wine'.[40] Such comments reveal ignorance of her subjects' position of subjugation, and a general lack of understanding of imperialist power structures. Despite her early sympathetic reference to 'poor conquer'd Poland', her documentation abstains from scrutinising or critiquing the social structure that positions Dashkova in control over the Jews. Martha relates Dashkova's explanations of the methods by which the Jews of 'White Russia' avoid paying 'tax to the Crown', hiding their wealth through 'incessant journeying from place to place' so that 'their power *really* [is] known only to themselves', thereby underlining a supposed miserliness and an ingratitude to the Russian Crown.[41] Writing in September 1804, she notes that Dashkova 'has 5,000 subjects' in Krouglo, and 'receives only 3 – roubles & *per skull*', despite the fact that 'Many Lords receive 8-9'.[42] 'Scarcely anything of this sort is demanded by Princess Daschkaw', writes Martha, 'whose consideration for her people is one of the first feelings of her heart, & surely a more noble one cannot be found' (p. 224). Yet, as Martha has earlier noted in a letter, Dashkova certainly profits from the estate, a 'pretty little smiling spot, which by the by brings the Princess a yearly revenue of 26,000 Roubles'.[43] Martha's description of Dashkova's feudal benevolence stands at odds with a later memorandum on serfdom written by the consistently more critical Katherine, which also outlines the dictatorial principles by which estates are governed in Russia.[44] 'With Lands, all the Peasants residing on them become the *Property* of the new possessor who has the right to sell them', she notes (p. 2). 'The Lord of the Estate gives what portion of *it he Chuses* to his Peasants to labour', and '[f]or this he taxes them *as he Chuses* from 3 to 15 Roubles a head' (p. 3).

[40] RIA MS 12 L 18, 'Friday 29th [August 1804]', p. 217.
[41] RIA MS 12 L 18, 'Wednesday 24th [July 1804]', pp. 184–185.
[42] RIA MS 12 L 18, 'Thursday 12th [Sep 1804]', p. 224; emphasis original.
[43] RIA MS 12 L 24, 'Krugla July 5th [1804]', p. 224.
[44] RIA MS 12 L 31, 'Journal of Katherine Wilmot in Russia', 1806–07, reverse inner board, pp. 2–4.

Katherine corroborates that 'Princess D only takes 3 Roubles' while 'many others Exact 15 [sic]' (p. 3). Yet she also deplores the 'abuse of ... power' that accompanies the system, and Dashkova's participation in it, relating the story that 'One of the P.'s Slaves [Zachary] who displeased her received the Whip for his punishment – & his daughter is to be sold [sic]' despite the fact that she is 'capable of being a Servant' (pp. 3–4). 'What is the administration of justice on an Estate?' Katherine wonders. '*The Will of the Lord* is the answer' (p. 3, emphasis original).[45]

Martha's presence in Krouglo is inextricably linked to Dashkova's role as the local feudal ruler, her power of observation contingent on the feudal patron's control, and she exploits this position to collect fodder for her travel writing. Her documentation of the Jews in Krouglo represents an early attempt to collect and synthesise a wide range of information abroad. While not, at this juncture, wishing to publish these observations, there is a palpable intensity and enthusiasm for accurately gathering information that can later be disseminated, if only within the parameters of the Wilmots' social circle in Ireland. As Martha writes in her journal, describing a song sung in the synagogue:

> The Chaunter sung, I only could distinguish the word '*Urusalem* ... Another time I heard the Word *Egyptian* ... the Chaunter as if to mimick ... squeak'd 'ba ba ba ba ba ba – bee bee bee bee be be be be – bu bu bu bu bu bu bu bu – *boi boi boi boi boi boi* – buu buu buu *bung, bwung*'. Oh dear, I hope I may be able to *sing* it whenever I chuse; the more discordant the more *terrific* the better [sic].[46]

These fragments will go on to form an important part of the Wilmot sisters' expanding corpus of travel writing that can be reiterated in performance and text. Martha's record of the song reflects a concerted attempt to distil a cultural example of Polish Jewish culture through her best possible means. Martha's wish to be able to sing the song in the future whenever she likes in all its discordant glory points to the ways in which she sees her documentations as fodder for later entertainment, enrichment, and education among her Irish-British audiences, much in the same way that her travel letters are already *en route* to Ireland for fulfilment of the same purpose.

---

[45] This incident echoes Martha's experience with 'Pashinka', a child serf gifted to Martha by Dashkova in 1804. Martha apparently intended to keep the eleven-year-old girl on leaving Russia, but she did not travel back to Ireland with her in 1808; see RIA MS 12 L 18, pp. 251–252.

[46] RIA MS 12 L 18, pp. 229–230, emphasis original.

'Living' Antiquities

The Wilmots' documentations of folk custom in Russia were shaped by their experiences yet also take specific cues from the books on Katherine's reading list, using them as a model for engaging with and responding to emerging national and cosmopolitan discussions surrounding the collection and documentation of antiquities, first in their letters and diaries, and later, in print. Women travel writers' antiquarian observations drew on both oral or eye-witness experience and existing literary source material. Srinivas Aravamudan writes of the 'empiricist epistemology' of the travelling 'woman-scholar'.[47] Seen through the observation of contemporary cultures, yet interpreted within a context of antiquarian mediation, the identification of living antiquities 'converts the focus from current identities to past ones, and displaces politics back into history'.[48] As Marilyn Butler has written, popular antiquarianism increasingly allowed 'early social historians and social scientists' to collect 'popular beliefs, customs, stories and ballads' from 'the lips of the peoples themselves'.[49] At the same time, the 'flourishing occupation' of popular antiquarianism drew on 'books' and 'manuscripts'. Nowhere can this modelling be more clearly established than in the instances of intertextuality between the Wilmots' own work and Matthew Guthrie's *Dissertations sur les antiquités de Russie* (1795).

It is unclear from Katherine's reading list where the copy of *Dissertations* is acquired, whether in Ireland or England, or following her arrival in Russia, as the list seemingly only references the provenance of a text when loaned by a person deemed significant to experiences of travel or friendship. For instance, beneath the entry for 'Rites and Ceremonies of the Greek Church in Russia by John Glen King', Katherine adds '(Dr Haliday lent me this very interesting Book)', Haliday having accompanied the Wilmot sisters on several journeys to and from Russia.[50] While no such record exists for Guthrie's text, an anecdote in Martha's journal in March 1808 makes clear that the book belonged to Katherine. While travelling between St Petersburg and Moscow, Martha comes across a familiar instrument at an inn. She identifies the instrument as 'a Gouslee, which is small, to hold in the hand like a Lyre & exactly such as Guthery has given a print of in the book

---

[47] Srinivas Aravamudan, 'Lady Mary Wortley Montagu in the Hammam: Masquerade, Womanliness, and Levantinization', *ELH*, 62:1 (1995), 69–104, p. 70.
[48] Ibid, p. 71.
[49] Marilyn Butler, *Mapping Mythologies: Countercurrents in Eighteenth-Century Poetry and Cultural History* (Cambridge, 2015), p. 124.
[50] RIA MS 12 L 34, p. 1.

on russian Antiquitys wch K. has got [*sic*]'.[51] Martha notes the instrument's ancestral connection to the guitar she is learning to play: 'the gouslee or horizontal harp, on which I play is a refinement on the other in which to say the truth its originality is almost lost – the one I see at present, is not a yard long – I rather think tis a Tartar instrument' (pp. 217–218). The gusli, a Russian folk instrument, detailed by Guthrie as *Gously*, is described in the first dissertation under the category of 'stringed instruments' as 'a very curious and very ancient instrument, which accompanies the peasants' choir'.[52] Guthrie's inclusion of a charming drawing of the object in *Planche II* allows an easy identification of the exotic instrument in situ, with Martha using his text as a cultural and material guidebook.[53]

Matthew Guthrie first travelled to Russia in 1769, staying in the country for nearly four decades and eventually rising to serve as a counsellor to the Russian royal family as well as a personal physician to Catherine II. His *Dissertations* was only ever published in French, the preferred language of the Russian nobility in St Petersburg, yet Guthrie continued to expand the original English-language manuscript of his study.[54] Guthrie's connections with Britain are emphasised through his dedication of the 1795 publication to the Society of Antiquaries of Scotland, a relatively young institution formed in 1780. The Royal Charter of the Society of Antiquaries of Scotland, published in 1783, heralds a new era of investigation in Scotland into 'both antiquities and natural and civil history in general, with the intention that the talents of mankind should be cultivated and that the study of natural and useful sciences should be promoted'.[55] The Society's mandate includes the study of antiquities 'not only in the kingdom of Great Britain but in other realms' as well (p. 30). Guthrie's *Dissertations* aims to

---

[51] RIA MS 12 L 21, 'Tuesday 22nd March N.S. 1807 [1808]', pp. 217–218.

[52] Matthew Guthrie, *Dissertations sur les Antiquités de Russie* (Saint-Petersbourg, 1795), p. 32; 'Instrumens à corde'; 'un instrument très-curieux & très-ancien, qui accompagne les choeurs villageois'; my translation.

[53] Martha had the instrument shipped back to Ireland when she departed Russia. In 1809, she wrote to her relative John Eardley-Wilmot lamenting its slow progress: the 'poor old *Gouslee*' had been 'sent up to Dublin to go thro' some forms & Ceremonys' at the Custom House. She asked Eardley-Wilmot to intervene and use his influence to ensure it reached her as soon as possible. See Beinecke OSB MSS 54, Box 3, Folder 151, '6th June 1809', recto.

[54] An English copy of the completed manuscript travelled to London by 1802, where it was made publicly available in the office of his publishers 'Messrs. Cadell and Davies', 'for the inspection of the curious', making clear his eager efforts to stay in dialogue with his British counterparts; see Guthrie and Guthrie, p. vi, fn.

[55] Society of Antiquaries of Scotland, *Account of the Institution and Progress of the Society of the Antiquaries of Scotland* (Edinburgh, 1783–84), p. 30.

answer this call by taking up what he interprets to be the most intriguing vestige of ancient life still apparent in Russia in the late eighteenth century: the music and culture of the peasantry, which he insists provides proof of a shared heritage between the Russians and the Ancient Greeks. Guthrie's text participates in widespread Scottish Enlightenment interest in the study and categorisation of difference among peoples '[t]hrough comparison of different societies, progress was shown to emerge from changes across economic, political, social and cultural spheres' among Scottish Enlightenment thinkers.[56]

In adopting Enlightenment methodologies of comparison between people by studying rural life and peasant culture, Guthrie seeks to reveal national identity. Yet he was certainly not the first to draw on analogy in an antiquarian capacity; Joseph-François Lafitau's 1724 study of indigenous North American populations served as a milestone for early comparative practices between the manners and customs of supposedly uncivilised populations and those of 'primitive' times.[57] As Noah Heringman notes, 'colonial ethnographers' frequently documented morals and customs as a form of 'antiquity' in the eighteenth century, in an attempt to locate 'the supposed origins of human civilization' among living people.[58] Guthrie asserts that the manners and customs of a nation are of antiquarian value, while also suggesting serfdom among the Russian peasants has maintained a type of stasis among the peasants worthy of attention.[59] The result of studying these preserved social group has exposed a 'resemblance between the Russians and Greeks', which 'becomes striking when one considers the musical instruments of the peasants' and 'their ancient mythology ... which is absolutely the same'.[60] As the proof for Guthrie's argument is rooted firmly in music and folk objects, his own illustrations and musical notations are embedded in the back of the text as an 'appendix', thereby allowing members of the Society of Antiquaries of Scotland, as well as all

---

[56] Silvia Sebastiani, '"Race", Women and Progress in the Scottish Enlightenment', in *Women, Gender and Enlightenment*, ed. by Sarah Knott and Barbara Taylor (Basingstoke, 2005), p. 75.

[57] Joseph-François Lafitau, *Mœurs des Sauvages Ameriquains Comparées aux Mœurs des Premiers Temps*, 2 vols (Paris, 1724).

[58] Noah Heringman, *Sciences of Antiquity: Romantic Antiquarianism, Natural History, and Knowledge Work* (Oxford, 2013), pp. 1, 2.

[59] Guthrie, p. 4; 'C'est parmi les paysans, surtout lorsqu'il ont été long-temps dans l'état de vasselage, & par conséquent attachés au même sol pendant plusieurs siècles, que l'antiquaire doit étudier les meours & les usages d'une nation'; my translation.

[60] Guthrie, p. 4; 'la ressemblance entre les Russes & les Grecs devient frappante, si l'on considère les instruments de musique des paysans ... leur ancienne mythologies ... qui est absolument la même'; my translation.

other readers – such as the Wilmots, who used it as a type of guidebook – to experience the antiquities he has collected by proxy.[61]

Guthrie's corresponding record of the women's premarital bathhouse ritual is included in the *Dissertations* as song 14, under the heading of '*Chansons de mariage, appartenant au bain*'.[62] Guthrie points to the ritual's antiquarian significance in his 'Remarque', stating '[t]his song is among the most curious and important'.[63] He further adds that the 'same song offers' a 'resemblance between the Russians and the Ancient Greeks', through 'the dress of the marital bath' and 'in that the participants put on white and rouge, in the style of the Athenians.[64] The extent to which the Wilmots' description of the ritual overlaps with Guthrie's in precise details raises further questions about relationality, authorship and agency. Katherine's manuscript and the version appearing in the supplement to *Memoirs* are strikingly similar to Guthrie's, with the Wilmot version offering an apparent line-by-line translation from French to English of Guthrie's original '*Chansons de mariage, appartenant au bain*'. The parallel nature of the text is potentially problematic, given that no attribution is provided for the translation of the song from the original Russian. Katherine's unattributed use of Guthrie's translation from the Russian should be interpreted as an act of borrowing common to the period particularly within the context of familial correspondence intended for the relatively closed parameters of the Wilmots' social networks. Katherine never claims to include an original translation of the song in her letter to Harriet of 1807, writing:

> A group of girls then set up what *sounded a sort of Requiem*, call'd *Pesni Swadbischnia* – As I was curious to *root* into the *marrow* of the business, I was resolved to comprehend the meaning of what was sung – which has been sung time out of mind, & many of these Allegoric compositions, still remain in the Sclavonian [*sic*] dialect – the change of name only being necessary to make it perfectly appropriate. – Here

---

[61] Guthrie's drawings are 'the only known drawings of musical instruments used by the Russian peasants of the times (albeit with some inaccuracies in the nomenclature)'; see K. A. Papmehl, 'Matthew Guthrie – The Forgotten Student of 18th Century Russia', *Canadian Slavonic Papers/ Revue Canadienne des Slavistes*, 11:2 (1969), 167–181, p. 178.

[62] Guthrie, p. 189.

[63] Guthrie, p. 190; 'C'est [*sic*] chanson est d'autant plus curieuse & importante'; my translation.

[64] Guthrie, p. 191; 'Je dois remarquer aussi que cette même chanson offre deux points de vue de ressemblance bien sensible, entre les Russes & les anciens Grecs: le premier, dans la coutume du bain nuptial; & l'autre, dans celle du *peuple*, de mettre du blanc & du rouge, mode athénienne'; my translation.

then is a specimen of *one* among *fifty* of the same nature, which was sung at the pitch of their voices.[65]

The inclusion of the recycled translation, which has helped Katherine to '*root* into the *marrow*' of the bathhouse ritual, can be read as her desire to document and share foreign experience. In this instance, the songs' insertion in the body of the letter evokes intertextual practices common among the Wilmot women's commonplace books, assemblages that frequently thread long selections of text without formal attribution.[66] Commonplace book practices were a widespread practice in the late eighteenth century, particularly among women with intellectual and literary interests and aspirations. The fact that the Wilmot women's commonplace books were frequently collaborative and apparently shared, paired with the established notion of closed sociable manuscript publication and performance, underlines Katherine's apparent intentions of entertainment and improvement of the family circle through her inclusion of the songs.[67]

Martha's failure to acknowledge her source for the English translation of Guthrie's French translation, later published as a supplement to *Memoirs*, however, involves further complications related to both authority and patronage. The neglected attribution can be read, in one light, as Martha's attempt to align the sisters' observations and collection practices to an antiquarian authority. Both Martha and Katherine seem to accept Guthrie's suggestion that the activities of the 'Vapour Bath' tie the existing rituals of the Russian peasants to customs of antiquity. Originally writing about the event to Harriet, Katherine declares that the ceremony is 'a living picture of the remotest age' whose 'origin may … be clearly traced to Pagan practices', adding that the ritual poses 'a strong similitude with the Greeks in these matters'; these are themes that Martha preserves and highlights in the 1840 publication.[68] Such instances point to the Wilmots' desire to legitimise their practices of observation through intertextual allusion to Guthrie. Martha's editorial positioning of the ritual in relation to Guthrie's interpretation can also be understood as a desire to posthumously honour

---

[65] RIA 12 L 30, p. 133.

[66] Commonplace books created by Katherine and Martha Wilmot, as well as their mother Mary, sisters Alicia, Dorothea and Harriet, and sister-in-law Eliza are present in the Blair Adam House Collection.

[67] See, for example, Katherine's commonplace book created during the exile of the female Wilmots to Brampton, Irish Rebellion, 1798: sister Dorothea Wilmot illustrated the back and front covers with lovely sketches; BAHC, Wilmot Box 1, Bundle 2, Item 2/6.

[68] RIA MS 12 L 30, p. 132; *Memoirs*, II, p. 410.

Dashkova's generous patronage. Dashkova's own mentor, Catherine II, supported Guthrie's *Dissertations*; Martha's mirroring might therefore be read as an act of homage. Guthrie's analogies between Russian peasant ritual and ancient Greek culture appear to be unique to the *Dissertations*, save for their appearance in the Wilmots' writing. By endorsing Guthrie's analogies, the Wilmots' own account of the Russian bathhouse ritual can be seen to validate Dashkova's support for Catherine II by extension, as well as supporting the work of both the Russian Academy to which both Catherine II and Dashkova were affiliated, and the work of the Society of Scottish Antiquaries.

Women travel writers could, at times, benefit from an advantage of gender that allowed them to enter spaces from which their male counterparts were precluded. While Guthrie's text documenting the closed feminine space of the ritual must be gleaned through second-hand information due to his gender, Katherine's account is, at least in part, an original narrative. Because historical writing 'was considered a masculine pursuit, men who researched and documented the past invariably emphasized the actions of men'.[69] By occupying an all-female space in her description, Katherine can extend and improve on Guthrie's account in a move that subverts the gendered hierarchies of institutionalised antiquarian practice.

Katherine's record of the Russian vapour bath also recalls Lady Mary Wortley Montagu's much discussed description of the Turkish bathhouse in the *Turkish Embassy Letters*.[70] Both Katherine and Montagu's accounts preface their visits to the bathhouse as essential foreign experiences founded on exotic voyeuristic travel. Montagu notes making special arrangements in order to visit the bathhouse: 'I must not omit what I saw remarkable at Sofia, one of the most beautiful towns in the Turkish empire, and famous for its hot baths ... I stopped here one day on purpose to see them.'[71] This resonates with Katherine's later description of the ritual 'Vapour Bath' as 'perhaps the most amazing circumstance arising from a Russian tour', an experience for which she is willing to 'suffer' the heat. These prefaces can be read through Edward Said's concept of the Oriental 'strategic location', or a space that has been configured in and between texts in order to manufacture a vision of the Orient for Western readers.[72] The description of the 'bagnio' that appears in *Turkish Embassy Letters* is written in a

---

[69] Crystal B. Lake, 'History writing and antiquarianism', in *The Cambridge Companion to Women's Writing in the Romantic Period*, ed. by Devoney Looser (Cambridge, 2015), p. 89.
[70] Lady Mary Wortley Montagu, *The Turkish Embassy Letters* (London, 1993), p. 77.
[71] RIA MS 12 L 30, p. 132; Montagu, p. 57.
[72] Edward Said, *Orientalism* (New York, 1978), p. 20.

sympathetic tone, with Montagu praising the women for their 'obliging civility' in welcoming her, as well as in their behaviour towards one another.[73] Montagu is unwilling to fully assimilate and join in the women's activity by disrobing completely, yet she does engage with the women to the point that they convince her to 'open' her garments and 'show' her stays:

> The lady that seemed the most considerable amongst them entreated me to sit by her and would fain have undressed me for the bath. I excused myself with some difficulty, they being however all so earnest in persuading me, I was at last forced to open my shirt, and show them my stays, which satisfied them very well, for I saw they believed I was so locked up in that machine, that it was not in my own power to open it, which contrivance they attributed to my husband.[74]

While still not orientalising herself with full nudity, therefore maintaining a level of propriety, Montagu bridges a gap that incites a role reversal: '[b]y maintaining the several senses of constriction that uphold her identity, the European aristocratic woman is momentarily rendered the slave, while the object of her reflection, Turkish ladies of quality, are seen as completely unfettered.'[75]

While Montagu's decision to bare herself suggests she is a participant, engaging primarily with 'the lady that seemed the most considerable amongst them', Katherine takes on the position of the detached observer, watching the ritual among the lower, serving class while seemingly not participating:

> They then took [off] their own clothes, & after scouring her to their hearts content, danced round about, (in all their national dances) clapping their hands, drinking wine, which was dispensed by another Eve, who sat with a bottle in one hand, & a glass in the other, her long tresses falling down about her shoulders, which, like all the others, was the only shadow of covering they cou'd boast.[76]

A sense of separation between Katherine and the bathers is made clear by her focus on their nudity. The purpose of the account as an illustration of Russian peasant life intended to entertain and educate Katherine's familial circle presupposes expectations of politeness and separation from the

---

[73] Montagu, p. 58.
[74] Montagu, pp. 59–60.
[75] Aravamudan, p. 85.
[76] RIA MS 12 L 34, p. 134.

foreign women she documents. It is perhaps for this reason that Martha and Katherine describe the 'Pagan' vestiges with equal parts censure and respect. Relating the participation of one elderly woman in the bathhouse, Martha notes that the application of the ritual paint incited 'a sudden transformation', 'a metamorphas that did not outlive the Bath scene [sic]'; instead, the woman 'drew in her horns, & return'd to her pacific natures [sic]'.[77] Both Katherine and Martha's descriptions remain aloof; participation would imply a breach of propriety, as well as an unusual and unacceptable engagement with pseudo-pagan rituals. Yet another and much more practical reason for this separation can be gleaned from one of Martha's journal entries from earlier the same month. '[I]t was in reality the *first* time of my seeing a Russian Bath', she writes, 'but I *could* not support the heat, for three seconds, and was oblig'd to come out, & stand at the Door, where I saw all the Ceremonys [sic]'.[78] Unable to withstand the climate, the Wilmots' viewpoint of the ritual is perhaps literally bordered by the doorframe, as outsiders looking in.

Martha's own description of an earlier bath scene echoes Katherine's in the evocation of both classical antiquity and feminine beauty, referring to the bathers as 'Bachanant [sic]', and deeming the leader '*Aquilina*', as if to denote her Roman qualities, while Katherine's language bears striking similarities to Montagu's description of the Turkish bathers as:

> without any distinction of rank by their dress, all being in the state of nature, that is, in plain English, stark naked, without any beauty or defect concealed. Yet there was not the least wanton smile or immodest gesture amongst them. They walked and moved with the same majestic grace which Milton describes of our general mother ... their skins shiningly white, only adorned by their beautiful hair divided into many tresses, hanging on their shoulders, braided either with pearl or ribbon, perfectly representing the figures of the Graces.[79]

All three accounts place heavy focus on the actions of the women bathers as vestiges of pre-Christian rituals, while simultaneously endowing the subjects with the qualities of figures from antiquity. Montagu's describes the Turkish women's behaviour as evocative of 'our general mother', or 'the Graces'; Katherine describes the woman dispensing wine to the other bathers as 'another Eve'. These representations are simultaneously classically biblical, drawing up allegorical images of the creation myth as if to illustrate

---

[77] RIA MS 12 L 20, 'Wednesday 7th [October 1806]', p. 181.
[78] RIA MS 12 L 20, 'Wednesday 7th [October 1806]', p. 180.
[79] RIA MS 12 L 20, 'Wednesday 7th [October 1806]', p. 180; Montagu, p. 59.

both the primordial purity, as well as the exotic quality, of the ceremony. As Cynthia Lowenthal suggests, by alluding to the women as living antiquities in the form of 'the Graces' or Eve, Montagu 'locate[s] the women in their proper non-Western geographical setting while simultaneously endowing them with the weight of Western classical culture'.[80] By imbuing living women with the classical roles of Eve and 'the Graces', both bathhouse accounts seek to cast dignity and respect onto the female subjects of the present day, as well as, presumably, their cultures. For women writing from abroad in the eighteenth century, 'their travels put distance between them and the gentleman's home turf, they seem emboldened to experiment with aesthetics' symbolic encoding of a social world viewed from the top down'.[81] The Wilmots' privileged position in Troitskoe as guests of Dashkova, the local feudal noblewoman, has given them access to the witness of this spectacle, placing them in a unique position of authority. As Anglophone women travellers who are placed in an upper-class position – even if only temporarily through their patron – their observation of the ritual, which is in this case performed by their own servant and her family, also highlights imbalanced power dynamics. For instance, Katherine refers to the Russian peasant women by generic titles such as 'another Eve', 'they' and 'her', despite her familiarity with the women through daily contact.

These bathhouse descriptions exemplify the ways that women writers synthesised their reading practices in Enlightened fields of knowledge with their lived experiences abroad. As Montagu boasts to her recipient at the conclusion of her own bathhouse narrative, 'I am sure I have now entertained you with an account of such a sight as you never saw in your life, and what no book of travels could inform you of, as 'tis no less than death for a man to be found in one of these places'.[82] Inspired and informed, in part, by Guthrie, the Wilmots extend his observations while circumventing the gendered exclusionary tactics of the antiquarian societies for which his text was produced. The description of the ritual signals the participation of women travellers in wider discourses and dialogues prevalent in travel writing and antiquarianism of the late eighteenth century, and their contribution to the formation and transmission of specialised knowledge.

---

[80] Cynthia Lowenthal, *Lady Mary Wortley Montagu and the Eighteenth-Century Familiar Letter* (Athens, 1994). p. 103.
[81] Elizabeth A. Bohls, *Women Travel Writers and the Language of Aesthetics, 1716–1818* (Cambridge, 1995), p. 18.
[82] Montagu, p. 61.

"'Tis likewise a dance': Folk Song and National Identity

Among the materials extant from the Wilmots' time in Russia is an olive-coloured silk notebook containing Russian songs gathered by Martha.[83] Many of the songs in the notebook are folk songs that display Martha's interest in the peasants' customs and rituals, while the paratextual commentary for each song indicates the substantial amount of time she spent immersed in and reflecting on her Russian surroundings. The first entry in the notebook documents 'A Russian Peasants Song [sic]' spread over three pages.[84] The preface points to her authoritative experience in having heard the song and dance performed repeatedly: "'Tis likewise a dance, I have heard the peasant girls women sing it while they danc'd their National dance, many & many a time [sic]' (p. 3). Martha's later revision, crossing out the word 'girls' in favour of 'women', adds maturity not only to the performance but also to her observation, refining the presentation of the song. The song encompasses eighteen verses, each of which is numbered and translated from the original Russian in parallel text with the English. Frequent marginalia provide a code for deciphering the content of the song at a later date: after the fifth verse, in which the singer promises 'I'll make two Goudotchkas [sic]', Martha scribbles 'a musical instrument a sort of flagelet'.[85]

Martha's olive notebook holds significance as a material representation of foreign travel. The songs in the notebook offer proof of learning acquired abroad, an essential aspect of travel for aspirational middle-class women such as the Wilmots. The folk songs that Martha gathers together in the notebook are, in one sense, used as linguistic exercises, allowing her to improve proficiency in French, Russian and Italian, all of which she notes studying while resident at Troitskoe. For example, a translation titled 'Song on the subject of the Offering made to the Dead, by the Russian Peasants' spans across four columns in Russian, French, English and Italian translation, the Italian being the crudest.[86] Only a small portion of songs in the notebook have not been translated by Martha herself, as she notes just below a song entitled 'Chanson – traduit de la langue Ruse [sic]', writing 'par – I don't know who'.[87] The inclusion of previously translated and unattributed songs by herself flags up the notebook's primary purpose as a collection site

---

[83] RIA MS 12 L 29.1.
[84] Ibid, pp. 3–5.
[85] Ibid, p. 4.
[86] Ibid, pp. 46–51.
[87] Ibid, p. 10.

Figure 9   Royal Irish Academy MS 12 L 29.1, 'Letters of Martha Bradford (née Wilmot) and Katherine Wilmot', p. 47: 'Song on the subject of the Offerings made to the Dead, by the Russian Peasants'. © Royal Irish Academy.

for Russian folk ballads and customs, with translation activities filling an ancillary didactic need. It also highlights practices of assembly reminiscent of the commonplace book, with knowledge amassed and collected for use at a later date. A. G. Cross has written about the pioneering importance of Martha's translation exercises in the silk notebook, noting that several of these exercises likely represent the first instance of the songs' translation from the original Russian.[88]

[88]   A. G. Cross, 'Early British Acquaintance with Russian Popular Song and Music (The Letters and Journals of the Wilmot Sisters)', *The Slavonic and East European Review*, 66:1 (1988), 21–34, p. 32. Cross reads the Wilmots' interest in Russian music within

A substantial portion of the entries in the notebook, however, appear to be the result of fieldwork, with Martha's paratextual commentary serving as a record of strange yet intriguing customs she encounters among the Troitskoe peasantry. A mourning song, for instance, is noted as being performed by the 'nearest relation making offerings to the Dead, *6 weeks* after their demise, *to release their souls from Purgatory*, & each year 4 times as a general Memorial Feast'.[89] Martha's underlining of '6 weeks' as well as 'release their souls from Purgatory' emphasises the exotic quality of her observations. Yet it is not only the foreignness of these traditions that she highlights, but also her own essential role in viewing and documenting them, as she writes: 'these verses are selected from above a dozen on the same subject & prove the custom which exists, & which I have witness'd [*sic*]'.[90] This paratextual note is concluded with her own signature, 'M. Wilmot 5th Nov'r 1807 – Troitskoe', as a means of stamping the song, and its collection, as an integral part of her foreign experience.

The collection of music played an increasingly significant role in travel literature of the mid to late eighteenth century. Many English and French travelogues in the period incorporated songs or musical experiences encountered abroad, even when the authors were not specifically interested in music.[91] Captain James Cook's *An Account of the Voyages* (1773) for instance, included songs heard among islanders in the South Pacific.[92] Other works placed musical encounter more firmly at the centre of their travel writing. Charles Burney's popular tours focused on music collection in France and Italy (1771), as well as Germany and the Netherlands (1773).[93] 'Prior to Burney', writes Vanessa Agnew, 'the pursuit of musical knowledge was not in itself a motivation for travel'.[94] For Martha, the collection of songs enriched her ability to relate her own foreign experience.

---

the framework of emerging Russian folk musicology of the late eighteenth and early nineteenth century; his article is therefore an insightful attempt to integrate their output within wider late Enlightenment knowledge discourses, despite only dedicating five pages of the total article to discussing the Wilmots' work specifically.

[89] RIA MS 12 L 29.1, p. 51, emphasis original.
[90] Ibid, p. 51.
[91] Ruth Rosenberg, *Music, Travel and Imperial Encounter in 19th-Century France: Musical Apprehensions* (New York, 2014), pp. 4–5.
[92] James Cook, *An Account of the Voyages in the Years MDCCLXVIII, MDCCLXIX, MDCCLXX, and MDCCLXXI*, 3 vols (London, 1773).
[93] Charles Burney, *The Present State of music in France and Italy* (London, 1771); Charles Burney, *The Present State of the Music in Germany, the Netherlands and the United Provinces* (London, 1773).
[94] Vanessa Agnew, *Enlightenment Orpheus: The Power of Music in Other Worlds* (Oxford, 2008), p. 4.

Careful documentation of the songs allowed their later performance, an accomplishment that would certainly be shared and drawn on for sociable purposes following her return to Ireland.

Martha's collection can also be read in the context of eighteenth-century folk song collection as a marker of cultural identity, mirroring trends in her host country, her native Ireland, as well as across Britain and wider Europe. The appearance of Thomas Percy's *Reliques of Ancient English Poetry* (1765) presented a turning point in the dissemination of musical and poetic antiquities as a vital element of national identity formation in Britain. The *Reliques* comprises 180 ballads, sonnets, songs and romances spread across three volumes. It aims, through recovery of the specimens of ancient poetry, to trace the progress of Britain's 'ancestors' from an 'unlettered people' into a modern society. As Nick Groom writes, 'Percy's *Reliques* ... is probably the finest example of the antiquarian tendency in later eighteenth-century poetry' because 'it dramatized the encounters between literate and oral media, between polite poetry and popular culture, and between scholarship and taste'.[95] Yet the interaction between the literate and the oral, between the polite and the popular, was underpinned by a primarily scholarly methodology. The works in *Reliques* were compiled 'from an ancient folio manuscript in the Editor's possession ... written about the middle of the last [17th] century'.[96] The ancient provenance of Percy's sources validated their appeal and quality by interacting with vociferous eighteenth-century preoccupations with the recovery of national antiquities. Antiquarianism and antiquities in Britain 'provided the raw material from which the narratives of history could be fashioned' by forming 'a sense of the past and historic identities' and thereby fashioning 'imagined communities of eighteenth-century nationalism'.[97]

Antiquarian interest in folk song was also proliferating in the Wilmot sisters' native Ireland in the second half of the eighteenth century, particularly among the Anglo-Irish. Energised by British and European movements to excavate and chart national identities from the ancient to the modern, the last decades of the century saw a burgeoning movement

---

[95] Nick Groom, *The Making of Percy's Reliques* (Oxford, 1999), p. 2.

[96] Thomas Percy, *Reliques of Ancient English Poetry, Consisting of Old Heroic Ballads Songs, and Other Pieces of our Earlier Poets, Chiefly of the Lyric kind Together with Some Few of Later Date*, 3 vols (Dublin, 1766), I, p. v; the manuscript in question is BL Add MS 27879, 'Collection of English metrical romances and ballads, with marginal notes by Thomas Percy, Bishop of Dromore'.

[97] Rosemary Sweet, 'Antiquaries and Antiquities in Eighteenth-Century England', *Eighteenth-Century Studies*, 34:2 (2001), 181–206, p. 181.

to capture Ireland's unique language, customs and culture.[98] Antiquarian pursuits were attractive to late eighteenth and early nineteenth-century Irish women, many of who took an interest in song collection.[99] Certainly the most notable example of a woman's participation in antiquarian folk song scholarship, as well as arguably the most influential collection in the eighteenth century, is Charlotte Brooke's *Reliques of Irish Poetry: Consisting of Heroic Poems, Odes, Elegies, and Songs Translated into English Verse* (1789).[100] Brooke's *Reliques* denote the first attempt to communicate Irish oral tradition into print culture. The *Reliques* made Gaelic-language popular culture accessible to the Protestant Anglo-Irish for the first time. At the same time, the text brought Irish folk poetry and songs to the attention of antiquarians. Brooke's own familiarity with native Gaelic tradition developed during her childhood in County Cavan and Country Kildare among the labourers resident on her family's estate.[101] She leveraged this linguistic knowledge by seeking out and translating Gaelic manuscripts previously inaccessible to the English-speaking population. The paratextual remarks accompanying songs and verses were gleaned both from scholarly research and oral tradition. Brooke's preface to *Reliques* presented the collection as 'the vital soul of the nation', offering them '[w]ith a view to throw some light on the antiquities of this country, to vindicate, in part, its history, and prove its claim to scientific as well as military fame'.[102]

While Martha's immediate exposure to folk songs can be more easily linked to the antiquarian practices of Irish society in the late eighteenth century, her use of fieldwork and her emphasis on the oral history of the rural peasantry resonates with collection practices on the Continent. Johann Gottfried Herder's (1744–1803) philosophical reflections on nationhood and indigenous peoples were highly influential to growing late eighteenth-century interest in what he classed as the *Volk*, or the folk/simple people. In particular, Herder argued for the collection and preservation of folk song, a preoccupation that resulted in the publication of his seminal

---

[98] See Clare O'Halloran, *Golden Ages and Barbarous Nations: Antiquarian Debate and Cultural Politics in Ireland* (Cork, 2004).

[99] Gerardine Meaney, Mary O'Dowd, Bernadette Whelan, *Reading the Irish Woman: Studies in Cultural Encounter and Exchange, 1714–1960* (Liverpool, 2013), p. 66.

[100] Charlotte Brooke, *Reliques of Irish Poetry: Consisting of Heroic Poems, Odes, Elegies, and Songs, Translated into English Verse: with Notes Explanatory and Historical* (Dublin, 1789).

[101] Joep Leerssen, 'Brooke, Charlotte (c.1740–1793)', *Oxford Dictionary of National Biography* (Oxford, 2004), <http://www.oxforddnb.com/view/article/3537> [accessed 20 December 2022].

[102] Brooke, pp. iv, v.

edited collection, *Volkslieder*, in 1778–79.[103] Folk song and ancient verse also occupied an important role in forming national identities in Britain and wider Europe in the second half of the eighteenth century. Herder's assertion that the national identity of a people could be traced to its peasant populations had widespread implications for the increasing value being placed on the oral history of rural populations. As he wrote in 1773, 'Unspoiled children, women, folk of a sound natural sense, minds formed less by speculation than by activity – these ... are the finest, nay the only orators of our time.'[104] Herder encouraged his countrymen to 'go in search of our local songs, each one of us, in our own provinces', in the hopes of gathering the living and active folk songs of the German people 'in Alsace, in Switzerland, in the Tyrol, in Franconia or Swabia', thereby drawing together 'German customs and German poems' to create a unifying collection of folk songs.[105] While Herder's project was assertively German-centric, he cited Percy's efforts to create a national body of the poems and songs of British 'singers, bards, and minstrels' as an essential inspiration for his theories, which would in turn have a significant impact on folk song collection and ideologies surrounding the rural poor in Russia (p. 138).

The late eighteenth century saw a surge of Russian interest in folk custom and song in intellectual and noble circles in St Petersburg as well, a trend that was invigorated by the publication of Ivan Pratch's *Sobraniye narodnikh russkikh pesen* ('A Collection of Russian Folk Songs') in 1790.[106] The title, as well as the content, is directly inspired by Herder's *Volkslieder* (1778–79).[107] Pratch, and his silent partner L'vov, are widely credited as the first composers to collect, translate and popularise the folk music of the Russian peasants for refined audiences.[108] Catherine II perceived the project as a valuable nation-building activity, and lent her patronage and support to his endeavours and publication. As Richard Taruskin writes, the songs in the collection are 'actively collaborating with the "folk", in the spirit

---

[103] Johanne Gotfried von Herder, *Volkslieder (Nebst Untermischten Andern Stücken)* (Leipzig, 1778, 79).

[104] *Eighteenth-Century German Criticism: Herder, Lenz, Lessing, and Others*, ed. by Timothy Chamberlain (London, 1992), p. 137.

[105] Herder, p. 140.

[106] Ivan Pratch and Nikolai L'vov, *Sobraniye Narodnikh Russkikh Pesen* (St Petersburg, 1790).

[107] Richard Taruskin, *Defining Russia Musically: Historical and Hermeneutical Essays* (Princeton, 2000), p. 16.

[108] Pratch is commonly listed as the primary author of this text in contemporary publications, though recent scholarship has asserted that the primary author was Pratch's employer, Nikolai Alexandrovich L'vov (1751–1803), a noble landowner and member of the Russian Academy of Sciences and the St Petersburg Academy of the Arts.

of the Enlightenment, to produce a new genre that purposefully mediated or transcended the borders between genres (read: social classes)'.[109] The reading list in Katherine's 1806 notebook proves the sisters' awareness of Pratch's publication, while Katherine's commentary points to a wider interest in the collection and dissemination of 'ancient' folk song in Russia in the late eighteenth century: 'Monsieur Pratch [A German] has collected Russian Music and published Ancient Songs at Petersborough [sic]'.[110] Pratch's text was never translated into French or English, though several of the songs in his collection appear in Guthrie's *Dissertations*, with appropriate attribution. Martha's ability to read and translate from Russian, if a work in progress, points to the likelihood that she drew on Pratch and Guthrie's respective song collections as a model, rather than a direct source.

Another example from Martha's music notebook, entitled 'Loptys vs Boots: A Christmas Song, of the Russ Peasants', captures one aspect of the multi-tiered social order of Russian village life:

> Cease dear Mother to torment yrself [sic]
> And make some Pyes [sic]
> For visitors will come to you, & suitors to me
> They'll come to you dress'd in *Loptys** (Peasants Shoes)
> And to me dress'd in *Boots*.[111]

Martha's notes imply that the songs have been collected from eyewitness encounter. She offers a range of supplemental information for this short folk song: '[t]he difference between Peasants shoes (made of the Birch tree & call'd Loptys) and Boots', she writes, is that 'the suitor dress'd in Loptys is a meer Peasant, liable to be taken as a soldier … or a sort of out House servant [sic]' (p. 53). Martha's interpretation of the song contains several interesting remarks, some of which imply a possible lack of sensitivity or a misunderstanding of the machinations of the class system among the peasants. For instance, a note at the bottom of her commentary elaborates on the class among which the song is sung: 'the race of maid servants are the daughters of this class. Who scorn to marry peasants & by degrees fill the shops & lower trades in towns [sic]' (p. 53). Martha's designation of the song as being sung by the 'Russ Peasants' is, therefore, slightly imprecise: rather than being solely the preserve of the peasants, the song reflects the members of local society situated slightly above the peasant class, who aspire above their station by trading peasant 'Loptys' for boots. Martha's understanding

---

[109] Taruskin, p. 17.
[110] RIA MS 12 L 34, p. 4.
[111] RIA MS 12 L 29.1, p. 53; emphasis original.

of the subtleties of the class structure among the lower orders may have improved over time; while the undated songs in the olive-coloured notebook were recorded as early as 1806, a diary entry from the end of 1807 indicates a growing sensitivity in the matter. There is, she writes, a 'strong line of distinction between the *Peasants* who wear *Loptys* (shoes made of the birch tree) and those who wear *boots*, the women who are dress'd in a National *Costume*, and those who dress as they please'.[112]

Despite her consistent attempts to grapple with the nuance of the culture, Martha's remarks often lack understanding. In the midst of her documentation and translation of 'Under the Dish', she interrupts the thirteen-verse stream to comment on a verse promising 'Great good luck & riches' (p. 58). In the verse, a bear swims across a river, wherein he is bitten by 'half a bushel of Fleas, & a Whole bushel of Lice [sic]'. Martha remarks:

> This filthy composition (wch is only sung by the Peasants) finds a place here, to show that the same superstition respecting these Vermine [sic] in *Dreams* & Sorcery, exists in Russia, & in Ireland, namely their portending *luck* & *riches*.[113]

Though the song is playfully crude, Martha expresses disapproval over the mystical viewpoint celebrated in the context of the song. Martha's reactions display her polite Irish Protestant sensibilities, a viewpoint that often leaves her scandalised by the pseudo-pagan practices of the Russian peasants, which evoke the habits and superstitions of the Irish, even as she documents their ways. While she placed herself among the peasantry, Martha's comments remain aloof: they are fragmentary elements of the exotic landscape to be documented, yet not particularly admired. The songs are recorded as they are performed in their native language, transforming them for future Irish or English readers and audiences, adds to her self-representation as an experienced Grand Tour traveller avidly collecting information for knowledge, improvement and Empire.

Women Antiquarians Beyond the Institution

In January 1808, Martha writes in her journal of a recent accomplishment:

> I have employ'd the Entire of last week, in translating from the russ, the curious manuscript which the Princess gave me, descriptive of

[112] RIA MS 12 L 21, 'Friday Eve'g 20th [November 1807] [sic]', p. 76.
[113] RIA MS 12 L 29.1, p. 58.

> the marriage of the Tzar Michael Fedrovitch, & Eudoxia, Grandfather & Gd Mother of Peter the Great – ... it has been a terrible piece of business, as the manuscript is written like the Bible, in a language out of common use ... the translation therefore tho' a comfort to have, cannot be scrupulously correct – I am thought mad, for giving myself so much trouble – but I was so anxious to finish it, that even my beloved Italian has lain Dormant.[114]

Martha notes receiving the assistance of two young Russian women who were visiting Troitskoe, describing them as the 'principle aids on this occassion' [*sic*], noting that they thought her 'mad' for choosing to take on the difficult translation project (p. 134). Translation work formed an essential part of gendered eighteenth-century travel writing, allowing women writers to 'transform' and 'transport' texts encountered abroad 'across different cultures'.[115] Martha's remark that the completed translation, though flawed, is still 'a comfort to have', points to the particularly important space that translations occupy among the textual exercises she engages in and textual objects she creates at Troitskoe as markers of linguistic accomplishment, as well as representative of experience abroad.

The notion of 'comfort' here may also spring from the acquisition of and engagement with the rare antiquarian object itself: a beautiful copy of an early eighteenth-century manuscript commissioned in the 1790s for the imperial library and containing more than one hundred pages of gold-leafed, hand-coloured illuminations depicting the Tsar's marriage celebration, which Martha is offered as a gift by Dashkova.[116] The manuscript binding has been altered from its original state, with Martha's translation inserted as an integrated form of paratext. Martha's translation is supplemented as an annex in the back of the binding, separated by a single leaf from the Russian manuscript pages. The translation is written on light blue sheets of paper of a slightly smaller size than the gilt-edged pages of the original, creating a visually conspicuous addendum. The handwritten English-language key references the pages by number, thereby elucidating the archaic textual contents that accompany the stunning images to future English readers. Plate 50, for example, offers a colourful representation of the moment 'the Tzarina' is presented 'to the Tsar'. While the image clearly shows the couple being united, Martha's supplemental codex provides a translation of the detailed dialogue from the original Russian, in which the

---

[114] RIA MS 12 L 21, 'Monday 24th [Jan 1808]', pp. 134–135.
[115] Mirella Agorni, *Translating Italy for the Eighteenth Century: Women, Translation and Travel Writing* (Manchester, 2002), p. 2.
[116] RIA MS 12 L 16.

presentation occurs 'By the Will of God' and the 'Trinity' in order 'to prolong thy race' and 'reign over this Empire' (n.d.).

The inscription on the inside cover of the volume emphasises the transformation of the manuscript. It reads: 'Martha Wilmot, Moscow. May 1807. The gift of Princess Daschkaw, my dear Russian Mother'; and further down the page: 'This book was in the possession of Katherine the 2nd for a week, and read by her Imperial Majesty [sic]' (p. 2). The interleaved manuscript is, of course, yet another material example of the many privileges that Martha and Katherine benefit from in Russia as Dashkova's guests and as recipients of her informal patronage, a position that affords seemingly unfettered access to the manuscripts and rare books in the noblewoman's extensive library. Dashkova's past role as Director of the Imperial Academy of Arts and Sciences in the 1780s filled her private collection with significant late eighteenth-century titles across a variety of knowledge genres. The many books at Troitskoe share space with printed broadsides of her own Russian-language speeches given during her time as Director. Several of these were brought back to Ireland with Martha as part of a growing collection of institutional and Imperial printed texts and manuscripts, including the 1765 *Privileges et Reglemens de L'Academie des Beaux-Arts*, a royal charter prefaced by Catherine II in celebration of the Academy's foundation in St Petersburg.[117] Dashkova's support of the Wilmots' historical interests can be seen as playing out within the bounds of the coterie, an effective alternative for the institutional affiliations focused on the formation of national antiquities from which women were barred in the late eighteenth and early nineteenth centuries. The rare nature of the artefacts available to the Wilmots, such as the manuscript of the Tsar's marriage, as well as Dashkova's patronage and support of their textual endeavours, gives the sisters' antiquarian efforts a sense of authority that was unusual, if not completely unique, for women in the era with antiquarian interests.

The Wilmots were undoubtedly aware of the existence and activities of the Royal Irish Academy in their native Ireland, as Dashkova had been elected the first honorary female member in 1791, following a visit to the Academy during her 1779 sojourn in Ireland as the guest of their aunt, Mrs Hamilton. The Royal Irish Academy was formed in 1785 for the purpose of promoting 'Science, Polite Literature, and Antiquities'.[118] Dashkova was the only woman granted the privilege of even an honorary membership

---

[117] *Privilèges et Reglemens de l'Académie Impériale des Beaux-Arts, peinture, Sculpture et Architecture, Établie à St. Petersbourg* (St Petersbourg, 1765); the copy in question is now part of the RIA Wilmot Papers Collection as RIA 12 L 35.

[118] *Charter and Statutes of the Royal Irish Academy: For Promoting the Study of Science, Polite Literature, and Antiquities* (Dublin, 1787), p. xi.

until the mid-nineteenth century, and her permanent residence in Russia precluded her active participation.[119] While all incipient institutional antiquarianism functioned as an exclusively male preserve in Ireland in the late eighteenth century, women nonetheless played a significant role in the development of the discipline. Those in elite circles were involved in facilitating antiquarian practices outside of the societies from which they were excluded. As Amy Prendergast has shown in *Literary Salons Across Britain and Ireland in the Long Eighteenth Century*, significant antiquarian discussion took place in the Moira House salon. Hostess Elizabeth Rawdon, Countess of Moira (1731–1808), more commonly known as 'Lady Moira', 'lent support to those who wished to promote such endeavours', and engaged in the activities of the Academy by proxy through the membership of her husband.[120] Lady Moira also engaged with local antiquarianism on her own estate, publishing an article in *Archaeologia*, the journal of the Society of Antiquaries of London, on the 'Particulars relative to a Human Skeleton, and the Garments that were found thereon, when dug out of a Bog ... in the Summer of 1780', an important, if rare, example of women's intervention with antiquarian institutional bodies in the period.[121] Lady Moira can also be linked to collaboration with Charlotte Brooke, author of *Reliques of Irish Poetry*, through Brooke's prefatorial acknowledgement that 'To the Right Honorable the Countess of Moira I am indebted for some valuable communications [sic]', indicating the importance that cooperation between women played in the text's publication. The circumstances surrounding the publication and reception of Brooke's *Reliques*, which enjoyed widespread popularity in antiquarian circles, remain poignantly ironic when her own story of institutional exclusion is considered. Brooke applied for the post of Housekeeper to the Royal Irish Academy in 1787 in an attempt to gain access under a guise that would be viewed as domestically appropriate to her gender. She later withdrew her request when unable to receive

---

[119] Mary Somerville was the second woman to be elected an honorary member in 1834, followed by Caroline Herschel in 1838 and Maria Edgeworth in 1842.

[120] Amy Prendergast, *Literary Salons Across Britain and Ireland in the Long Eighteenth Century* (Basingstoke, 2015). p. 112.

[121] Countess of Moira, Elizabeth Rawdon, 'Particulars relative to a Human Skeleton, and the Garments that were found thereon, when dug out of a Bog at the Foot of Drumkeragh, a Mountain in the County of Down, and Barony of Kinalearty, on Lord Moira's Estate, in the Autumn of 1780', *Archaeologia, The Society of Antiquaries of London*, 7 (1785), 90–110. For more on Lady Moira and other women archaeologists in Ireland in the period, see Madeleine Pelling, 'Digging Up the Past: Contested Territories and Women Archaeologists in 1780s Britain and Ireland', *Open Digital Seminar in Eighteenth-Century Studies* (2021), <https://www.youtube.com/watch?v=VBtLx5QiA_s> [accessed 15 January 2023].

support from a sufficient number of the existing members despite the fact that twenty-seven members of the Academy subscribed in support of the publication. The fact that both she and Lady Moira contributed significant antiquarian knowledge from beyond the bounds of the Royal Irish Academy signals much about women's tactics of collaboration and subversion of exclusion. Butler has written about the ability of 'the stories of other people and other times' to become 'an appropriate topic for those writing out of the provinces', away from 'the centres of power'.[122] So too might the work of women engaging in antiquarian study of the physical and oral remnants of ancient myth and folklore from the people and the landscape surrounding them be interpreted as an attempt to decentralise institutionally gendered authority. In other places, however, antiquarian women trailblazers are less easily identified. For instance, no female names are included among the many pages listing the members of the Society of Antiquaries of Scotland, the institution with which Guthrie was affiliated. The document does reveal, however, that women took an interest in the activities of the society, as evidenced in the donations list, which includes 'Mrs Drummond of Blairdrummond. 290. A silver penny of King William the Conqueror'.[123] Women were eventually admitted into the Society of Antiquaries of Scotland as Lady Associates in 1870, and as Lady Fellows in 1900, while the Royal Irish Academy's first full female member was elected in 1949.

Martha's interleaved manuscript now occupies a prized place in the archives of the Royal Irish Academy, an institution that devotes an entire special collection to the Wilmots' manuscripts, which are today cherished as emblems of the agency and prowess of eighteenth-century Irish women travellers. The 1796 illuminated manuscript, which documents the seventeenth-century marriage of Peter the Great's grandparents and was once read by Catherine II, is forever stamped with the imprint of Martha's antiquarian textual intervention. It stands to illustrate the ways in which women collaborated and intervened with antiquarian practices from beyond the closed borders of institutional practice. The dedicatory page, which is the first to greet the modern reader, contains Dashkova's forward-slanting French scrawl, identifying the manuscript as a 'copy of an ancient manuscript in the Moscow Imperial Archive'.[124] Below this, written nearly sixty years later in 1864, a note of inheritance bequeaths the manuscript to Martha's daughter, 'Catherine Anne Daschkaw Brooke', named for the Imperial

---

[122] Butler, p. 19.
[123] Society of Antiquaries of Scotland, '1782. June 25', p. 52.
[124] RIA MS 12 L 16, n.d; 'copie d'un ancien manuscript de L'archive Imperiale de Moscou'; my translation.

Russian women with whom the trajectory of the manuscript is bound up. Martha's interleaving of the old text with her new translation, as well as the dedication recognising her friendship with Dashkova, reconstitutes the old text into something new. By adding her own paratext and translation, Martha transforms the rare and potentially indecipherable early manuscript into a consumable object of literary antiquarianism, mediated and packaged with a preconfigured interpretation. This new text is inextricably linked to her own antiquarian endeavours, while also being inscribed with the intimacy of the transnational and transgenerational coterie.

For the 'further edification' of the Public

The Wilmots' activities can be seen as an expression of the growing role that British women played in the preservation of antiquities and the emergence of ethnographic pursuits. While the first audiences for the practices discussed in this chapter can be found in the sisters' immediate coterie and sociable circle in Ireland, the subsequent publication of much of the material as a supplement to Dashkova's *Memoirs* shifts the trajectory and purpose of the Wilmots' manuscripts, offering a legitimacy and importance to the work that the sisters themselves likely did not anticipate.

The eighteenth-century fad for popular antiquarian collecting continued to be a 'pervasive influence during the Victorian period and after upon more successful academic specialisms – anthropology, social history, religion and culture studies'.[125] George Catlin's wildly successful 1839 exhibition of Native American artefacts and paintings at the Egyptian Hall, as well as his 1841 *Letters and Notes on the Manners, Customs and Conditions of the North American Indians* provides useful contemporary context for the interest of British audiences in foreign civilisations.[126] Catlin's efforts 'mapped onto Romantic inflected narratives about the noble savage' and mediated onto mid-nineteenth-century 'developments in racial theory, human taxonomies, and ideas about degeneration'.[127] The print afterlife of the folk songs and rituals documented and collected by the Wilmots foreshadowed this mid-nineteenth century increase in the categorisation and interrogation of branches of science.

---

[125] Butler, p. 125.
[126] George Catlin, *Letters and Notes on the Manners, Customs, and Condition of the North American Indians* (London, 1841).
[127] Kate Flint, 'Counter-Historicism, Contact Zones, and Cultural History', *Victorian Literature and Culture*, 27:2 (1999), 507–511, 507.

The ever-increasing nineteenth-century enthusiasm for information about exotic cultures can be located in Martha's own practices as editor of Dashkova's *Memoirs*, published in 1840. Odd textual exclusions make more sense in light of the increased public interest in foreign customs and ancient ways of life; for instance, a song originally collected and translated by Martha in the silk olive notebook is mysteriously transposed within Katherine's supplement in *Memoirs*.[128] The song is prefaced with a fictionalised note from Katherine: 'Here, for your further edification', is half-a-dozen of these mystic songs' (II, p. 418). By crediting a folk song, which she herself has collected, to her by-then deceased sister, Martha posthumously imbues Katherine's writing with ethnographic interest for the Victorian mid-nineteenth-century reader. This subtle editorial choice prepares the way for the subsequent chapter, which discusses Martha's editorial work in envisioning and forming a much-delayed legacy for Dashkova, as well as for the sisters themselves, as inscribed on the pages of *Memoirs of Princess Daschkaw*.

---

[128] *Memoirs*, II, p. 418–419.

4
Collaborative Women's History

In 1809, Martha Wilmot was back in her native Ireland. She had been abroad in Russia for a period of more than six years. Far from wishing to settle down after a momentous period of travel, returning had inspired Martha to continue to travel domestically. In September, she and her sister Alicia set off on a tour of Ireland that would last for almost a year, repeating some of a journey Martha had taken nearly a decade earlier during the bloody aftermath of the failed Irish Rebellion.[1] Now, as she had then, Martha kept a journal of her experiences.[2] The earlier tour of 1802 had been written from the perspective of a tourist, with Martha preoccupied by documenting remnants of the violent uprising, such as seeing 'the head of one of the rebel leaders, placed over the jail a most shocking & disgusting memorial of those melancholy times'.[3] By contrast, the 1809–10 tour journal turns towards Martha's role as a literary and social participant in the places she travels through. Her time as the special guest and protégée of Princess Dashkova in Russia had enriched her education through intensive study of the arts, languages, and intellectual practices. She had experienced an up-close view of the political conflicts of the day as they unfolded, particularly as she sailed home through the tumultuous bombardments of the Anglo-Russian war. Martha came back to her own country with an array of new talents, interests and experiences. And to show for these efforts, she now possessed a trove of literary works produced by

---

[1] Martha notes in a letter to her cousin John Eardley Wilmot that the journey began in Bantry, as her sister with whom she travelled 'had been unwell & was recommended sea bathing'; Beinecke OSB MSS 54, Box 3, Folder 151, '10 August 1809', recto.

[2] The earlier tour can be found in BAHC, Bradford Wilmot Box 2 Item 8, 1802, beginning from page 15. Martha used the earlier pages of the same slim brown leather-bound notebook to document her family's flight from Ireland to Brampton, England at the outset of the 1798 Irish Rebellion (see Chapter 1, pp. 36–37); a typewritten transcript of the later tour can be found in BAHC Wilmot Box 1 Bundle 2, 2/8. Only a typewritten copy of this second tour remains in the Blair Adam House Collection, having been transcribed by Martha's twentieth century descendants.

[3] BAHC, Bradford Wilmot Box 2, Item 8, 1802, p. 26.

herself and her sister Katherine while abroad, including their own compiled travel letters and fair-copy journals, which she was determined to put to good use in Irish society.[4]

Staying in the houses of relatives and friends throughout the country, Martha shared these manuscript treasures liberally, reading out 'Kitty's Journal, thro' France, Italy, etc' to her hosts ('Wednesday 4th [October 1809]', p. 3) and later 'Kitty's Letters from Russia', which sent 'the society assembled in the drawing-room ... in extacys' ('Wednesday 22nd [November 1809]', p. 17). When the occasion called for it, she shared the customs and practices she had witnessed, including 'dancing my Gypsy and Russian dances, which after all I succeeded in but badly, however all pass'd off very well' ('Thursday 21st [November 1809]', p. 25). As she travelled, Martha persevered with the daily literary practices she had begun as Dashkova's mentee, working on the coterie's papers nearly every day, as she noted in October 1809: 'I am copying Kitty's letters from Russian into a book, I write a page or two every morning before breakfast' ('Sunday 15th [October 1809]', p. 5).

In addition to carrying these prized personal papers, Martha possessed the manuscript of Dashkova's memoirs, having filled the role of Dashkova's amanuensis and confidante throughout the writing process at the Princess' Troitskoe estate. Martha and Katherine had laboured over the course of their respective stays in Russia to create fair manuscript copies of the volume to bring back to Ireland. While Martha was forced to leave her own copy behind due to suspicion from Russian border officials, Katherine carried the other home safely to Cork, with a view to its eventual publication. Dashkova had declared that the work could not be published until after her death, an event that the small literary coterie hoped lay long in the future. From Ireland, Martha continued to write to her friend, hoping that she might be able to travel to Russia again in the future, perhaps after the conclusion of her present tour. Dashkova's final letter, which was directed to Martha from Cork, encapsulated the intensity of their connection, and the pressure on Martha to return. Dashkova wrote in October 1809, beginning in the French language in which she had composed her memoir as well as in which she had mentored the two sisters: 'I am sad, I cry every day and I can't get used to your absence', later adding in her imperfect English, 'Thank you thousand time [sic] my sweet Angel for the promise you give me that ... you will come to me'.[5]

---

[4] See Chapter 2.
[5] 'Je suis triste, je pleure tout les jours et je ne saurai m'accoutremer à votre absence'; my translation; BL Add MS 31911, '1809, ce 25 octobre N.S.' p. 302r; '3 Novembre N.S.,

But Martha's second journey to Russia would never come about. As she wrote in her journal in May 1810, 'I receiv'd Letters from Russia giving me the fatal intelligence of my beloved Princess Daschkaw's death. I cannot express the variety of painful sensations which have press'd on my heart ever since'. The scale of Martha's grief put an abrupt end to her second Irish tour. Her journal captures a shift in her focus away from socialising, as Martha immediately travelled home to Cork:

> Ever since my return I have been employ'd in reading over with Eliza Wilmot, the Memoir of her life, which my beloved Princess had written for me, while I was in Russia. Whether it is to be publish'd or not, I do not know, but I must now set about copying it in order to shew [sic] it to a bookseller. This will probably cause me to take a journey to London.[6]

Martha's journal captures her urgent wish to reassess Dashkova's manuscript for publication. Faced with the enormity of the task, she marshals help from her sister-in-law Eliza, one of several women in her provincial Irish family circle with whom she had previously shared and worked on literary projects.[7] Drawing on well-established habits, she begins to create a new copy, which can be shown to a 'bookseller', so that her own sole copy of the manuscript may remain safely at home. This new task implies further travel, as well as the assumption of a new role: that of editor. Martha's apprenticeship at Troitskoe was intended, in large part, to prepare her for this moment. Yet her journal entry gives away a sense of uncertainty, embodied in the lines, 'Whether it is to be publish'd or not, I do not know'. This trepidation was not unfounded. Despite Martha's good intentions, the memoir's pathway to print would be full of challenges, both anticipated and unforeseen.

This chapter discusses the obstacles faced by transnational women editors and writers of biographical history in the late eighteenth and early nineteenth centuries, as seen through the microcosm of Martha Wilmot's experience. I trace the difficulties overcome by Martha in achieving her

---

pp. 303r–v.
[6] BAHC Wilmot Box 1 Bundle 2, 2/8 'Sunday 27th. May, 1810'.
[7] Chapter 2 details the dynamics of manuscript production and exchange within the Wilmot family circle. Eliza's commonplace book, held by Blair Adam, provided the source for identification of Lady Mount Cashell's anonymously printed broadside poem, 'The Bard of Erin'. See Wolf, 'Identity and Anonymity in Lady Mount Cashell's 1798 Rebellion Broadside', *Journal for Eighteenth-Century Studies*, 45:2 (2022), 259–276.

and Dashkova's dream of publishing the manuscript. Martha's relative inexperience and lack of connections in the publishing world would come to bear on her editorship. She would be forced to contend with persisting concerns surrounding the work's authorship and authenticity, given the unusual relationship between herself, a middle-class Irish woman with no credentials, and a Russian noblewoman with ties to the Empress of Russia. These issues were made worse by aspersions cast by and a lack of support shown on behalf of Dashkova's surviving relatives, who expressed their own doubts on the veracity of the manuscript and disapproved of the nature of its contents. Further, the manuscript itself was not of a high literary quality. The flawed text, as it existed in its original form, would require translation, amendment and perhaps supplementation to make it fit for a public readership. As a result of these many hurdles, three full decades would elapse between the time of the Princess' death and the publication of her manuscript as *Memoirs of the Princess Daschkaw, Lady of Honour to Catherine II. Empress of All the Russias. Written by Herself: Comprising Letters of the Empress, and Other Correspondence. Edited by Mrs. W. Bradford* (1840). It is difficult to imagine a formation that would have better pleased Dashkova: including her filial ties to the late Empress as well as raising the profile of her beloved protégée – using her later married name – the title showcases how female friendships sit at the centre of the book.

In its original printed form as it appeared in 1840, *Memoirs* spans 850 pages across two volumes, only a few hundred of which are occupied by Dashkova's original narrative. The extensive paratext in *Memoirs* provides fertile ground for painting a more positive posthumous character for Dashkova than she enjoyed in life, while also aligning the work with contemporary publishing trends, and highlighting the relationships shared by its subject and editor. In what follows, I reconstruct the publication history of the book within the context of transnational literary practices of the period in which it was produced. I do so by following the structure of the book itself: first, in its background to publication; next, its paratext and prefatory material; then, work associated with preparing and editing the central narrative. I also examine how the nexus of British, European and Russian literary worlds converged to influence Martha Wilmot's choices for the final shape of the text. As I will show, for women authors and editors of historical, biographical and travel writing of the late eighteenth and early nineteenth centuries, both national and foreign interests play an essential role in validating their choices, concerns which can be traced in the pages of the books they created.

Making Women's Literary History

Dashkova's written permission enabled Martha to act as editor of *Memoirs of Princess Daschkaw*, both through the dedication and in the gift of her story into Martha's care. Despite this explicit consent, Martha's choice to publish the text meant assuming a precarious role. Martha's unwavering claim to the title of editor, a statement that is reiterated repeatedly throughout the pages of *Memoirs*, is not only reflective of her protective attachment to Dashkova's manuscript, it is also an attempt to hold firm control of a historically important manuscript, a space not typically overseen by an unknown, middle-class woman.

Considering the reasons behind Martha's firm claim to authority has led me to untangle a long-standing mystery surrounding the 1840 publication: while she is clearly identified as the work's *Editor* on the title page, no *Translator* is attributed there, nor anywhere else in the lengthy published book. The manuscript was originally composed in French, the preferred language of intellectual correspondence and publication in Imperial Russia, yet the 1840 first edition appears in flowing English. This missing attribution of a translator is curious, particularly given the Wilmot sisters' efforts to create a cohesive English translation of the manuscript. During their time at Troitskoe, Martha and Katherine both write of 'copying' the manuscript and 'trying' to translate it from the French. For instance, in October 1806 Katherine declared in her diary 'I finish'd the translation completely'.[8] The labour of translating the manuscript, once an absorbing preoccupation for the Wilmot sisters, is notably hidden from public consideration in the 1840 publication, despite Martha's desire to highlight her by-then late sisters' achievements.[9] In fact, no mention of the original French manuscript is ever made, save for an indirect allusion in the preface to Martha's '*English*' version, which Dashkova sanctioned to one day be created in order to publish her story for a public readership.

The English version, as it would finally appear in the 1840 print edition, is fluid and convincing, disguising its origins as a translation to the extent that, for several decades, it was more or less accepted as Dashkova's original. The English text from the 1840 publication was subsequently translated back into French in 1859, as well as into German (1857), Russian (1859) and Czech (1911).[10] The French subtitle further misconstrues the provenance

---

[8] RIA MS 12 L 18, '29 March 1804', p. 99; RIA MS 12 L 31, 'Oct 26 1806', p. 3.
[9] Katherine Wilmot died in 1824.
[10] Eketerina Romanovna Dashkova, *Princess. Mémoirs de la Princesse Dashkoff, dame d'honneur de Catherine II ... Publié sur le manuscrit original par Mistress W. Bradfort*

of the text by indicating Martha as the original author: 'published from the original manuscript by Mrs W. Bradfort [sic]'.[11] Martha appears to have participated at least somewhat in the production of the retranslated 1859 French edition, evidenced by surviving handwritten French drafts of her 'Introduction, by the Editor'.[12] Her failure to highlight the original French version, or to contradict the French subtitle, if such things were in her power, points to a choice to conceal information with the potential to erode her authority as editor.

Biographers and critics have erroneously cited Katherine's English translation as the likely source for the later publication of the central narrative in *Memoirs*, despite the fact that it is absent from the archives. Dashkova's biographer Alexander Woronzoff-Dashkoff writes, for instance, that it is 'safe to assume ... Catherine had also drafted an English-language translation while still in Russia'.[13] This provenance is understandable in light of the dispersed and multilayered nature of the Wilmots' existing manuscripts. However, new and previously overlooked archival evidence points to Martha's husband, Reverend William Bradford, as the translator of the 1840 *Memoirs*. Bradford and Martha had married in 1812. They shared intellectual interests and both had experience as Anglo middle-class travellers. Bradford's journey as the chaplain to an expedition in Portugal and Spain during the Peninsular War resulted in the 1809 publication of *Sketches of the Country, Character, and Costume in Portugal and Spain*.[14] In 1850, he published *Correspondence of the Emperor Charles V and his Ambassadors at the Courts of England and France, ed. by the Rev. William Bradford*, a collection of letters transcribed and translated from the Royal Archives in Vienna.[15] Bradford's interests as a historical biographer and experience

---

[sic] (Paris, 1859); E. R. *Dashkova, Memoiren der Fürstin Daschkoff: zur Geschichte der Kaiserin Katharina II* (Hamburg, 1857); E. R. *Dashkova, Zapiski kniá'gini E. R. Dashkovoĭ, pisannyiáèiú samoĭ* (London, 1859).

[11] 'Publié sur le manuscrit original par Mistress W. Bradfort'; my translation.

[12] These are bound within manuscript volumes held by the British Library and at Blair Adam; BL Add MS 31911, pp. 12r–22v; BAHC, 'Contents of the Letter File of Princess Dashkoff', n.d.

[13] A. Woronzoff-Dashkoff, *Dashkova: A Life of Influence and Exile* (Philadelphia, 2008), p. 271.

[14] Rev. William Bradford, *Sketches of the Country, Character, and Costume in Portugal and Spain ... engraved and coloured from the drawings by W. Bradford* (London, 1809).

[15] Rev. William Bradford, *Correspondence of the Emperor Charles V and his Ambassadors at the Courts of England and France, ed. by the Rev. William Bradford* (London, 1850); Bradford prepared this project while serving as Chaplain to the British Ambassador in Vienna between 1819–29, during which time he and Martha lived in

with languages and translation complemented Martha's skills in preparing Dashkova's manuscript for publication.

Several archival records prove that the translation should be attributed to William Bradford. The first is found in Martha's 1813 correspondence with Lord Glenbervie, a politician and diarist. Glenbervie had been loaned Martha's copy of the manuscript, and wrote to offer guidance on how to proceed. Given the manuscript's many grammatical and structural imperfections, Glenbervie suggests that the manuscript 'be submitted to the supervision of some native Frenchman, of honour and taste, & established reputation for literature'. Though Martha's reply to this suggestion is absent, Glenbervie's return is telling: after receiving a response, he retracts the advice of hiring a Frenchman to translate the manuscript, having been informed that the Bradfords are set on the appearance of an English version, and that Reverend Bradford is to play a central role in the translation process. As he writes: 'By knowing that Mr Bradford has himself undertaken the revision of the English translation, all apprehension on the score of pure idiomatic language, or the more important points of composition, must cease.'[16] The overall exchange implies that Martha is either unable or unwilling to carry out the work herself.

Further proof of the translation's provenance can be found in several newly uncovered letters sent by William Bradford to publisher John Murray in 1814 in an attempt to secure a contract for publication. Describing the original French manuscript, he writes, 'I have been persuaded to proceed with the translation … I will send you what is already done, that you may form some idea of what the performance may be.'[17] Bradford sends the manuscript to Murray only to request it back the following month, as 'it is the only fair copy we have & … the one I use in translating.'[18] Bradford's letters, along with much of the other correspondence relating to publication attempts for the memoir, make no mention of Katherine's English translation, instead identifying himself as translator.

A third piece of archival evidence is most explicit. Confirmation of the translation's provenance can be found in an undated letter fragment written by Martha. The contents of the letter make clear that it was composed in the period directly prior to the appearance of the 1840 publication.

Vienna. For Martha's collected letters from this period, see Martha Wilmot, *More Letters from Martha Wilmot: Impressions of Vienna 1819–1829*, ed. by Edith Marchioness of Londonderry and H. Montgomery Hyde (London, 1935).

[16] RIA MS 12 M 18, 'Brighton, Jan 7, 1813'.
[17] NLS, Edinburgh, The John Murray Archive, MS.40140, Fol 111v, Storrington March 9th 1814'.
[18] NLS, MS.40140, Fol. 113r, 'Storrington April 18th. 1814'.

Martha writes to the addressee that the memoir 'is at length going to see the light ... I now consent to what I have so long wished'.[19] Martha states that Bradford's 'translation is certainly admirable & the whole thing, I should suppose, likely to be an object of much interest'.[20] It is surprising to see this detail revealed casually to the anonymous recipient, noted only as 'E', given that the 1840 publication appears to intentionally conceal the translator's existence.

Though William Bradford apparently completed the final version of the translation, essential decisions for the publication's presentation remained under Martha's control, as shown through a note scribbled on the back of the undated letter. In the fragment, Martha tests the possibilities of biography as a genre, scribbling: 'the translation is sometimes enlivened by conversations & anecdotes fresh from her own lips, but which she did not think it worthwhile to introduce'.[21] This fragment provides an important contrast to the printed version of the same statement, which appears in the preface: 'Had I thought it right to do so, I might have added to the princess's manuscript, by introducing, here and there, conversations and anecdotes fresh from her own lips, which she did not think it worth while [sic] to insert.'[22] The transition from the first to second statement traces Martha's line of thinking as she seeks her own editorial style. But most importantly, it shifts the description of the work from a 'translation' to a 'manuscript', effectively erasing her husband's work. The decision not to attribute the translation to Bradford represents a choice not to allow a male voice to infringe on the text, which, in its printed form, is a carefully crafted artefact of women's lives and literary communities.[23]

---

[19] BAHC, 'Contents of the Letter File of Princess Dashkoff', Item 35, n.d., recto; this letter fragment is interesting for a number of reasons, including its placement in the Blair Adam family archive. It is tucked into the back of a large album containing dozens of mounted original and transcribed letters. These letters form the bulk of the paratext in the 1840 publication, and appearances suggest that the album was prepared as a prop for typesetting. However, there are several pages that have been cut out, apparent from the binding. These may have once contained the transcriptions of Catherine II's letters, created by Katherine Wilmot at Troitskoe in 1805, and now located in the British Library (BL Add MS 31911). There is also one additional manuscript bound within the album that did not appear in the 1840 publication: a scribal copy of Dashkova's 1770 tour of the Highlands, prepared by Martha at Troitskoe in 1804. It is likely, therefore, that this tour was originally considered for inclusion in the paratext, yet excluded at a later stage.

[20] BAHC, 'Contents of the Letter File of Princess Dashkoff', Item 35, n.d., r.
[21] BAHC, 'Contents of the Letter File of Princess Dashkoff', Item 35, n.d., r.
[22] *Memoirs*, I, p. xix.
[23] This strategy echoes the choices of late eighteenth-century communities of women writers and translators working on one another's literature due to friendship and

Martha's editorship can also be read within the context of a burgeoning field of women-authored historical texts, which were reshaping the boundaries of publication opportunities for women editors, authors and translators in Britain. While not encouraged to write about such topics beyond the range of their everyday experience, women had been, from the mid-eighteenth century, encouraged to read history. The act of reading history could stand 'in for those parts of the world that "ladies" should not see', giving them 'understanding [of] aspects of life they were not supposed to have access to without encountering problems of decorum in experiencing them'.[24] Women's limited opportunities to live through historically imbued experiences clearly continued into the nineteenth century, as 'historiography … traditionally treated the major events of the public world: courts, not hearths; wars, not romances; treaties, not engagements; the births and deaths of empires, not of children'.[25] Aspiring women authors of history were generally barred from academic societies and scholarly archives, being allowed into institutions such as the Bodleian Library on visiting days during holiday periods, if at all.[26] Subsequently, 'the writing of English history has been understood in relation to the male historians who produced it, and to the masculinist institutions that fostered it'.[27]

Still, in spite of these limitations, and potentially in response to societal pressure to adhere to subjects considered appropriate for feminine morals, the late eighteenth and early nineteenth centuries saw an increase in the number of popular publications of women-authored biographies focused on the lives of women through the development of the genre of royal female biography. The act of writing royal biography, whether focused on a male or female ruler, can also be linked to collective efforts to provide a cohesive and comprehensive record of the British monarchy and, by extension, the British Empire. Contrary to the clichéd idea that men dominate historical representation due to their central role as agents in its creation, 'such a picture neither tells a complete story nor proves that such a division

---

love, including Anna Seward and Eliza Hayley, as recently detailed in Francesca Blanch-Serrat, 'Women Translating Women: Resisting the Male Intellectual Canon in Eliza Hayley's Essays on Friendship and Old-Age, by the Marchioness de Lambert (1780)', *Enthymema*, (2023), 78–90.

[24] Devoney Looser, *British Women Writers and the Writing of History, 1670–1820* (Baltimore, 2000), p. 18.

[25] Rohan Amanda Maitzen, *Gender, Genre and Victorian Historical Writing* (New York, 1998) p. 6.

[26] Rosemary Ann Mitchell, '"The Busy Daughters of Clio": Women Writers of History from 1820 to 1880', *Women's History Review*, 7:1 (1998), 107–134, p. 116.

[27] Mary Spongberg, *Women Writers and the Nation's Past 1790–1860: Empathetic Histories* (London, 2018), p. 1.

is necessary or natural.'[28] Women authors of royal biographies sought to co-opt a shared, public space of empire-building through their historical writing, and they began to do so with relative prominence in the late 1830s and throughout the 1840s.

The rise of women-authored royal biographies has previously been characterised as an embodiment of the rising 'moral influence that gave women power' in the late eighteenth and early nineteenth centuries.[29] By focusing on the behaviour of royal women as a model, women found an acceptable avenue for serious scholarly engagement, while also questioning gendered roles pertaining to domestic and public life.[30] A sampling of titles of women-authored royal biographies of the period gives a sense of the emerging trend. Between the late 1830s and the mid-1840s several lives of individual royal women appeared, including Hannah Lawrence's *Historical Memoirs of the Queens of England* (1838), Katherine Thomson's *Memoirs of Sarah, Duchess of Marlborough, and of the Court of Queen Anne* (1839) and Martha Freer's *Marguerite of Angouleme, Queen of Navarre* (1854).[31] Group biographical studies also gained momentum with the publication of Agnes and Elizabeth Strickland's highly acclaimed, multi-volume work, *The Lives of the Queens of England* (1840–48).[32] The popularity of the project inspired the Strickland sisters to follow up with *The Lives of the Queens of Scotland* (1850–58), and provided a model for Mary Anne Everett Green's *Lives of the Princesses of England* (1849–55).[33] The focus on the lives of not only individuals, but also groups of royal women, points to a growing desire for aspiring women historians not only to exploit the opportunity to enter historical dialogues using female subjects, but also to create a lineage

---

[28] Phillipa Levine, *Gender and Empire* (Oxford, 2004), p. 8.

[29] Mary Spongberg, 'The Ghost of Marie Antoinette: A Prehistory of Victorian Royal Lives', in *Clio's Daughters: British Women Making History, 1790–1899*, ed. by Lynette Felber (Newark, 2007), pp. 71–96; pp. 72, 73.

[30] *Clio's Daughters: British Women Making History, 1790–1899*, ed. by Lynette Felber (Newark, 2007), p. 18.

[31] Hannah Lawrence, *Historical Memoirs of the Queens of England from the Commencement of the Twelfth Century* (London, 1838–40); Katherine Thomson, *Memoirs of Sarah, Duchess of Marlborough, and of the Court of Queen Anne* (London, 1839); Martha Walker Freer, *The Life of Marguerite D'Angouleme, Queen of Navarre* (n.p., 1854).

[32] Agnes and Elizabeth Strickland, *Lives of the Queens of England, from the Normal Conquest*, 12 vols (London, 1840–48).

[33] Agnes and Elizabeth Strickland, *Lives of the Queens of Scotland and English Princesses, Connected with the Regal Succession of Great Britain*, 8 vols (Edinburgh, 1852–59); Mary Anne Everett Green, *Lives of the Princesses of England*, 6 vols (London, 1849–55).

of women's historiography leading back throughout the centuries. Still, it is important to note that the number of these publications were relatively limited in comparison with the huge volume of male-authored historical writing being produced by the mid-nineteenth century.[34] Additionally, many women readers (and writers) disapproved of women-authored history books: 'Although history is one of the most useful studies which a woman can pursue, her powers of mind are hardly fitted to enter this field for the sake of instructing others', M. A. Stodart argued in *Female Writers: Thoughts on their Proper Sphere and on their Powers of Usefulness* (1842).[35]

While it is not strictly accurate to classify Martha as an aspiring woman historian, her role in publishing a work of historical significance does associate her activities with the growing number of women who were producing and publishing female biography around the period of the 1840 publication of *Memoirs*. Clearly, Martha's desire to publish is prompted by the relationship that she shared with the author, rather than by an independent desire for enquiry and research; likewise, her reasons for solidifying a legacy through publication are motivated by the interests of the coterie and the desire to rectify negative public opinion of Dashkova's reputation. The special access to rare material that Martha benefited from, both in the form of the core manuscript written by Dashkova, as well as the large body of letters and documents copied by the Wilmots in Russia, also separates Martha from contemporary women historians. However, the similarities between her own edited publication and those proliferating in the marketplace at the same time is significant, as Martha was able to assimilate her text within the popular tide of her contemporaries.

Other publications released by Henry Colburn, publisher of *Memoirs*, provide further evidence of the gender politics and legal challenges encountered by women authors in the literary marketplace of the 1830s–50s. Colburn's dealing with the Strickland sisters show his techniques and ethos when dealing with women authors. John Southerland notes that Colburn often unscrupulously pressured authors for increased profitability, citing that he 'bullied an unwilling Miss Agnes Strickland into rushing out the abysmal pot-boiler *Queen Victoria From Birth to Bridal* for the royal wedding in 1840'.[36] In the same year the Stricklands were negotiating an agreement with Colburn for the publication of their massive project, *The Lives of Queens*. After Colburn offered them a miserly £100 in exchange for

---

[34] Miriam Elizabeth Burnstein, 'Royal Lives', in *Companion to Women's Historical Writing*, ed. by Mary Spongberg (Basingstoke, 2009), p. 497.
[35] M. A. Stodart, *Female Writers: Thoughts on their Proper Sphere and on their Powers of Usefulness* (London, 1842), p. 124.
[36] John Sutherland, 'Henry Colburn Publisher', *Publishing History* (1986), 59–84, p. 59.

the copyright against the £2,000 they demanded, the sisters were forced to bring in a male friend to conduct business with the publisher on their behalf. The sisters attributed the inadequate offer to their gender, with Elizabeth writing in a letter in 1840 that if Colburn were forced to 'deal with gentlemen the whole matter would come to a dead stop'.[37] These incidences occurred in the same year as the publication of Dashkova's *Memoir*.[38]

Although Martha's dealings with Colburn are not documented, her husband's involvement was legally necessary. Indeed, it was impossible for married women authors to enter independently into contracts prior to the Married Women's Property Act of 1882.[39] The contemporary publishing records of Richard Bentley, Colburn's former business partner, show this involvement in practice, in the form of a memorandum of sale signed by Sir T. C. Morgan, on behalf of his wife, Lady Sydney Morgan, author of *The Wild Irish Girl*. Bentley agrees to buy 'the entire copyright of a novel written by Lady Morgan entitled "The Princess of Schaffenhausse"', which was later published as *The Princess* (1835).[40] However, this practice was apparently not ubiquitous, as several other women authors in the Bentley volume, including the widowed Mary Shelley, add their own signatures to their agreements.[41] In Martha's case, as a married women, it can be assumed that Bradford also filled a further silent role in the publication process by conducting business transactions associated with publication.[42]

[37] 'Letter: 20 December 1840, Elizabeth Strickland to Sir Thomas Phillips', in Mitchell, p. 118.

[38] It is also possible that Martha may have had a pre-existing connection to Colburn's publishing house through her extended family's literary networks. Angela Byrne has linked two novels published by Colburn to members of Martha's family. Byrne identifies the anonymous author of *Blue Stocking Hall* (1827) and *Tales of My Time* (1829) as being either Anna Maria Chetwood (1774–1870), Martha's sister-in-law, or Alicia Wilmot (1776–1860), her younger sister. *Blue Stocking Hall* enjoyed success and was published in a second edition in 1829, yet Colburn was unwilling to publish a third novel by the same anonymous author. See Angela Byrne, 'Anonymity, Irish Women's Writing, and a Tale of Contested Authorship: Blue-Stocking Hall (1827) and Tales of my Time (1829)', *Proceedings of the Royal Irish Academy Section C: Archaeology, Celtic Studies, History, Linguistics and Literature*, 119 (2019), 259–281.

[39] Only married women authors required their husbands' support to enter into legal contracts. As such the unmarried Strickland sisters were not beholden to the same constraint; National Archives, Married Women's Property Act <http://www.legislation.gov.uk/ukpga/Vict/45-46/75> [accessed 15 August 2023].

[40] BL Add MS 46612, vol. LIII (ff. 350), f. 118 'Sidney Jane Morgan, née Owenson; wife of Sir T C Morgan; novelist: Agreement on behalf of, with R. Bentley: 1834'.

[41] BL Add MS 46612, vol. LIII (ff. 350), f. 7 Mary Wollstonecraft Shelley, author: Agreement with R. Bentley: 133: Signed.

[42] Lee Holcombe writes that, prior to the Act of 1882, 'technically a married woman could not enter into contracts in her own name, for she had no property under her control out of which her contracts could be satisfied … rather, her agency arose

William Bradford's participation in the publication appears to have gone no further than these specific roles: nothing in the multiple Wilmot archives reveals his hand in any other stage of the editorial process. The necessity of his involvement, however, sheds light on Martha's careful positioning of herself as sole editor. Her voice as editor is conspicuous in the text, whether announcing herself repeatedly in the paratext as Dashkova's assistant and inspiration, by moving more subtly through the interstices of chapter titles, notes and postscripts, or through the insertion of her lengthy Russian travel narrative as a supplement. These interventions are justified through the affective bond of female friendship, and therefore, Bradford's concealment must be read as a gendered exclusion: for the woman editor to thrive, the male collaborator needs to be invisible.

The Paratext of Friendship

Ornate frontispieces adorn each of the two volumes of *Memoirs of Princess Daschkaw*. The original paintings from which the engravings were made passed into Martha's hands in Russia so that the memoir could 'be illustrated with Portraits of the Princess'.[43] Both images are subtitled 'From an original painting in the possession of the Editor'. Gérard Genette famously defined literary paratext as 'a privileged place of a pragmatics and a strategy, of an influence on the public, an influence that ... is at the service of a better reception for the text and a more pertinent reading of it'.[44] In the case of *Memoirs of Princess Daschkaw*, these interventions repeatedly emphasise a reading embedded within two sets of relationships: the first being between Dashkova and Catherine II, the second between Dashkova and Martha as well as the Wilmot family.

Despite the visual appeal of the attractive frontispieces to each volume, their purpose is not to 'look nice', but 'rather to ensure for the text a destiny consistent with the author's purpose'.[45] The inclusion of an engraving of the author on a book's frontispiece from the seventeenth century onwards, often surrounded by intellectual paraphernalia, persisted throughout the

---

from her husband's express or implied consent'; Lee Holcombe, *Wives and Property: Reform of the Married Woman's Property Law in Nineteenth-Century England* (Toronto, 1983), p. 27.

[43] RIA MS 12 L 30, p. 148.

[44] Gérard Genette, *Paratexts: Thresholds of Interpretation*, trans. by Jane E. Lewin (Cambridge, 1997), p. 2.

[45] Genette, *Paratexts*, p. 407.

Figure 10 British Library, *Memoirs of Princess Daschkaw*, vol. I, frontispiece.
© The British Library Board.

Figure 11 British Library, *Memoirs of Princess Daschkaw*, vol. II, frontispiece.
© The British Library Board.

eighteenth and nineteenth centuries.[46] Perhaps as a result of their near-universal inclusion, as well as thanks to the rich clues they afford the reader, frontispieces have endured as a popular site of paratextual investigation for eighteenth-century scholars.[47] The paratextual engravings' function is to underscore Dashkova's place in Russian Imperial history.

The caption to the first frontispiece stages its scene: 'Princess Daschkaw, Lady of Honour to Catherine II'. Dashkova is here portrayed in the prime of her life in the centre of the portrait wearing the elegant eighteenth-century garments of a Russian lady-in-waiting. Her chair is draped with a fur cape that evokes her wealth and noble power. She sits at a ninety-degree angle, turned halfway between her writing desk and the viewer; her fixed gaze is simultaneously feminine and unabashedly confident. A bust of Catherine II is half-shadowed in the background, just behind the small library on the desk, as if the Empress is mentoring Dashkova's scholarly pursuits. Dashkova's reputation as an intellectual woman is reinforced by the learned accessories that populate the image. On the desk in front of her is a stack of weighty tomes, one of which is open, as if captured in the midst of study. A small library forms a line in the background. A globe is positioned in the foreground, representing Dashkova's extensive international travels amidst the literati of Europe, as well as the many state excursions within Imperial Russia that she undertook at Catherine II's request.

The portrait's regalia specifically associate the sitter with the court.[48] Across her bodice she wears the sash of the Order of St Catherine, and the star of the Order is also pinned over her heart. The order had been instituted by Peter the Great in 1714 at the time of his marriage to Catherine I in honour to the Empress's patron, Saint Catherine of Alexandria. The Order of St Catherine was the only chivalric award that could be given to women in Imperial Russia. Most members received the order by birth or position, but it was awarded to Dashkova to honour her services during the *coup d'état* following Catherine II's elevation as Empress. In addition to the star, Dashkova has a miniature painting of Catherine II pinned to her gown in the centre of her chest, thus including her in yet another incarnation. Dashkova is depicted as a young woman in the prime of life, yet the provenance

---

[46] David Piper, *The Image of the Poet: British Poets and their Portraits* (Oxford, 1982), p. 36; Helen Cole, 'From the Familiar to the New: Frontispiece Engravings to Fiction in England from 1690 to 1740', *Journal for Eighteenth-Century Studies*, 39:4 (2016), 489–511, p. 491.

[47] See Corrina Readioff, 'Recent Approaches to Paratext Studies in Eighteenth-Century Literature', *Literature Compass*, 18:12 (2021).

[48] See Christopher Rovee, *Imagining the Gallery: The Social Body of British Romanticism* (Stanford, 2006).

of the portrait is not clear. No artist or date is supplied in *Memoirs* indicating the original painting from which the engraving was taken. Neither is the original painting extant in any of Wilmot archives, despite Katherine's comment that portraits were carried back to Ireland for the purpose of illustrating Dashkova's memoir. Martha noted Dashkova's thirst for historical portraiture in her Russian diary: 'at the Painters this morng Princess D: plann'd some historical pictures of the reign of the Empress Kath. & invited Sign. Vigonee to Troitska to begin the execution there, to sketch the ideas'.[49] This example raises the possibility that the portrait may have been retrospectively commissioned as late as 1804, and that its complex iconography was arranged by the sitter herself.

The second frontispiece, captioned 'Princess Daschkaw in Banishment', illustrates the most dramatic event of Dashkova's later life: her experience of exile. Catherine II's death in 1796 placed power in the hands of her son, Emperor Paul I. The new emperor's interest in avenging his father Peter III's early death during the coup of 1762 resulted in the banishment of members of the court who had been faithful to his mother. Dashkova's perceived role in the coup, as well as her long-standing association with Catherine II's court, resulted in her exile to the northern province of Novgorod, where she was instructed by the emperor to 'recollect the epoch of 1762'.[50] In the memoir, Dashkova treated her recent loss of courtly favour with fortitude and faithfulness to Catherine II's memory by affirming to the emperor that she 'should never forget that year, and would punctually obey his majesty's orders, in reflecting on what I never thought of with either grief or remorse' (I, pp. 387–388). Though she experienced tremors and spasms on learning of the death of Catherine II, Dashkova comforts herself with the knowledge that her 'despair … was not aggravated by any feelings of self-reproach from reflections on my own conduct, and the part I had uniformly acted' (I, p. 391). She then retired into a period of exile with her daughter and three *femmes de chambre*, living in a 'peasant's cabin, in upwards of sixty degrees northern latitude, situated amidst morasses and impervious forests' (II, p. 17). The situation was relatively short-lived thanks to her own petition for release, as well as her powerful friends in Moscow, who questioned the emperor's choice to send a fragile and aged woman to the northern wilds. Though the experience of exile was isolating and alarming, Dashkova noted that she remained 'easy and contented', an affirmation that she accepted any punishment for her support of Catherine as a further badge of honour for her former sovereign (II, p. 10).

---

[49] RIA MS 12 L 18, Journal of Martha Wilmot, 'Monday 26th [Feb 1804]', p. 73.
[50] *Memoirs*, I, p. 387.

The engraved frontispiece representing this incident in the narrative conveys significant differences in the age and social status of the subject compared to the frontispiece of the first volume. Rather than meeting the viewer's gaze directly, as in the first portrait, Dashkova's eyes are averted; she looks into the distance up and beyond the frame of the portrait. Her face lacks the youthful charge of the earlier image, replaced by an expression mingling melancholy with thoughtful longing. In place of her fashionable silken gown and draped furs, she is presented in peasant's clothing, her perfectly coiffed hair traded for a scarf loosely wrapped around her head. The elegant curtains and expensive furniture framing the first frontispiece have given way to the low-ceilinged confinement of a rustic cottage, presumably in the remote northern corner of Russia to which Dashkova was banished. The dog sleeping at her feet adds a sense of domestic retirement to the quiet scene. Yet in spite of the noticeable differences between the two images, the second frontispiece bears significant similarities to the first by means of iconography and intent. Here, too, books are piled on the table before Dashkova, and line the shelf above her head, implying her continued pursuit of knowledge. New instruments of learning have been introduced, the quill, sealed letters and ledger representing a desire to engage with intellectual communication, even in exile. Most importantly, the Star of the Order of Catherine is present here, too, pinned to Dashkova's breast over her heart. This symbol, granted to Dashkova in honour of her service to Catherine II, ties her not only to the court, but to the service of the Empress that she claims to love so dearly throughout her narrative.

The caption to the second frontispiece, 'Portrait of the Princess Daschkaw in Banishment', leads the reader/viewer to believe that it is an illustration of Dashkova's experience of exile, conveying her noble sacrifice. It was, however, created at a later period at Troitskoe, long after the end of her banishment. Martha records the Princess sitting for the portrait by the Italian artist Salvatore Tonci in a cottage on Dashkova's estate, writing in her diary in 1804:

> I accompanied her there, & spent an uncommonly agreeable morng – Tonce [sic] is charming and the picture promises to be lovely, a striking likeness, dress'd in her every day costume of great coat, mans nightcap, seated in the cottage to which Paul exil'd her [sic].[51]

The painting was devised, then, as a representation of Dashkova's exile, an event that she recalled with pride and that she wished to commemorate

---

[51] RIA MS 12 L 18, Journal of Martha Wilmot, 'Mon.y 30th [Dec 1804]', p. 295.

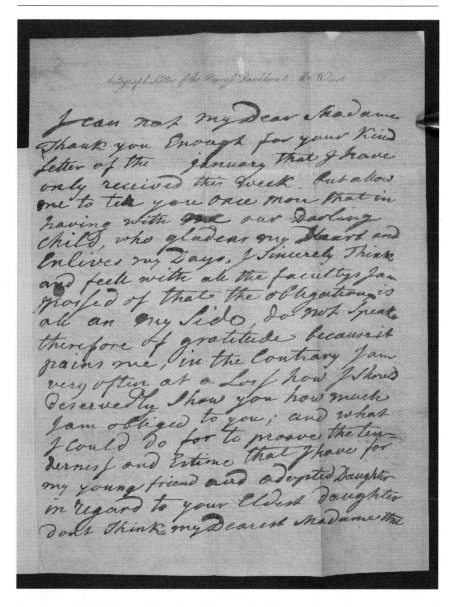

Figure 12   British Library, *Memoirs of Princess Daschkaw*, vol. I, n.d., recto: autograph letter to Mrs. Wilmot. © The British Library Board.

through an almost hagiographic depiction of her own pseudo-martyrdom. No allusion is made to the portrait's later creation date in *Memoirs*, allowing the image to give the sense of Dashkova's captivity and suffering. Tonci's work is given no attribution despite the fact that the engraving was taken from his original painting, his absence maintaining the illusion of exile. The exile portrait's *mise en scène* was perpetuated by the publisher in his promotional publication, *Colburn's New Monthly Magazine*, which notes that the forthcoming book contains a portrait of Dashkova 'taken during her exile in Siberia'.[52]

The 1840 publication also contains two 'Autograph Letters', or facsimile reproductions of original letters. The first replicates a letter sent by Dashkova to Martha's mother, 'Mrs Wilmot', during Martha's Russian residence. It is inserted between Martha's editorial *Introduction* and Dashkova's 'Letter Dedicatory to Miss M. Wilmot, by the Princess Daschkaw'.[53] The second autograph letter replicates the third entry of the original 'notes' sent from Catherine II to Dashkova (II, pp. 64–65). It precedes 'Letters and Notes of the Empress Catherine to the Princess Daschkaw, with Four Letters to Mademoiselle Leoffschin', a section containing twenty-five fragments of letters or entire letters from Catherine II (II, pp. 63–112). The two autograph letters are listed under the table of 'Illustrations', not incorporated as textual paratext within the volume, and therefore not included in the table of contents (I, p. i). The categorisation of the letters as illustrations highlights their performative nature: the facsimile reproduction of each letter is designed to connect the reader directly with its author. The date markings at the heading have been removed, whereas the signatures at the bottom have been maintained. The autograph letters subvert the book's structure by changing the orientation of text on the page, because they are printed on long sheets of paper arranged at a perpendicular angle to the rest of the text; when folded out, they interrupt the linear reading experience, creating a stunningly realistic effect and a sense of immediacy.

Other publications by Colburn, Martha's publisher, similarly drew on the autograph letter as a mode of celebrity encounter, exploiting popular interest in autograph collecting as a means of authenticating the text. *Diary and Letters of Madame D'Arblay, author of Evelina, Cecilia, & C., Edited by her Niece* (1842) provides an interesting bibliographical comparison with *Memoirs*.[54] Frances Burney's death in 1840 inspired renewed interest in her life and work, a result that the author herself anticipated by preparing her own heavily edited papers and 'consigning them to the editor, with full permission to publish whatever might be judged desirable for that purpose'

---

[52] 'Literature of the Month. Autobiography of the Princess Daschkaw', in *Colburn's New Monthly Magazine and Humorist, Edited by Theodore Hook Esq.*, III, 1840, pp. 562–565, p. 562.

[53] *Memoirs*, I, pp. xvii–xxxi; I, pp. xxxv–xxxix.

[54] *Diary and Letters of Madame D'Arblay, author of Evelina, Cecilia, & C., Edited by her Niece, Vol. I 1778–1780* (London, 1842).

(pp. xxxi–ii). Burney's role in curating her own papers is highlighted early on by her niece, Charlotte Barrett, in the *Introductory Memoir* as a means of validation: 'She herself arranged these Journals and Papers with the most scrupulous care' (p. xxxi). This strategy bears similarity to the one used by Martha in the preface, where she asserts that 'the portrait here presented is drawn by [Dashkova's] own hand' (I, p. xxii). In both these texts, autograph letters written by the author are included in facsimile as physical proof corroborating the editor's possession of original papers. Proving the authenticity of the text is critical for Martha, whose authority as editor is less straightforward than that of a blood relative like Burney's niece.

Dashkova's letter to Mrs Wilmot, the first of the two autograph letters, is wedged between Martha's editorial introduction and Dashkova's dedicatory letter. This letter, unlike the later facsimile by Catherine II, is not transcribed. It does not shed any new light on the composition process of the central memoir to follow. This lack of transcription highlights the letter's peripheral nature as one that is particularly illustrative of Dashkova's interactions with the Wilmot family. It is solely concerned with Dashkova's intense attachment to Martha. As Dashkova writes to Martha's mother:

> allow me to tell you once more that in having with me our Darling Child, who gladens [sic] my Heart and Enlivens my Days, I sincerely Think and feel with all the facultys [sic] I am possessed of that the obligation is all on my side ... I am very often at a loss how I should deservedly show you how much I am obliged to you; and what I could do to prove the tenderness and Estime [sic] that I have for my young friend and adopted daughter.[55]

The selection of this particular autograph letter by Dashkova from among Martha's collection is a calculated choice. Any letter written by Dashkova would have been sufficient to prove the authenticity of Martha's manuscript collection, and others in her possession would likely have been more historically instructive to readers. Martha's positioning of this letter between the two prefaces serves as an indicator of her own importance very early in the prefatory material.

The autograph letter reproducing correspondence written by Catherine II to Dashkova is a pointed continuation of the framing initiated by the title choice for the text, *Memoirs of Princess Daschkaw, Lady of Honour to Catherine II*. The inclusion of the autograph letter indulges the history reader's desire to 'place our hands on the spot where theirs once rested' as

---

[55] Memoirs, I, n.d.

John Gough Nichols wrote in 1829, in order to 'pursue their very thoughts and feelings', by shedding light on the life of the Empress.[56] The direction of Catherine II's 'thoughts and feelings' in the autograph letter are also important. She writes affectionately to Dashkova, whom she describes as an indispensable ally:

> I am sensible, so sensible, indeed, of all your kindness, that I have been the victim of ennui ever since you left me. Difficult, indeed, would be the search to find your equal here, when, throughout Russia, the person I am sure does not exist worthy to replace a friend like you.[57]

The letter offers a positive picture of the two women's long but often-troubled association. As Martha notes in her micro-preface to Catherine's letters, 'The following Notes from the Empress Catherine the Second ... were for the most part written whilst she was still Grand Duchess, a little before the revolution of 1762' (II, p. 61). Prior to the Coup of 1762, Catherine II and Dashkova were frequent correspondents. Once Catherine II rose to power, however, their relationship became considerably more complicated, as Dashkova outspokenly disapproved of the political power the Empress granted to her lover, Gregory Orlov. Catherine II went so far as to claim publicly that Dashkova had played no substantial part in the coup. Martha notes that the letters written prior to the 1762 coup exist only because they 'accidently escaped the flames; as, during their correspondence at this period, almost all their writings on either side were carefully destroyed', thereby heightening the sense of political collaboration and classified information shared between the two women (II, p. 61). Catherine II later appointed Dashkova as the President of the Imperial Academy of Arts and Sciences, only to humiliate her by stripping her of the post for a perceived lack of loyalty, demanding that Dashkova travel abroad indefinitely. Dashkova nonetheless saw herself as an essential participant in the success of the coup and framed her life narrative accordingly. Martha accepted Dashkova's version of events as an editorial prerogative.

The facsimile of Catherine II's letter serves an illustrative purpose: it evokes the manuscript originals of the typeset pages to follow, as if to give the reader the sense of viewing private correspondence sent from Catherine II to Dashkova. It is interesting, then, that the twenty-five letters written by Catherine II in the pages that immediately follow are not, in fact, printed

---

[56] John Gough Nichols, *Autographs of Royal, Noble, Learned and Remarkable Personages Conspicuous in English History* (London, 1829), p. iii.
[57] *Memoirs*, II, p. 64.

from originals in Martha's possession, but rather from copies created by Katherine Wilmot during her residence at Troitskoe.[58] Once again choosing a style of subtle concealment, the fact that the majority of the letters are printed from copies is never mentioned in the text, an important omission given Martha's eagerness to foreground the textual accomplishments of her late sister. Maintaining the illusion of authenticity, however, is apparently more important. Pointing out the scribal mode of copying that produced the letters might also lead the reader to question their selection, and skew the true nature of Dashkova's relationship with Catherine II, on which the integrity and validity of the publication rests.

The multiple prefaces of *Memoirs* also play a critical role in continuing the messages outlined by the frontispieces and autograph letters. In the preface, writes Genette, 'it is no longer precisely a matter of attracting the reader ... but of hanging onto him with a typically rhetorical apparatus of persuasion'.[59] Martha and Dashkova both exploit this influential space in their individual prefaces, which immediately precede the core memoir: 'Introduction, by the Editor' (I, pp. xvii–xxxi) and 'Letter Dedicatory to Miss M. Wilmot, by the Princess Daschkaw' (I, pp. xxxv–xxxix). While the dates of the prefaces are separated by a period of thirty-five years, written in 1840 and 1805, respectively, their agendas function in harmony. The prefaces stage the connection between Martha and Dashkova as a key foundational element of the 1840 publication as a whole.

The 'Introduction, by the Editor' is the first narrative element to introduce readers to the book. Edward Said describes the beginning of any book as 'crucial, not only because it determines much of what follows, but because a work's beginning is ... the main entrance to what it offers'.[60] One might expect that the opening lines of the introduction to the memoir of a major Imperial figure of the Russian Enlightenment would begin with verbose professions regarding the late subject's individual accomplishments or character. Instead, Martha shifts the focus towards herself. She relates the particulars of her journey to Russia 'to pass some time ... with the Princess Daschkaw, who had been acquainted with my family during her residence in

---

[58] BL Add MS 31911, pp. 214r–235r. Interestingly, these letters are translated and printed in *Memoirs* inclusive of the numbering, notes and arrangements apparently assigned them by Katherine Wilmot in her transcription work at Troitskoe. For example, Letter #2 in *Memoirs* (II, p. 64) includes the note 'Written with a pencil', a comment corresponding to Katherine's original note 'ecrit avec un crayon' (Add MS 31911, p. 214v). This shows an interesting example of distanced collaboration on the text between herself and Reverend Bradford, who chose to retain these attributes.
[59] Genette, *Paratexts*, p. 198.
[60] Edward Said, *Beginnings: Intention and Method* (New York, 1985), p. 3.

England and Ireland' (I, p. xx). She makes clear the substantial nature of her acquaintance with Dashkova by stating 'my stay with her was protracted to five years' before transitioning into a discussion of the relationship between the two women (I, p. xxi). At Troitskoe, writes Martha, 'I experienced all the affectionate distinction and kindness which a fond parent could shew [sic] to the most beloved child' (I, p. xxi). This exchange of 'affectionate distinction and kindness' leads to the composition of the memoir:

> She appeared to me a being of so superior an order, that I listened earnestly to every word she uttered which threw any light on her early life, and longed to hear more of it in detail ... I had not been more than a year under her roof when I ventured to express my wishes, and to urge her warmly to write the events of her life.[61]

In directing attention to 'so humble an individual' as herself, Martha draws on a formulaic apologia common in women's writing of the period. The preface can, and in this case does, serve as a place where women engage in what Cheryl Nixon identifies as 'character-creation', suggesting that 'close examination' of the messages behind the female author's modesty 'reveals how this marginal space encourages self-definition that blurs' distinctions.[62] Martha begs for patience with Dashkova's praise towards Martha herself in the last pages of the memoir, which she has decided to retain in the text: 'I must entreat the reader ... to bear with them, as proofs only of the princess's warm affection and too great partiality for those whom she loved' (I, p. xxvi). She asserts that her 'motives' for doing so 'are far different from any feelings of personal vanity, that those testimonies are still dear, most dear to my heart' (I, p. xxvi). Addressing her own misgivings for the thirty-plus year delay in publication, she states that 'my consolation ... is that without me the Memoirs now before the reader would never have been written' (I, p. xxx).

Martha paraphrases Dashkova's verbal permission that she may do what she chooses with the manuscript following Dashkova's death:

> My dear, I have no pride of the author, so you can put in and write of me, or in your preface, or at the end of your English, whatever you like to tell of your Russian mother.[63]

---

[61] *Memoirs*, I, pp. xxi–xxii.
[62] Cheryl Nixon, '"Stop a Moment at This Preface": The Gendered Paratexts of Fielding, Barker, and Haywood', *Journal of Narrative Theory*, 32:2 (2002) 123–153, pp. 123, 124.
[63] *Memoirs*, I, p. xix.

This statement softens the boundary between the editorial and authorial. On one hand, Dashkova, in stating that she has 'no pride of the author', merely underlines her own self-identification as an amateur, thereby separating her own aristocratic identity from the lowly trade of authorship prevalent in the late eighteenth-century context from which she is speaking.[64] This statement also raises questions regarding the shape and structure that Dashkova anticipated for the printed text. The quotation grants that Martha may freely 'put in' and 'write' extra details about Dashkova's life in the author's own manuscript, yet it also implies that Martha may occupy other territories around the text. While the preface is a clear categorisation with understandable boundaries, the phrase 'at the end of your English' suggests more complex possibilities. 'Your English' may simply point to a translation of the full text following publication in the manuscript's original French. However, this statement may also suggest that the English version was authorised to contain *extra* information not available in the original French. 'Your English' might also allude to Martha's own writing, in the form of a supplement to the memoir. The ambiguity of this statement may have been intentional: rather than coming from Dashkova in writing herself, the reader must trust Martha's second-hand reporting. If the permission is accepted, however, the reader is left to believe that Dashkova envisaged the memoir project as a vehicle for Martha's entrance into respectable forums of public intellectual life. These possibilities enhance the dynamic of transnational – and translingual – collaborative authorship between the two friends in their conceptualisation of the project.

Correcting Dashkova's long-blighted reputation is a key objective taken up in both prefaces. Negative portrayals of Dashkova persisted in public consciousness: as late as 1832, long after her death, she appeared as a villain in a short story published by Mary Shelley in *The Court Magazine*, where she was depicted as a murderer 'wholly destitute of a sense of honour'.[65] The scapegoating of Dashkova 'as a vain, designing, ambitious, and sometimes profligate woman' by the abstract authors of Russian history is tied to her allegedly vicious role in the coup of 1762 (I, p. xxii). In contrast, Martha presents Dashkova's benevolence as unquestionable. Writing of Dashkova's

---

[64] For more on gentile 'amateur' pursuits, see Kim Sloan, *A Noble Art: Amateur Artists and Drawing Masters c.1600–1800* (London, 2000); Lucy Peltz, 'A friendly gathering', *Journal of the History of Collections*, 19:1 (2007), 33–49.

[65] "The Pole", in Mary Shelley, *Collected Tales and Stories with Original Engravings*, ed. by Charles E. Robinson (Baltimore, 1976), pp. 347–364, p. 364. Robinson outlines the likelihood that this story was actually written by Claire Claremont, who wished to preserve her anonymity by publishing under the moniker 'By the Author of "Frankenstein"'; see fn. p. 391.

request that she be viewed as Martha's '*Russian mother*', Martha notes it was 'a name of tenderness' given in 'boundless kindness' (I, p. xxvi). At the same time, this maternal characterisation evokes associations of the parental relationship between a benevolent sovereign and his or her people.[66] Dashkova's ability to embody sentimental affection is invested, too, in her filial and patriotic duty. Martha describes Dashkova as 'actuated ... by an almost unbounded love, and the most enthusiastic admiration, of Catherine the Second' (I, p. xxiii). Martha acknowledges that while Dashkova has become 'a subject of history' due to her ties to the Empress, 'history has in some particulars foully misrepresented her, and in none has it done her justice' (I, p. xxx). 'Enough will certainly appear in the following pages', she writes, 'to correct the false impressions of those who have known the Princess Daschkaw only through the medium of some popular works' (I, p. xxii). The absence of details in the memoir concerning that 'great and bloodless change effected in the dethronement of a powerful monarch', Martha notes, will likely be met by 'surprise or disappointment' (I, p. xxiv). This is notable considering that Dashkova's negative public image was widely linked to her participation in the coup, whether by followers of Paul I, who held her partially accountable for Peter III's death, or by supporters of Catherine II, believing she infringed on the Empress's claim to glory in the coup. Martha explains Dashkova's silence on the events of the coup as a means of enhancing her heroic fidelity to the Empress while simultaneously imbuing her character with integrity:

> It was never, it will further be seen, the habit of the princess to magnify herself; and in speaking of the revolution which placed her friend and idol upon the throne, although she considered her own share in the work as the proudest circumstance of her life, she expresses herself uniformly with unaffected simplicity ... [as] one who certainly never exaggerated or coloured a fact for the purpose of heightening its effect.[67]

Dashkova's own dedicatory letter is ostensibly addressed to Martha and corroborates the younger woman's claims of centrality by stating that 'my friends and relations have for many years urged me to the task which you now require. I have resisted their solicitations; but I find myself incapable of refusing yours' (I, pp. xxxv–xxxvi). However, Dashkova's intention that the letter should reach a wider audience is clear. 'Whoever the official

---

[66] For the origins of this concept, see Robert Filmer, *Patriarcha, or The Natural Power of Kings* (London, 1680).
[67] *Memoirs*, I, p. xxv.

addressee', notes Genette, 'there is always an ambiguity in the destination of the dedication, which is always intended for at least two addressees: the dedicatee, of course, but also the reader'.[68] Dashkova describes her narrative as 'the history of my life, – a painful story, which I might have worked into a touching romance', a comment that emphasises that she has portrayed events truthfully (I, p. xxxvi). Like Martha, Dashkova acknowledges that she has 'passed over, it is true, or but lightly touched on, some occasions', presumably referring to the absence of her own account of the 1762 coup (I, p. xxxvi). Such details have been omitted due to 'the ingratitude' of unnamed enemies, 'whom I would justify, were it possible, at the expense of my life' (I, p. xxxvi). Dashkova hopes that her memoir might serve as a counterpoint to the 'tissues of falsehood and vile imputations which some French writers had been pleased to fabricate and propagate, against the great Catherine' (I, p. xxxvii). She attributes her maligned public persona primarily to her support of the Empress, writing 'I have become a victim of the malicious frenzy of her enemies' (I, p. xxxviii). Dashkova refuses to dwell on slander, hoping that it, 'like everything else in the world, will pass away' (I, p. xxxviii). Instead, she focuses on her 'dear young friend', and the 'tender friendship which binds' them together (I, p. xxxviii). Moving seamlessly between her devotion to Catherine II and her devotion to Martha, Dashkova's dedicatory letter further strengthens the bonds that link herself, the Empress of Russia and the unknown Irish travellers.

Framing the Life Narrative

The heart of the 1840 printed edition of *Memoirs of Princess Daschkaw* is the life narrative composed at Troitskoe from 1804–06. The smooth cohesion of the central memoir invites readers to easily engage with the text, and therefore with Dashkova's history. For Roger Chartier, 'writing deploys strategies ... It lays traps, which the reader falls into without even knowing it'.[69] The original manuscript, when compared with this readable tome, appears rather different: it is riddled with scratched out lines and ink markings, and written in the halting French of a foreigner. Yet Martha's editorial practices, which guided the preparation of the imperfect manuscript for print in this elegant format, were not easily settled upon. The archives portray Martha as an editor disenfranchised by a lack of professional textual

---

[68] Genette, *Paratexts*, p. 134.
[69] Roger Chartier, *Forms and Meanings: Texts, Performances, and Audiences from Codex to Computer* (Philadelphia, 1995), p. 1.

experience, as well as by her status as an unknown woman trying to enter the literary market, as this section shows.

From the early days of the memoir's drafting process at Troitskoe in 1804, Martha notes in her journal that the process has been a disorganised affair:

> [Dashkova] writes half a page, then perhaps she settles a law suit between two peasants, then writes again, in short, she does not stop half a minute to consider what she shall say, or to compose her sentences, every word flows as naturally from her pen, as in her common conversation.[70]

Martha's description implies that composition was squeezed in amidst an abundance of other distractions, resulting in an informal style. Katherine wrote to a friend about her plan to carry a fair copy of the manuscript back to Ireland at the time of her departure in 1807, joking that in transporting the complete and original version of Dashkova's work she was in fact not bringing back anything of 'value': 'you need not expect to find it intelligible, till it has undergone a complete dislocation from begining to End [sic]'.[71] Dashkova was also aware of the limitations of her own writing, corroborating the Wilmot sisters' early concerns that the manuscript was not fit for publication in its original form by writing in her dedicatory letter that the memoir was essentially unliterary, 'written as I speak, without preparation, and with a frankness unsubdued even by the warnings of unhappy experience'.[72] Dashkova's comment is intended to imply a lack of artifice in her writing style, yet it also underlines the problems with the manuscript that posed substantial obstacles to an immediate publication following her death.

Dashkova's passing leaves Martha, according to her daughters, 'anxious to publish the memoir'; however, she is discouraged from doing so 'by the objections of many people to its defective style'.[73] This criticism on the part of outside readers during the preparation of the core manuscript can be traced to Martha's surviving letters, which indicate that she shares the

---

[70] RIA MS 12 L 18, 'Sunday 25th [August 1804]', p. 211. For a full discussion of this statement, and its later partial omission from the Wilmot archives due to its damaging nature, likely by Martha or her daughters, see Alexis Wolf, 'Introduction: Reading Silence in the Long Nineteenth-Century Women's Life Writing Archive', *19: Interdisciplinary Studies in the Long Nineteenth Century* (2018), 27, <https://doi.org/10.16995/ntn.841> [accessed 15 April 2024].

[71] RIA MS 12 L 30, 'To Anna Chetwood, Moscow, Feb.ry the 2d 1807', p. 148.

[72] *Memoirs*, I, p. xxxvi.

[73] Add MS 31911, p. 6v.

Collaborative Women's History   159

manuscript with multiple readers during 1810–13. Her circulation of the material has various motivations and consequences. Through sharing the manuscript, Martha is able to gain the advice of friends or acquaintances with significantly more practical literary or public experience than herself, discussing with them both the obstacles of publication as well as the merits of the manuscript, which is held to be of important literary and historic value by the positively responding readers.

Not long after Dashkova's death Martha begins circulating the manuscript. Writing to her cousin John Eardley-Wilmot in June 1810, she mentions 'the memoir I am engaged in transcribing', as well as her 'wish to have some conversation … in *your study*, before the subject is spoken of in a general way'.[74] If her cousin's advice is to proceed, Martha hopes to be connected with his 'bookseller *Cadell*', surely referring to the publisher Cadell and Davies. She anticipates 'going to London for a few days' will be 'quite necessary'.[75] However, Martha delayed her visit to Eardley-Wilmot, instead travelling to Cheltenham at the request of Elizabeth Morgan, who Martha described as 'the only survivor of the long tried friendship which had united my beloved Princess, Mrs. Hamilton, & Mrs. Morgan for more than thirty five years'.[76] Dashkova had met the two women at Spa while travelling in Europe in 1770, an important milestone in her life. She describes the meeting in her memoir, writing that the three women's shared 'intimacy soon grew into a friendship which has stood the test of time and absence' and that the pair had helped Dashkova to learn English.[77] Martha travels to Cheltenham planning to let Mrs Morgan 'read the manuscript', something that she feels must be done before she can take 'any steps whatever, towards its publication'.[78] The manuscript's first reception is not a positive one. As Martha soon after writes to Eardley-Wilmot, 'the result of my first communication of the Manuscript induces me decidedly to *postpone* for many months *at all events*, its publication'.[79] Morgan's appraisal of the work, or perhaps her concerns that its publication would be improper, causes Martha to suspend her planned trip to visit booksellers in London.

---

[74] Beinecke OSB MSS 54 Box 3 f.151, 'Hinckley 21st June 1810, p. 1.
[75] Ibid, p. 2; John Eardley-Wilmot had, in 1802, published a biography of his late father, *Memoirs of the Life of the Right Honourable Sir John Eardley Wilmot*, which was printed by Hansard and sold by Cadell and Davies.
[76] Beinecke, 'Sapcote Bath 2nd August 1810', p. 1.
[77] *Memoirs*, I, pp. 158, 159.
[78] Beinecke, 'Sapcote Bath 2nd August 1810', p. 1; Elizabeth Morgan was the daughter of Philip Tisdall (1703–77), who held the office of Attorney-General for Ireland and served in the Irish House of Commons for nearly four decades.
[79] Beinecke, 'Cheltenham, 23rd September 1810', pp. 1–2; emphasis original.

Nonetheless, she seems less than fully convinced of this negative appraisal, hedging her full abandonment of the project by asking her cousin to also lend his opinion as well. If it does not 'throw some new light on the affair, I know not whether it will ever see the light of day'.[80]

By 1813, however, Martha returns to circulating in hope of finding favourable readers, giving the manuscript to Anne Seymour Damer. The letters exchanged between the two women offer insight into Martha's early editorial work. Damer was a controversial British sculptor with strong ties to literary and artistic circles, both in England and abroad. She was the niece of Horace Walpole, who bequeathed his Strawberry Hill estate to her, and a friend of Sarah Siddons, Mary Berry and Joanna Baillie. Martha's choice to share the manuscript with Damer, who is twenty-five years her senior, may have been encouraged by the sculptor's brief and positive appearance in the work itself, for Damer had met Dashkova in Rome in 1780:

> I had here the good fortune to form the acquaintance of Mrs. Damer, a lady so justly celebrated for her skill in sculpture, and no less to be admired for her profound information and good sense, which, under the veil of a particular modesty, sought rather the disguise than the display of her acquisitions.[81]

Martha apparently encounters Damer during a visit to London and leaves the manuscript in her care in order to collect feedback from her at a later date. Damer writes to Martha thanking her for 'the infinite satisfaction all that I have red [sic] of this interesting Manus-t [sic]', entreating her to return to visit again: 'I trust … whenever you return to London, it will not be without your giving me the pleasure of seeing you.'[82] Damer advises Martha to develop an editorial strategy, recognising Martha's individual ability and skill, and commending her for the start that has apparently already been made on minor modifications to the text:

> it is the duty of an Editor to correct such inaccuracies as can in any way alter a phrase as the tense of the verbs & c – indeed this seems already nearly done, by the alterations of the sort made in pencil in the first Vol: … under your Eye such correction might be completed without the Slightest alteration in style [sic].[83]

Martha's choice to share the manuscript with Damer points to her continued interest in female collaboration following Dashkova's death. It

[80] Ibid, p. 2.
[81] *Memoirs*, I, p. 245.
[82] RIA MS 12 M 18, 'April 17 1813', pp. r–v.
[83] Ibid, p. v.

also highlights the sociable power that the circulation of the manuscript could supply, increasing Martha's intellectual profile as she worked towards publication.[84]

Not all of Martha's readers during this period, however, provide her with encouragement. A series of letters exchanged in 1813 with Count Simon Woronzow, Dashkova's elder brother and the former Ambassador to England, illustrate his opposition to the project. While Martha had the support of Dashkova's older brother, Michael Woronzow, she appears to write to Count Woronzow as a polite formality, expecting his approval. Their correspondence begins in a civilised manner; however, it quickly develops into a hostile dialogue over the potential publication of the manuscript, displaying a minefield of conflicting interests rooted in gendered, political and proprietary objections. In his first response, Woronzow minimises the importance of the memoir, implying that there will be no public interest in its contents. Yet he also states that he will not meddle with Martha's decisions on whether to publish it, due to the circumstances under which the manuscript was composed: 'It is a record of confidential information entrusted to you by friendship'.[85] Woronzow declares that Dashkova, as a woman, should have written only about domestic rather than political matters:

> If my sister had only written of her domestic life, there would be no difficulty in publishing the manuscript, but she has been driven by the circumstances of a political whirlwind which rendered her life a part of history.[86]

Woronzow states the manuscript should be put aside for a period to avoid offending both living people and the memory of those recently deceased, encouraging Martha to withhold publication for at least thirty years.

---

[84] As noted earlier in the chapter, Martha also circulated the manuscript to Lord Glenbervie of Brighton, himself a diarist. He advised Martha to omit long-winded passages and replace these with 'incidents, anecdotes, & reflections of more general interest as must have been communicated' to Martha by Dashkova. While Martha eventually heeds some of this advice, for instance, by omitting Dashkova's lengthy account of the constitution of the city of Lucca, she stops short of his suggestion that she create new content entirely from her own memory. See RIA MS 12 M 18, Letter from Lord Glenbervie, 'Brighton, Jan 7 1813'.

[85] RIA MS 12 M 18, 'Londres ce 26 Janvier 1813'; 'c'est un dépot de confiance remis à l'amitié'; my translation.

[86] RIA 12 M 18, '26 Jan 1813'; 'Si ma soeur n'avoit écrit que sa vie domestique, il n'y aurait aucune difficulté à publier ses mémoires, mais elle a été entrainée par les circonstances dans un tourbillon politique qui rend sa vie comme appartenante à l'histoire'; my translation.

Though Woronzow uses gracious language to validate Martha's position as literary executor of the papers, writing 'it is your property, and I have no right to meddle with it', he also undermines her authority.[87] In a letter that is now lost, Woronzow apparently suggests that the memoir was not authored by Dashkova, but rather by the Wilmots. Martha's response to the accusation details the contents of the now-absent letter, as she reminds Woronzow of the provenance of the manuscript:

> Checking your own memory, sir, should have corrected this shocking error. I never stated that the manuscript which I possess was 'created from memory, after another which was made by Princess Daschkaw, the first having been burned'. I would have found that a truly embarrassing deceit.[88]

Woronzow is invested in suppressing the manuscript for a variety of reasons. Given his established position in England as a former ambassador, Woronzow sees a renewed public interest into his own family's early life as unwelcome, not wishing to drag up recollections of Dashkova's complicated political manoeuvrings. His objections to Dashkova's narrative appearing in print are all the more pointed when considered in light of the autobiography he penned himself: while never published, the manuscript was incorporated into the *Russky Arkhiv* in St Petersburg in 1881. This resonates with his request that publication be delayed for a period of thirty years and underscores a sentiment of propriety surrounding life writing available only in limited manuscript form, rather than in print.

Count Woronzow's implication that the manuscript is a forgery emphasises the significant risks facing Martha as editor. Any attempts at publication might result in the memoir being denounced as a fake if not properly presented, or indeed if appearing to be a poorly written assemblage of incoherent materials. For example, a collection of Catherine II's letters and papers were presented as a memoir shortly after her death in 1797, titled *Authentic Memoirs of the Life and Reign of Catherine II. Empress of all the Russias. Collected from authentic MS's. Translations, & c. of the*

---

[87] RIA 12 M 18, '26 Jan 1813'; 'c'est votre proprieté, et je n'ais aucun droit de m'en méler'; my translation.

[88] *Vorontsova Archives*, Tom. 21, (Moscow, 1880), pp. 372–376; 'Un retour sur votre mémoir, monsieur, aurait dû corriger cette étonnante erreur. Je n'ai jamais dit que le manuscrit que je possède a été 'fait de mémoire, après d'un autre fait par la princesse Dashkaw, lequel avait été brûlé'. J'aurais trouvé bien embarrassante une pareille tromperie'; my translation.

Kind of Sweden ... and other indisputable Authorities.[89] This publication was derided in *The Critical Review* almost immediately, offering a brutal comparative case study that Martha, having a great interest in the life of Catherine II, would almost certainly be aware of:

> When the death of the imperial Catherine was announced, we expected some hasty compilations would be obtruded on the world ... Such a production we now have before us. The compiler observes in his Preface that 'the authenticity of all that is mentioned is certainly the greatest recommendation.' ... But we have no reason to believe that the work possesses that recommendation, or that it flows from the purest sources ... the *book-maker* has executed his task with so little skill or judgment, that we do not hesitate to pronounce this performance unworthy of public encouragement.[90]

Martha's clash with Woronzow over the manuscript was not enough, however, to cause her to put the project aside completely. The 1814 attempt to publish with Murray indicates the level of prestige that Martha and William Bradford hoped to achieve for Dashkova's memoir.[91] Murray's contemporary publications include Walter Scott's *Marmion* (1808) and Byron's wildly popular *Childe Harold's Pilgrimage* beginning in 1812.[92] Murray may have seemed an obvious choice to publish Dashkova's foreign life narrative due to his extensive catalogue of books centred on international exploration: his 1813 designation as 'Official Bookseller to the Admiralty' also allowed him 'to monopolise the authorship of discoveries in an entire geo-imaginary region'.[93] Murray's predominance as a publisher was also noticed by contemporary women authors, who sought to place their books with his publishing house: Jane Austen's *Emma* was released by Murray in 1815, while Mary Shelley's *Frankenstein* was also rejected for publication in May 1817.[94]

---

[89] *Authentic Memoirs of the Life and Reign of Catherine II. Empress of all the Russias. Collected from Authentic MS's. Translations, & c. of the Kind of Sweden ... and Other Indisputable Authorities* (London, 1797).

[90] *The Critical Review: Or, Annals of Literature* (London, 1797), p. 452.

[91] NLS, Edinburgh, The John Murray Archive, MS.40140, Fol. 110r, Storrington March 9th 1814.'

[92] Walter Scott, *Marmion: A Tale of Flodden Field* (Edinburgh & London, 1808); George Gordon Byron, Baron, *Childe Harold's Pilgrimage. A Romaunt* [Cantos I and II. With fourteen other poems.] (London, 1812).

[93] Adriana Craciun, 'What is an explorer?', *Eighteenth-Century Studies*, 45:1 (2011), 29–51, p. 32.

[94] Jane Austen, *Emma; A Novel*, 3 vols (London, 1815); *The 'Frankenstein' Notebooks: A Facsimile Edition of Mary Shelley's Manuscript Novel, 1816–17*, ed. by Charles E. Robinson, 2 vols (New York, 1996), I, p. lxxxvi.

Bradford first makes contact with Murray on 9 March 1814, introducing the manuscript and its history, and offering to send it for Murray's perusal.[95] A second letter sent the following week details the paratext as an added enticement, including letters by Catherine II, citing that 'it may be possible to publish this Spring' (Fol. 111v). Whether Murray read and rejected the manuscript due to its untidy state, or whether he simply had no interest in publishing the work, remains unknown, as his replies to Bradford are missing from the archives. This failed effort, coupled with the disapproval of Woronzow and his family, the closest blood relatives to Dashkova, may have led to the shelving of the project for several decades. Woronzow's comments, as well as possibly John Murray's apathy towards the project, cast a shadow over Martha's hopes for the memoir's early appearance, raising concerns about the potentially negative reception that the text may face from those with an interest in discrediting it. Over the lengthy period between Woronzow's accusations, and the date of publication, these problems would come up against and influence Martha's editorial choices – the need for legitimisation of both the manuscript and her authority to present it – remaining always at the forefront of her concerns.

Omissions: 'some unimportant anecdotes'

Martha's editorial choices include the omission of several fragments from Dashkova's narrative prior to its publication. In their handwritten introduction to the bound manuscript deposited in the British Museum in 1882, Martha's daughters Catherine and Blanche insist that few substantial changes were made between the manuscript at hand and the 1840 publication:

> In comparing the translation with the memoir, it will be found that it is perfectly exact, & that nothing extraneous has been inserted in it – There are however, several pages in different parts of the work, which have been *condensed, & a few transposed, frm the order originally written*, in order to make the style clearer.[96]

Martha's daughters state that only 'some unimportant anecdotes have been left out', and they provide a list of these. Scholarly revaluations of Martha's interventions to Dashkova's memoirs have been more critical than

---

[95] NLS MS.40140, Fol. 109r–110r.
[96] BL Add MS 31911, p. 6v, emphasis original.

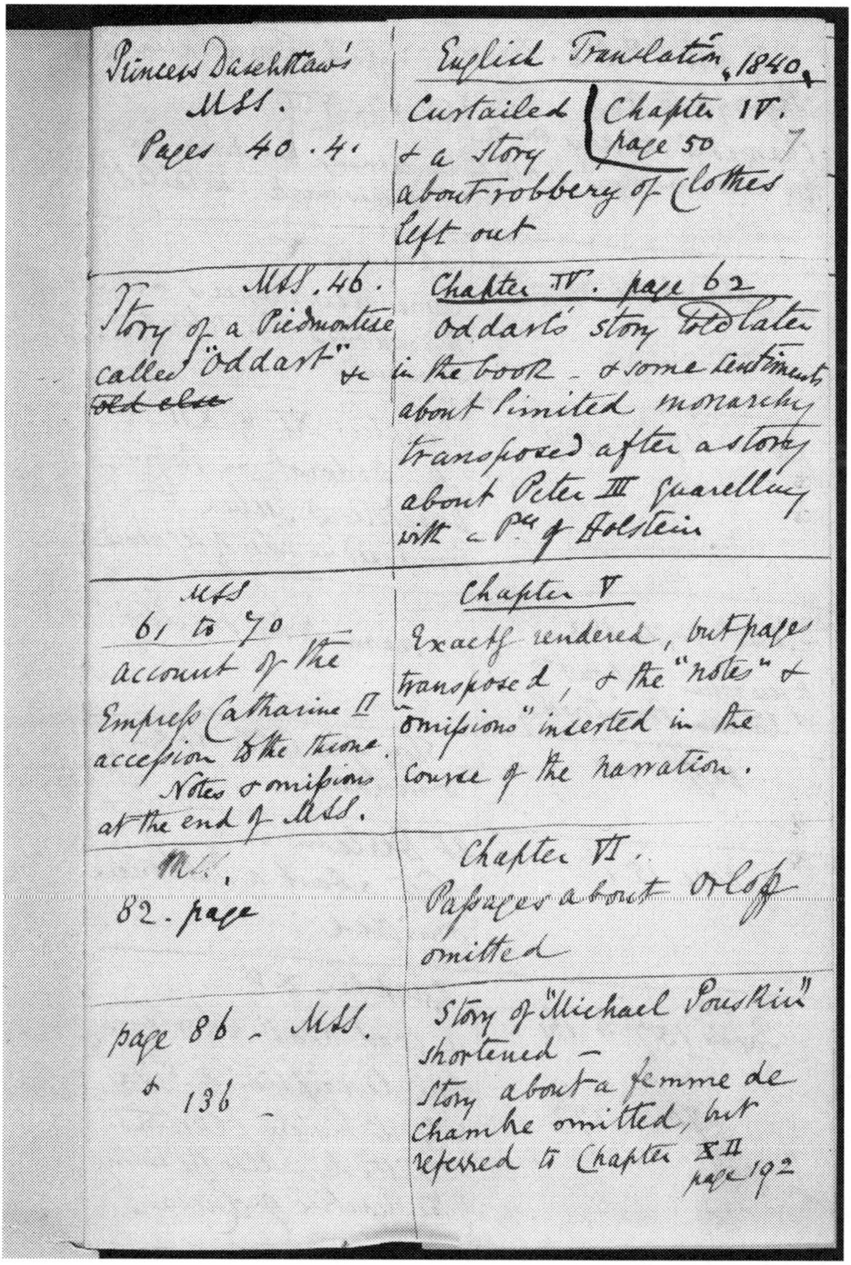

Princess Dashkhaw's MSS. Pages 40.41.	English Translation, 1840. Curtailed Chapter IV. page 50 & a story about robbery of clothes left out
MSS. 46. Story of a Piedmontese called "Oddart" &c ~~&c &c~~	Chapter IV. page 62 Oddart's story told later in the book – & some sentiments about limited monarchy transposed after a story about Peter III quarelling with a P[rin]ce of Holstein
MSS 61 to 70 account of the Empress Catharine II accession to the throne. Notes & omissions at the end of MSS.	Chapter V Exactly rendered, but page transposed, & the "notes" & "omissions" inserted in the course of the narration.
MS. 82. page	Chapter VI. Passages ~~about~~ Orloff omitted
page 86 – MSS. & 136	Story of "Michael Pouskin" shortened – Story about a femme de chambre omitted, but referred to Chapter XII page 192

Figure 13 British Library, Add MS 31911, f.007r. © The British Library Board.

she and her daughters might have liked. 'Unfortunately', Kyril Fitzlyon noted in the introduction to his 1958 retranslation of the memoir, 'Martha Wilmot applied her own censorship to Princess Dashkova's document, cut out or summarised sentences and paragraphs she considered indelicate or trivial … added little touches of her own'.[97] Far from interpreting Martha's editorial interventions in a positive light, Fitzlyon concludes that they 'considerably lowered the value of her [Dashkova's] work'.[98] More recently, Woronzoff-Dashkoff has referred to the 1840 publication as 'a highly edited, greatly condensed literary reworking' of the original manuscript.[99]

The omission of scenes represented in the manuscript from the 1840 publication of *Memoirs* seem to have gone unnoticed by Russian literary scholars and historians interested in tracing the textual trajectory of Dashkova's memoir. Since the appearance of Martha's 1840 publication, several new Russian editions have been prepared from the manuscript copy held in the Vorontov family archive.[100] In his 1991 summary of the long and varied publication history of Dashkova's *Memoirs*, Woronzoff-Dashkoff notes that Russian editions consistently fail to consult the British Library copy of the manuscript, resulting in substantial content discrepancies. Woronzoff-Dashkoff lists nineteen instances of divergence between the 'British Museum' manuscript and the one held at the Vorontsov archive in Moscow.[101] These nineteen divergences are later additions made to the British Library copy, which were not transcribed into the copy retained by Dashkova. Martha comments on these additions in her travelogue supplement

---

[97] *The Memoirs of Princess Dashkova [with Plates, Including Portraits]*, trans. and ed. by Kyril Fitzlyon (London, 1958), p. 22.

[98] Ibid, p. 22.

[99] A. Woronzoff-Dashkoff, 'Additions and Notes in Princess Dashkova's "Mon Histoire"', *Study Group on Eighteenth-Century Russia Newsletter*, 19 (1991), n.d., <http://www.sgecr.co.uk/1991-woronzoff.html#17> [accessed 18 April 2022].

[100] I have chosen to use the transliteration supplied by the archive itself, hence the differentiation between 'Vorontov' and 'Woronzow'. For a facsimile of the original manuscipt, see E. R. Dashkova, *Бумаги княгини Е. Р. Дашковой, урожденной Графини Воронцовой. (Mémoires de la Princesse Dashkaw. D'après le manuscrit revu et corrigé par l'auteur.)* [The original French version of Princess Dashkova's memoirs from the manuscript in the Vorontsov archives. With letters and other documents.] (Moskva, 1881). For subsequent editions prepared from the Russian manuscript, see Екатерина Дашкова, Записки 1743–1810. Подготовка текста, статья о комментарии Г. Н. Моисеевой (Leningrad, 1985); Н. Д. Чечулин, Записки княгини Дашковой (St Petersburg, 1907); Петр Бартенев (ed.), Архив князя Воронцова, 40 vols. (St Petersburg, 1870–97); Е. Р. Дашкова, Литературные сочинения (Moscow, 1990), pp. 31–262.

[101] Woronzoff-Dashkoff, *Dashkova*, n.d.

to *Memoirs*, attributing them to Dashkova's disorganised composition process at Troitskoe:

> She committed to paper rapidly what her memory furnished … In a few instances, when she recollected some circumstance which had escaped her memory in the proper place, she wrote it at the end of the volume, under the title of 'omission', with a reference to the page where it ought to have appeared.[102]

These late additions, which were embedded into the 1840 publication as part of the central text, are noted throughout the British Library manuscript with a convoluted system of symbols whose function is not clearly indicated: lengthy footnotes at the bottoms of pages marked with '+' or '#' signs, and extracts later incorporated into the text on pages added at the end of each volume with the heading 'omit'. Woronzoff-Dashkoff laments the fact that 'a systematic, textual comparison of the Brooke and Vorontsov copies has never been undertaken … nor has any attempt been made to define and describe thoroughly the additions contained in the Brooke copy' against the lacunae of the Vorontsov copy (n.d.).[103] While focusing on the late additions detectable between the two extant manuscripts, Woronzoff-Dashkoff overlooks a different and fascinating type of textual ellipses present in the publication history of Dashkova's *Memoirs*, which has never been previously addressed.

Catherine and Blanche Bradford acknowledge that, 'Two or three quite immaterial & uninteresting details, & short anecdotes have been omitted' from the 1840 publication.[104] Yet the content of the omitted sections points to a system of representation that is far from 'unimportant'. Studying the content of these omissions, which are listed in a chart following the manuscript's preface, provides a valuable lens for interpreting Martha's editorial agenda concerning the core manuscript. At first glance, some of these cuts are indeed rather benign in nature. For example, one of the most visually dramatic examples of omission performed on the manuscript is found in the full-length crosses blotting out several sheets descriptive of a visit to Tuscany (pp. 114r, 116r–117v). The contents of this passage are relatively inconsequential to the trajectory and aims of the central narrative. Removal

---

[102] *Memoirs*, II, p. 240.
[103] The 'comprehensive comparison' of the two extant manuscripts that Woronzoff-Dashkoff calls for differs from the aims of this study. Here I seek to examine Martha's textual manipulation in specific reference to British Library Add MS 31911, which was the only version available to her for editorial purposes.
[104] BL Add MS 31911, p. 6v.

of the long-winded and impersonal passage is apparently performed to improve overall readability while reducing redundancy.[105] However, more often Martha's interventions display efforts to preserve Dashkova's respectability through a reframing of events. This is particularly clear with regard to representations of gender. The omitted incidents often linger in the banality of daily life or include frivolous and immature emotions.

In the first significant passage omitted from the memoir, Dashkova recounts an ill-fated visit to St Petersburg that Dashkova undertakes as a young woman (pp. 47r–v). The story centres on the theft of clothes and money by a band of local sailors. The objects taken from Dashkova's room cause her notable distress. Although only approximately 200 words in length, multiple sentences appear out of place in a political memoir. For example, Dashkova begins by writing that the incident occurs 'As I did not have anyone with me', implying that a lack of protection made her feel vulnerable.[106] The incident takes place very close in the narrative to her participation in the political coup of 1762, so it is likely that Martha did not wish for Dashkova's bravery or independence to be questioned by readers. The robbery leaves Dashkova 'without money and with no underwear besides that which I was wearing.'[107] She turns to her sister Elizabeth to request 'one or two shirts while I waited for mine to return from the laundress' and is dispatched a beautiful piece of Holland silk by that 'good sister' right away.[108] Focus on Dashkova's body and reference to her personal garments in particular might have appeared superfluous or vulgar to critical eyes in the context of the wider narrative. This incident verges on indelicacy by skirting taboo territory, particularly in light of the climate of early Victorian sensibility during which it is first made public.

The passage's melodramatic conclusion also poses a problem, as Dashkova writes: 'I mention this little misfortunate as the first lesson in misery and want that I experienced, and it hasn't been the last in my life.'[109] Drawing on future instances of misery still to come in the narrative, Dashkova appears

[105] The decision to cut this lengthy section on Dashkova's trip and her subsequent retelling of the history and custom of Tuscany recalls Glenbervie's editorial advice to Martha in 1813: 'Might not the work be improved by omitting the details ... of your illustrious Friend's [sic] journeys and travels ... [of] what is to be found more at large, & therefore with more instruction or amusement, in various books of geography?', RIA MS 12 M 18, 'Brighton Jan 7 1813', n.d.
[106] 'Comme je n'avais gardé que peu de monde avec moi'; my translation.
[107] 'sans argent et sans linge que je puisse porter'; my translation.
[108] 'une ou deux chemises pendant que les miennes reviendront de la blanchisseuse'; 'bonne soeur'; my translation.
[109] 'Je cite ce petit malheur comme la première leçon de misère et besoin que j'aie éprouvée et qui n'a pas été la seule dans ma vie'; my translation.

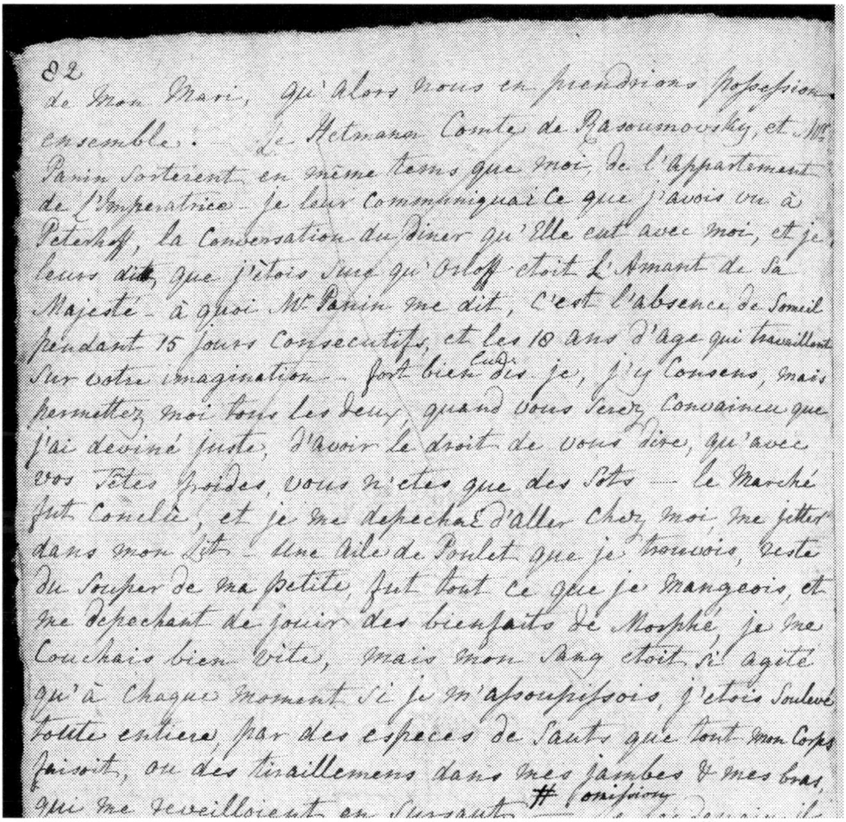
82
de Mon Mari, qu'alors nous en prendrions possession
ensemble. Le Hetman Comte de Rasoumovsky, et Mr.
Panin sortèrent en même tems que moi, de l'Appartement
de l'Imperatrice je leur Communiquai Ce que j'avois vu à
Peterhoff, la Conversation du Diner qu'Elle eut avec moi, et je
leurs dit, que j'étois sure qu'Orloff étoit L'Amant de Sa
Majesté à quoi Mr. Panin me dit, C'est l'absence de Someil
pendant 15 jours Consecutifs, et les 18 ans d'age qui travaillent
sur votre imagination fort bien dis je, j'y Consens, mais
permettez moi tous les deux, quand vous serez Convaincu que
j'ai deviné juste, d'avoir le droit de vous dire, qu'avec
vos Têtes froides, vous n'etes que des Sots — le Marché
fut Conclu, et je me depechai d'aller Chez moi, me jetter
dans mon Lit — Une Aile de Poulet que je trouvois, reste
du Souper de ma petite, fut tout ce que je mangeois, et
me depechant de jouir des bienfaits de Morphé, je me
Couchais bien vite, mais mon sang etoit si agité
qu'à Chaque moment si je m'assoupissois, j'étois soulevé
toute entiere, par des especes de Sauts que tout mon Corps
faisoit, ou des tiraillemens dans mes jambes & mes bras,
qui me reveilloient en sursaut # convulsions

Figure 14 British Library, Add MS 31911, f.047r. © The British Library Board.

to conflate the misfortune of losing her personal belongings with her later life experiences of suffering, such as during her time of political exile. The incongruous comparison diminishes the impact of Dashkova's exile on the narrative as a whole, a topic that Martha particularly highlights through the inclusion of Tonci's illustration of Dashkova in exile as an engraving at the start of the second volume. In other sections of the narrative, which have been cleverly reorganised for clarity, editorial changes are at times apparent by lines crossed out and reinserted in other locations, or by conjugational revisions on certain incorrect verbs. Here, however, a large pencilled 'X' blots out the long paragraph on both sides of the leaf. The pettiness of the incident marks it as irredeemable, its content not only unnecessary to the overall value of the memoir, but also blighting Dashkova's potential for strength and poise by exposing aspects of feminine weakness.

Further omitted passages appear to reflect poorly on Dashkova's political integrity. The manuscript records an exchange between Dashkova and some of her compatriots, the Hetman Count Razumovsky and the Empress's mentor, Nikita Panin, in the days immediately following the *coup d'état* that raised Catherine II to power. Following a private visit with the newly crowned Catherine II at the palace, during which the politically dangerous Gregory Orlov was present, Dashkova tells the men 'that which I saw at Peterhoff [and] that I was certain that Orloff had become the Empress's lover'.[110] Her companions either do not believe her, or do not wish to speculate on such claims. Panin attributes her accusation to 'the lack of sleep for the past 15 consecutive days, and your 18 years of age working upon your imagination'.[111] To this Dashkova responds:

> Very well, I said, I agree, but both of you must permit me, as soon as you are convinced that I guessed correctly, to have the right to say to you, that you with your cool heads are nothing but fools.[112]

This omitted anecdote is, in one sense, redundant: the incident at the palace, during which Dashkova realises that Orlov is Catherine II's lover, is documented in greater detail in the preceding narrative.[113] Martha's choice to cut the exchange, however, is more likely due to the ungenerous nature of Dashkova's remarks. Far from depicting Dashkova as a loyal and unfaltering servant to Catherine II, which is one of the central goals of the overall publication, this anecdote portrays Dashkova talking behind the Empress's back. While Dashkova intended to underline her own intuitive nature and shrewd political sense, she instead appears acrimonious and indiscreet. The nature of the exchange casts a shadow over Dashkova's exulted place as the closest woman in Catherine II's inner circle, leaving her potentially undeserving of the role. In the manuscript, a large 'X' crosses out the passage in blue pencil. A similar outburst detailed in a later scene has also been omitted. During a visit to France, Dashkova initially refuses to visit Versailles, as she feels it would be a disgrace to her sovereign to appear in the French court in a position beneath the French ladies in waiting. Martha

---

[110] 'ce que j'avois vu à Peterhoff ... que j'étais sure qu'Orloff était L'Amant [sic] de sa Majesté; my translation; p. 69v.

[111] 'l'absence de sommeil pendant 15 jours consecutifs, et les 18 ans d'age qui travaillent sur votre imagination; my translation; p. 69v.

[112] 'Fort bien, dis-je, j'y consens, mais permettez moi tous les deux, quand vous serez convaineu que j'ai deviné juste, d'avoir le droit de vous dire, qu'avec vos Têtes froides, vous n'etes que des sots'; my translation; p. 69v.

[113] *Memoirs*, I, pp. 98–99.

omits Dashkova's vitriolic description of the French ladies in waiting: 'I can certainly look with some indifference upon a French duchess, the daughter of a man who has made his fortune from farming, sat upon the seat of honour ... in the Court of Versailles'.[114] Both of these anecdotes highlight Dashkova's lack of humility in political situations; they were therefore omitted due to incongruity with the representation of Dashkova embodied by the rest of *Memoirs*.

Another brief omission relates to Dashkova's affection for a small dog during a visit to Scotland, in which she writes 'I love dogs very much'.[115] The incident is likely cut due to its sentimental and inconsequential nature, as it gives a feeble sense of the elderly age of the author at the time of writing. While these omitted anecdotes may at first appear unsubstantial, their cumulative effect is to improve Dashkova's character on the page. The resulting depiction of Dashkova is tidier, less abrasive and less hindered by the shortcomings of her age or gender. The omissions may be read as part of an editorial agenda that is primarily protective in order to recuperate Dashkova's public persona. These lacunae, then, raise questions about the integrity of the author's original self-representation. The text that disappears silently between the pages of the manuscript and the publication can only be interpreted as a deliberate intervention that takes control of the legacy of the memoir's subject.

'Notice pour l'histoire': The Wilmots in Print

In the summer of 1840 Maria Edgeworth sent a letter to Martha Wilmot Bradford, expressing gratitude for the recent publication of her edited volumes of *Memoirs of Princess Daschkaw*. The book, Edgeworth writes, 'is one of the most entertaining pieces of Biography' that she and her family have ever read, giving them 'the most agreeable idea of the Writer'.[116] The character of the author, Princess Dashkova, 'would have been sufficient to make the book very interesting'. However, it is the additional narrative supplied by Martha, as well as Katherine's collected Russian letters, which make the book truly stand out. 'There is a variety of entertainment in your accounts ... which no other English traveller or writer that I am acquainted

---

[114] 'Je pourrai certainement voir avec indifférence une duchesse française, fille d'un homme qui à fait sa fortune par les fermes, assise sur le siège d'honneur ... à la cour de Versailles'; my translation; p. 108v.
[115] 'J'aime beaucoup les chiens'; my translation; p. 103v.
[116] BL Add MS 41.295 M, Letter from Maria Edgeworth to Mrs. [William] Bradford (née Martha Wilmot), 'Edgeworth Town, July 27th, 1840', 121r.

with ever enjoyed or enabled the public to enjoy', Edgeworth writes, asserting that the Wilmot sisters' supplements will have lasting impact as 'Notice pour l'histoire'.[117] Edgeworth clearly admires *Memoirs*' editorial mixture of genres, drawing in biography, history and, through the inclusion of the Wilmot sisters' narratives, two independent travelogues.

The Wilmot sisters' supplements absorb the final 228 pages of the second volume, or 28 per cent of the overall page counts of both volumes combined. Martha offers an apology for the inclusion of her own supplement on the first page of her editorial introduction to *Memoirs*. She writes of having 'ventured, not without great reluctance and diffidence, to subjoin to the princess's work, a narrative, which I wrote many years ago, of my residence in Russia'.[118] She also defends the validity of her appendage by implying that she has special insight to share concerning Dashkova. She writes, 'I am induced to believe that my own personal narrative, connected as it is with circumstances concerning the Princess in the evening of her life, may supply some notices of her later history'.[119] Her justifications occupy a significant portion of the text, greeting the reader on the very first page, and continuing to discuss her own writing and identity for several paragraphs. Martha's introductory remarks are similarly refocused away from the noblewoman's life by an interjected justification for the inclusion of her sister Katherine's travel writing. An (anonymous) suggestion was made to Martha to print Katherine's writing; unlike her reticence to append her own, to this idea she 'readily concurred' (I, p. xxvii). Katherine's supplement will 'supply a fund of further and very animated illustration, to the subject of this Memoir' (I, p. xxviii). Martha takes the opportunity to specifically praise her late 'beloved' sister, drawing attention to 'the sprightly sallies of [Katherine's] pen, published at the conclusion of these volumes', her 'traces of imagination, and originality of thought and humour' (I, p. xvviii).

While Martha and Katherine's narratives do offer substantial biographical anecdotes of Dashkova's later life, they also depart from this stated intention by documenting their own experiences abroad through the presentation of rich and lengthy Russian travelogues. As I have argued throughout this chapter, the 1840 publication of *Memoirs of Princess Daschkaw* allowed Martha to discharge her duty to her late, great friend by offering the world an ambitious literary work that corrected her disparaged reputation, cemented her legacy as an Enlightenment thinker, and outlined her life as one devoted to Catherine II. Through the mediation of manuscript

---

[117] BL MS 41.295 M, 1840, pp. 122r–v, 123r.
[118] *Memoirs*, I, p. xvii.
[119] *Memoirs*, I, p. xviii.

and print, Martha can connect her Irish and Russian worlds. In the republic of letters, her name can figure alongside Dashkova's, and even Catherine II, albeit by proxy. Yet the Wilmot sisters' supplements are of particular interest to Edgeworth not for this association – but rather due to their ability to shed light on 'the customs & manners and the bits of life in different classes in town & country in Russia'.[120]

Edgeworth's letter makes clear that interest existed on the part of readers to consume travel literature written about cultures beyond the bounds of Europe. While the Wilmot sisters' writing follows in the tradition of a few British women travel authors to the East who published their writing, for instance Lady Craven, personal narratives by women written in such locations were a relative rarity.[121] Despite the enormous popularity of travel literature in the late eighteenth and early nineteenth centuries, women authored only a small percentage of it; the *Database for Women's Travel Writing 1780–1840* estimates that 4 per cent of travel writing published during the period is women-authored.[122] The publication of the supplements is not included in this figure, as the texts are embedded within the volumes of Dashkova's *Memoirs*. In the chapter to follow, I consider how the inclusion of their writing in the book fashions an important identity for the Wilmot sisters, joining them to a burgeoning tradition of women writing about culture, politics and Empire for a British public readerships while travelling in lesser known and exotic lands.

---

[120] BL MS 41 295 M, 1840, 122 r–v.
[121] Elizabeth Craven, *A Journey Through the Crimea to Constantinople* (London, 1789).
[122] Benjamin Colbert, *Women's Travel Writing, 1780–1840: A Bio-Bibliographical Database*, <www.wlv.ac.uk/btw> [accessed 1 August 2023].

5
Women Writers and the Transnational Imagination

On 14 June 1807, Alexander I signed the Treaty of Tilsit with Napoleon at the Battle of Friedland, an agreement that stipulated that Russia end maritime trade with Britain, thereby instigating the Anglo-Russian War (1807–12). By the time hostilities broke out, Martha Wilmot had been living as a guest of Princess Dashkova for more than four years, residing between the noblewoman's home in Moscow and her country estate of Troitskoe. In July 1807, as Martha later wrote in her 'supplement' to Dashkova's *Memoirs*, 'peace was proclaimed between Russia and France – the probable forerunner of war between England and Russia'.[1] These hostilities quickly disrupted the idyllic, if unusual, familial arrangement between Dashkova and Martha. Dashkova's daughter, Anastasia Shcherbinina, long suspicious of Martha's place in her mother's life, seized the opportunity of 'mutual jealousy' between their two countries to spread rumours that the Anglo-Irish protégée 'might be dangerous to the state' (II, pp. 255–256). The sudden threats that Martha perceived rattled her deeply, leading her to conclude that '[t]he face of everything is now changed' (II, p. 256). This included her ability to remain with Dashkova in Russia: '[t]he declaration of war between England and Russia interrupted our … domestic bliss' (II, p. 264).

In her narrative published decades later, Martha recalls the sudden danger and displacement felt by the British then resident in Russia, writing that every day she remains in the country is 'one of torture scarcely to be endured' (II, p. 265). All around her, 'the English were beginning to quit Russia as quickly as they could obtain passports' (II, p. 264). Martha's own first attempt to gain passage in October 1807 is a failure. Disheartened, she returns to Dashkova until a letter arrives in August 1808 alerting her of a ship preparing to sail for England. Following one final 'agonizing embrace and fervent blessing', Martha departs from Troitskoe and Dashkova (II, p.

---

[1] *Memoirs*, II, p. 263.

275). However, as Martha sails away from Russia, she focuses on the emotion of her own upcoming repatriation. Sitting quietly on the deck, Martha watches 'the sun setting in majestic splendour for the last time over a country so long' her home, a country 'where some of the warmest affections of [her] heart still lingered' (II, p. 289). Martha falls into a 'profound reverie', filled with intense feelings of 'calm and melancholy', her thoughts occupied by Dashkova. As the Russian coastline fades away, Martha experiences a reawakening, marking the divide between her adopted country, and her true home to the West:

> I shall never forget being aroused from this reverie by the man at the helm beginning to sing an English song – music which I had not heard for above five years, and which at that moment brought with it a thousand affecting associations. It seemed to reproach me for the melancholy and regret in which I was absorbed, and to awake the dear remembrance of home, of the friends I was now going to rejoin, and anticipation of the happiness yet in store for me.[2]

Shifting her thoughts and her orientation towards 'home' rather than 'abroad', this passage realigns Martha with the 'friends' she is 'going to rejoin'. Literally adrift at sea in the liminal space between two separate points of identity – being the self that was abroad and the self that is returning home to England – Martha's poignant reconnection to her own patriotism comes across in the voice of an English sailor singing a familiar song, drawing along 'a thousand affecting associations' of her British roots. The remainder of the supplement is taken up by Martha's difficulties in the Finnish sea, experiencing not just one but two shipwrecks.

Martha Wilmot's supplement, included in the back of volume two of *Memoirs of Princess Daschkaw* (1840), takes the form of one extended letter that spans ninety-two pages in total. Of these, forty-nine pages are devoted to the time she spent as a guest of Dashkova, thereby fulfilling the duty that she lays out to 'supply some notices of [Dashkova's] later history', casting the noblewoman as loyal, morally upright, loving, and respectable (I, p. xviii). Sara Mills has written of the centrality of the personal and relational in women's travel writing, a paradigm that can be seen in Martha's early focus on the bond she shared with Dashkova.[3] By highlighting her intimacy with her 'Russian mother', Martha implies that the primary motivation of her supplement is rooted in prevalent notions of sensibility. Martha also uses

---

[2] *Memoirs*, II, pp. 289–290.
[3] Sara Mills, *Discourses of Difference: an Analysis of Women's Travel Writing and Colonialism* (London, 1991).

her supplement to highlight the practices of collaboration and scribal publication that sprang from the affectionate coterie at Troitskoe. She writes of her 'utter astonishment' at the work being dedicated in her name, and her daily practices of copying the manuscript.[4] Yet, as noted above, Martha's supplement is a work of two parts. In the first half, Martha justifies her connection to Dashkova. The second half, by contrast, positions Martha's own patriotic affinities, as well as those of Dashkova, through the narration of a lengthy return journey at the outbreak of the brief Anglo-Russian War. Martha's foray into the narration of her wartime return at sea literally sends her away from her professed subject, Princess Dashkova, infusing her work with adventure and personal agency as a female traveller in the Napoleonic period, and one able to supply a unique view of British national identity abroad during a time of conflict. The supplement in the second volume of *Memoirs* containing Katherine's Russian travel writing follows on immediately from Martha's own. While Martha's travelogue is edited into one cohesive narrative written years after the events it describes, Katherine's supplement is an assemblage of letters, which are selected by Martha to highlight her late sister's deft observations of transnational political circumstances at the time of her travels, for example through a critique of the hypocritical Russian adulation of French culture during a time of war with that country.

Both Martha and Katherine's supplements offer the reader representations of a country beyond the conventional bounds of the Grand Tour, though a 'northern variant' of the route was not unheard of.[5] Russia was a somewhat unusual destination for young, middle-ranking female travellers at the end of the eighteenth century, particularly those without diplomatic or military family ties to the region.[6] Yet the sisters' choice to travel to

---

[4] *Memoirs*, II, pp. 239, 240–241.

[5] Anthony Cross has identified a grouping of late eighteenth-century narratives that took in Russian travel, including travel texts by Nathaniel Wraxall, John Richard, Thomas Randall, and Andrew Swinton. See Anthony Cross, *Anglo-Russica: Aspects of Cultural Relations between Great Britain and Russia in the Eighteenth and Early Nineteenth Centuries: Selected Essays by Anthony Cross* (Oxford, Providence, 1993), pp. 17–18.

[6] Maria Guthrie, for instance, travelled to the region with her husband, Matthew Guthrie, a Scottish physician with ties to Catherine II (see Chapter 3). Guthrie's epistolary tour of Crimea was published posthumously. Some elite women travelled the route for pleasure: Lady Elizabeth Craven made Russia and Crimea her destination as she crossed Europe, which she also described in great detail. See Maria Guthrie, *A Tour, Performed in the Years 1795–6, through the Taurida, or Crimea* (London, 1802); Elizabeth Craven, *A Journey through the Crimea to Constantinople* (London, 1789).

Russia and then write about their journeys was not completely unique within the context of eighteenth-century print culture, particularly among women writers.[7] Considered exotic and foreign to British travellers and readers thanks, in part, to its feudal system, its association with European courts and use of French as a diplomatic language also sustained a sense of familiarity and curiosity. While British attitudes towards the country had long been characterised by notions of barbarism and corruption, the 'image of a new Russia' that was embodied by the more Enlightened reigns of Peter I and Catherine II throughout the eighteenth century had 'captivated the popular and scholarly imagination in Britain.'[8] Still, prejudices remained. The Wilmots' narratives embody an increased level of contact between the Britain and Russia by offering moments of geopolitical connection that reframe both counties. In what follows, I interpret the Wilmots' manuscript and published travel writings on Russia to show how women travellers communicated national affinities and mediated imperial prerogatives in the late eighteenth-century British imagination. I do this, in part, by comparing the Wilmot sisters' authorial strategies with those of Maria Graham (Lady Callcott), a notable contemporary. Graham and the Wilmots all draw on first-hand experiences to articulate complex geopolitical affinities relative to Empire in their travel writing, often doing so through paratextual strategies. Throughout the chapter, I argue that the inclusion of the Wilmots' supplements alters the overall meaning and enduring value of Dashkova's *Memoirs* as it appeared in 1840 before a public readership, transforming it from an individual life-writing record to a collective embodiment of women's transnational literary relationships and networks, while also fashioning the sisters as writers of political, historical and national narratives.

Beyond the Grand Tour: Anxieties and Strategies

Travel writing as a form invites the reader to relive aspects of a personal experience, a prospect which is inherently subjective. The reader 'cannot avoid filtering any description through a sceptical lens', given that it is often difficult to discern the difference between 'fiction, non-fiction, or

---

[7] A notable, if small, field of eighteenth-century women travel writers publishing popular accounts of Russia emerged from the 1730s onwards, including Elizabeth Justice and Jane Vigor; see Katrina O'Loughlin, *Women, Writing and Travel in the Eighteenth Century* (Cambridge, 2018).

[8] Cross, pp. 1–2.

autobiography'.[9] What's more, 'travel writing often reveals the lives of women at times of particular difficulty, danger, excitement, or achievement' (p. 183). For women travel writers of the late eighteenth century, particularly those documenting less familiar foreign nations, such writing required a delicate balancing act. Women writers needed to not only justify the importance of their own narratives, but also to prove their trustworthiness and authenticity, particularly in a print marketplace flooded with male-authored texts.[10] While usefulness to the British nation state had long been a key validation of travel writing as a genre in the late eighteenth century, women's roles in the collection and circulation of such knowledge was an evolving matter.[11] Moving between foreign spaces during an era of immense global upheaval, women travel writers of the period aimed to articulate what they witnessed abroad without understating their gendered perspectives. Linda Van Netten Blimke's valuable scholarship shows how British women travel writers of the late eighteenth century 'actively resist conventional definitions of femininity and envision a place for women within the British polity' by drawing on widespread political and revolutionary change as 'a momentary aperture ... that allowed for their greater inclusion'.[12] The resulting narratives thus offer a specifically female view of unfolding geopolitical events, doing so through a range of literary strategies that intervene into discussions of national – and transnational – identity at critical moments.

These strategies and anxieties are often most clearly on display in the paratext of women's travel texts. The prefaces to the works of the popular travel writer and illustrator Maria Graham showcases some of the concerns of representation that preoccupied women writers of the period. Graham wrote a wide range of travel books covering places both well-known to

---

[9] Maureen Mulligan, 'Women Travel Writers and the Question of Veracity', in *Women, Travel Writing, and Truth*, ed. by Clare Broome Saunders (New York and Abingdon, 2014), pp. 171–184, p. 172.

[10] Eye-witness accounts could offer a powerful validation for publication of women's travel narratives, and such strategies persisted in popular examples well into the nineteenth century, particularly in the realm of the arts; for a good discussion of these strategies, see Caroline Palmer, '"I Will Tell Nothing that I Did Not See": British Women's Travel Writing, Art and the Science of Connoisseurship, 1776–1860', *Forum for Modern Language Studies*, 51:3 (2015), 248–268.

[11] Beyond its entertainment value, late eighteenth and early nineteenth-century travel writing was simultaneously viewed as an invaluable tool for spreading knowledge. See Robin Jarvis, *Romantic Readers and Transatlantic Travel: Expeditions and Tours in North America, 1760–1840* (Farnham, 2012).

[12] Linda Van Netten Blimke, *Political Affairs of the Heart: Female Travel Writers, the Sentimental Travelogue, and Revolution, 1775–1800* (Lewisburg, 2022), pp. 2, 16.

British readers and travellers accustomed to the bounds of the Grand Tour, such as Italy, along with guides, narratives and histories on countries further afield. These included India, more familiar due to Britain's colonial control, as well as Brazil and Chile. Her first and perhaps most well-known book, *Journal of a Residence in India* first appeared in 1812. Graham travelled to India in 1808 with her father, George Dundas, a former naval officer who had been appointed head of the naval works at the Bombay dockyard of the British East India Company, along with her sister. On their outbound journey, she met and married her first husband, Thomas Graham, a Scottish naval officer aboard the same ship. Initially written as a diary over a two-year period, Graham's Indian journal was worked into a narrative and published not long after her return to Britain in 1811. The book is more than 250 pages long, replete with personal experiences and several beautiful illustrations made by Graham herself. Yet it is the preface that is the most interesting for how it succinctly frames the previously unknown woman writer as uniquely positioned to serve as author of the text. Graham acknowledges that India has indeed previously 'been the subject of innumerable publications' by many 'intelligent Englishmen', but argues that previous to the appearance of her book there was nothing available 'in our language containing such a popular and comprehensive view', despite the fact that such texts are commonly furnished ... by travellers in countries comparably less deserving of notice'.[13] Graham ties what she sees as a paucity of existing travel narratives on India to the country's status as a British colony rather than a place of tourism. As an extension of Britain through the colonial bonds of Empire, Graham views this oversight as one worthy of correcting, writing that, unlike herself 'few people go to this remote region as mere idle or philosophical observers' (p. v). Instead, 'the multitude of well-educated individuals' to be found in India 'are too constantly occupied with the cares and duties of their respective vocations as statemen, soldiers, or traders' to observe and document what may be intriguing to the 'contemplative spectator' (p. v). Her own *Journal* will take in new views and subjects that stand in opposition to 'all our modern publications on the subject of India', which 'are entirely occupied with its political and military history – details and suggestions upon its trade and commercial resources, – and occasionally discussions upon the more recondite parts of its literary or mythological antiquities' (p. vi). Graham's Preface in *Journal of a Residence in India*, then, seeks to fill a gap created by the plethora of masculine authorial voices writing from within British India. Rather than looking inwards to further the male military or trade ambitions of the Empire, Graham promises to document the country's

---

[13] Maria Graham, *Journal of a Residence in India* (Edinburgh, 1813).

'scenery and monuments, and of the manners and habits of its natives and resident colonists', areas of observation and study which are apparently positioned within an acceptably gendered realm (p. v).

As Graham quickly makes clear, she has a wider stake in the project, rooted in ideas of nationhood, identity, and history – but also in reform. She acknowledges that 'her character of the natives' is 'more unfavourable than that of some other writers' (p. viii). Instead of the 'innocence, benevolence, and voluptuous simplicity' that 'the imaginations of some ingenious authors have peopled the cottages of the Hindoos', Graham's encounters resulted in 'a very opposite picture' (p. viii). While she accepted that her *Journal* described 'a people whose laws, whose religion, whose arts, whose habits of reasoning and notions of politeness, all differ from ours, as radically as their language or complexion', she was nonetheless' unable to 'reconcile herself, even by these considerations', to the lower 'morals' and 'decencies of social life' that she had met with (pp. vii; ix).[14] Yet Graham's text does not take leave of solutions. She offers her book as a form of 'mediation' for the disturbing social differences detected among her Indian subjects, writing due to a hope that 'she may perhaps contribute … to direct the attention of those in whose hands so much of their destiny is placed, to the means of improving their moral and intellectual condition, as well as of securing them from political or civil injuries' (p. ix). Graham's assumption of the role of colonial arbitrator is fairly blatant in her preface, a self-fashioning theme that continues in her subsequent book. *Letters on India*, which appeared in 1814, only two years later, due in part to popular demand, serves as a kind of sequel-come-handbook by offering further information on aspects of life in India. Writing in the Preface, Graham builds on her earlier legacy, writing that 'the indulgence with which the Public received the "Journal of a Residence in India," induced the writer to hope, that the curiosity concerning our oriental possessions was still sufficiently alive to promise a favourable reception to the following little work.'[15] Graham again focuses on the practicality of her text, stating that 'it is written solely with the design of being useful to such as are called upon to go at an early period of life, to India,' with a hope of assisting those who 'cannot have had time to make themselves acquainted with even the general outline of the history, religion, or science of that country' (p. iii). Regina Akel, Graham's biographer, notes

---

[14] Onni Gust describes Graham's focus on the social and productive inadequacies of the people she encounters on her tour as an extension of European Colonialism that justifies 'the subordination of India as a space and society'; see Onni Gust, 'Mobility, Gender and Empire in Maria Graham's *Journal of a Residence in India* (1812)', *Gender & History*, 29 (2017), 273–291, p. 274.

[15] Maria Graham, *Letters on India* (London, 1814), p. iii.

that her 'vision of India was clouded by her own shadow', as her Indian texts deliver a view of power structures 'mostly in compliance with the directives of her time, as in her representation of British colonialism as benign'.[16] It is important to remember that Graham's own travel to and residence in India was contingent on her father's, and later her husband's, roles as agents of both military might and trade in the country under British imperial rule. Graham's self-fashioning as guide and spectator, but also as moral and social critic, can therefore be interpreted through Philippa Levine's work on the dynamic connections between gender and empire. While 'the British Empire always seems a very masculine enterprise ... that reality only tells a fraction of the story': books such as Graham's show how 'the building of empires themselves cannot be understood without employing a gendered perspective'.[17] With a final apology in the preface of her *Letters on India*, Graham 'takes leave of her little book to send it forth to the world', criticising its own faults while 'trusting that the motives of the undertaking will cancel some of its many faults' (p. v). Graham's motives are an interesting question to contemplate, given the repeated focus on the British men and women engaging in the colonial government and occupation of India. While she repeatedly states her desire that the texts should be useful, they also grant her a unique agency as a British woman traveller intervening in expansion and the concerns of Empire.

In her earliest works on the country, Graham had acknowledged that India had already been relatively well-documented by male travel writers, even if their narratives may have been lacking on the points of society, the arts and scenery, particularly in comparison to what was in print on countries along Europe's Grand Tour. Graham's later travel narratives, however, delve into locations that would be less familiar to the British reader. Her *Journal of a Residence in Chile, during the year 1822 And a Voyage from Chile to Brazil in 1823* was published in 1824.[18] Graham travelled to Chile in the aftermath of the Chilean War of Independence, which saw the country undergo a rupture from Spain and an end to the colonial period. Beginning in 1808 with the Napoleonic forces' capture of King Ferdinand VII of Spain, ensuing conflicts between Patriot and Royalist factions continued beyond the Chilean declaration of Independence in 1818, only fully resolving in 1826 with the defeat of the remaining royalist forces. Her personal situation was a tenuous one. She had travelled to Chile accompanying her husband on

---

[16] Regina Akel, *Maria Graham: A Literary Biography* (Amherst, 2009), p. 63.
[17] Philippa Levine, 'Introduction: Why Gender and Empire?', *Gender and Empire*, ed. by Philippa Levine (Oxford, 2007), pp. 1–13, p. 1.
[18] Graham also published her *Journal of a Voyage to Brazil* (London, 1824) in the same year.

the *HMS Doris*, which was under his command, in order to protect British mercantile affairs in the country. His shocking death by fever *en route* to Valparaiso left her in a precarious position. Despite offers to return her to Britain, Graham chose to stay in Chile. She lived independently for a year while carrying out research and writing her new book.

It is clear from the outset of the preface of *Journal of a Residence in Chile* that Graham considers her volume on Chile to be her most impactful work to date, and one that departed, in some ways, from her earlier studies. Graham points out that 'of the first six years of the revolution in Chile, no account is to be procured, either from the offices of the secretaries of state, or among the papers of the actors in the scene.'[19] Yet she also understates the great effort that she has put into the composition of her book, writing that it was her 'good fortune, while in Chile, to become acquainted with … actors or spectators in the great event', who 'were kind enough to allow her to write down' their experiences' (p. iii–iv). Carl Thompson writes that Graham's 'self-deprecating disclaimers do not adequately convey the sophistication, depth and ambitiousness' of her South American journals; rather than being 'merely the impressions of a woman caught up in interesting events', her writing instead 'reflects a level of knowledge that is at once historiographic, ethnographic, and inherently political.'[20] Indeed, the volume includes, immediately after the preface, an approximately 100-page history of the political situation in Chile, containing all of the revolutionary activities of recent years through to the present day. Yet once again, Graham uses the uniqueness of her position, as well as her now-established expertise as a traveller and reporter on foreign lands, to intervene on the country's behalf. 'There is so much of good' in Chile, she writes, 'so much in the character of the people and the excellence of the soil and climate, that there can be no doubt of the ultimate success of their endeavours after a free and flourishing state' (p. iv–v). Yet 'there are no ordinary difficulties to get over, no common wants to be supplied' (p. v). Her Chilean *Journal*, she hopes, may in the 'smooth those difficulties, by calling attention to that country either as one particularly fitted for commercial intercourse, or as

---

[19] Maria Graham, *Journal of a Residence in Chile, during the year 1822. And a Voyage from Chile to Brazil in 1823* (London, 1824), p. iii.

[20] Carl Thompson, 'Sentiment and Scholarship: Hybrid Historiography and Historical Authority in Maria Graham's South American Journals', *Women's Writing*, 24:2 (2017), 185–206, p. 186; Claudia Georgi also focuses on Graham's 'thirst for knowledge and self-fashioning as an expert in disciplines as diverse as Orientalism, botany, geology, and politics'. See Claudia Georgi, 'Maria Graham, Travel Writing on India, Italy, Brazil, and Chile (1812–1824)', in *Handbook of British Travel Writing*, ed. by Barbara Schaff (Berlin & Boston, 2020), pp. 313–334.

one whose natural resources and powers have yet to be cultivated' (p. v). Delivering her extensive and erudite text to the British reader as a means of promoting 'commercial intercourse' with Chile through exploitation of its 'natural resources and powers', Graham's preface subtly steps away from some of the gendered prerogatives of women's travel writing by suggesting new frontiers for trade and the expansion of Empire. If her pages achieve these aims 'in the slightest degree', then 'the writer will feel the truest satisfaction' (p. v).

As Graham's prefaces show, while women writers use these spaces to offer a formulaic feminine apology for offering their experiences in print, they also carefully draw on the expertise of their first-hand knowledge of both social life and political events abroad as a means of justifying their texts. Like Graham, the Wilmot sisters' supplements – a type of paratext themselves, following Dashkova's memoir – use a series of framing strategies to situate their expertise as foreign travellers, allowing them to write on politics and empire at pivotal historical moments. They do so through the lens of personal experience and relationships, all while balancing feminine reticence, tactics which link their published writing to the wider canon of women's travel literature of the late eighteenth century.

Supplementing National Affinities

The Wilmot sisters' lengthy travelogues within *The Memoirs of Princess Daschkaw* begin with a simple title page. Primarily blank, but containing in bold the subtitle, 'Supplement: Containing a Personal Narrative by the Editor, and Letters of her Sister, Miss Wilmot' (II, p. 211), it indicates a turning point in the latter half of the second volume, and introduces a new set of voices that will now fill the remaining pages. Curiously, however, the appearance of the dual travel narratives within the volumes is prefaced by more than just paratextual apparatus. Martha's supplement, placed first ahead of Katherine's, is also framed and introduced narratively through the organisation of the material that immediately precedes it: five letters written to Dashkova from 'the Empress Elizabeth', or Elizabeth Alexeievna, Louise of Baden, consort of Emperor Alexander I (II, pp. 201–205).

Written primarily between 1801–02, when Empress Elizabeth was resident in Moscow, the letters lean towards the personal while maintaining an air of propriety. In them, Elizabeth thanks Princess Dashkova for the gift of two small dogs, and later describes her shock and heartbreak at the death of her infant child (II, pp. 202–203). The final letter, not written until 1807, maintains the tone of the earlier letters yet relates directly to Martha.

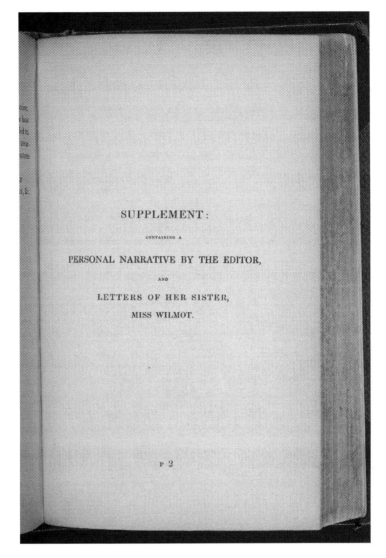

Figure 15 British Library, *Memoirs of Princess Daschkaw*, vol. II, p. 211. © The British Library Board.

Elizabeth responds to Dashkova's request (not included in the volume) that she protect Martha – whether in the scenario of Dashkova's death, when Martha might be left alone without a patron or protector in a foreign land – or perhaps even under the circumstances of international hostilities. The letters take on a political undertone and the Empress writes, 'under every circumstance, Miss Wilmot may rest assured that nothing shall be wanting which it may be in my power to do for her' (II, 205). The inclusion of the

Empress' letters is intriguing, as they foreshadow Martha's difficulties in leaving Russia at the outset of the Anglo-Russian War, a conflict of which the letter writer's husband, Alexander I, sat at the heart.

A further exchange of letters between Dashkova and the Dowager Empress Mary, widow of Emperor Paul, reiterate a similar request for and promise for Martha's protection, along with Dashkova's effusive expressions of affection towards Martha and a financial wish to settle 'five thousand pounds sterling in favour of my young friend Miss Wilmot … to be guaranteed for her use' (II, 206–210, p. 208.) Martha's micro-preface to this particular letter, the final entry, begs for patience and understanding. 'The Editor must once more disclaim all personal feelings' in including it, she writes, adding that 'it would ill become her to withhold so touching a proof of the noble nature of her revered friend.'[21] These Royal letters, as well as her discussion as a subject within them, frames and situates her own writing in both political and sentimental terms. The careful arrangement of these correspondence records reminds the reader of Martha's simultaneously privileged and delicate status in Russia, casting a light on the precariousness she experienced as a British subject. They also highlight the uniqueness of her position as Dashkova's companion, while subtly justifying the inclusion of the Wilmots' narratives as central to the noblewoman's late-life concerns. In the events that soon followed, and which are detailed in her supplement, Martha did in fact come under suspicion of the government, leading to a fraught return home, regardless of promises of protection, financial support and friendship from the highest women in Russian society.

At the outset of her supplement, Martha's editorial micro-preface to her travelogue continues to evoke ideas of patronage and a validation of the inclusion of her own writing. 'The motive for publishing the following narrative has been sufficiently noticed in the Introduction to Princess Daschkaw's Memoirs', she writes (II, p. 213). Martha states that the narrative originally took the form of a letter addressed to Lord Glenbervie.[22] 'Several additions have been lately made to it', yet she has maintained the epistolary form rather than 'cast it into a different shape'. Finally, in a typically reticent register for a woman-authored travelogue preface, Martha offers an 'apology for its extravagant length'. No manuscript copy of Martha's original epistolary description of her journey for Lord Glenbervie survives, though she states that this source text was written in 1814. However, some correspondence between them from around the same period shows that Glenbervie, a politician and lifelong diarist, was discussing Dashkova's

---

[21] Ibid.
[22] Sylvester Douglas, 1st Baron Glenbervie (1743– 1823).

memoir manuscript with Martha, and that he suggested she add her own travel stories to its eventual publication.[23] It can be assumed, then, from these varying parameters, that the earliest composition date for the supplement may have been 1814, and 1840 the latest, given the publication date of *Memoirs*. The epistolary format chosen by Martha for her narrative was a common convention in eighteenth century women's travel writing. It allowed the author to present their travels as a series of informal sociable documents that were perhaps not originally intended for a public readership, and only later worked up for circulation in manuscript form, as with Katherine Wilmot's Peace of Amiens epistolary travelogue addresses to her brother, or for a public readership in print, such as with Lady Mary Wortley Montagu's 'Turkish Embassy Letters', Helen Maria William's *Letters Written in France* (1790–96), and Eliza Fay's *Original Letters from India* (1817).[24] Martha's use of the letter as a framing device at the start of her lengthy narrative, rather than as a repeated intervention taking the form of a series of letters, is also reminiscent of Maria Graham's *Journal of a Residence in India* (1812), which the author claims 'were really and truly written ... for the amusement of an intimate friend'.[25]

The opening paragraphs of Martha's narrative position the Wilmot family's collective identity as subjects of the British Empire and contributors to its presence in the world, in both formal and informal ways. She begins by situating herself physically in the moment of writing while also framing the act as a difficult task, remarking 'I have wasted at least half an hour in thinking how I ought to begin the history which your lordship asks of me'. She also positions her identity and reasons for travelling in order 'to make my narrative the more intelligible', but also as a means of justifying her journey as a young single female traveller to Russia. Martha recounts her depression following the death of her 'beloved brother' in 1802, which left her feeling as if 'every wish of my soul was buried in his grave' (II, 215). The death of Martha's brother, Charles, is framed through the lens of the British Empire's losses and gains at sea. 'He was appointed at the age of nineteen to the command of a sloop of war', Martha writes. Once 'stationed in the West Indies and ere he had taken possession of her, he fell a victim to

---

[23] RIA MS 12 M 18, 'Brighton, Jan 7, 1813'. For more on this, see Chapter 4.
[24] For more on Katherine's Peace of Amiens tour (RIA MS 12 L 32) see Chapter 1; Lady Mary Wortley Montagu, *Letters of the Right Honourable Lady M—y W—y M—e: Written During her Travels in Europe, Asia and Africa*, 3 vols (London, 1763); Helen Maria Williams, *Letters Written in France* (London, 1790–96); Eliza Fay, *Original Letters from India: Containing a Narrative of a Journey through Egypt and the Author's Imprisonment at Calicut by Hyder Ally* (Calcutta, 1817).
[25] Graham, *Journals*, p. vi.

the yellow fever which then raged at Jamaica' (II, 216). Rather than feeling a sense of caution about sea travel or its consequences as a result of his death abroad, Martha next recounts how her sister Katherine's journeys in France soon after 'revived a desire for travelling', leading her relation Catherine Hamilton to renew her old friendship with Princess Dashkova on the young Martha's behalf (II, 217). Due to her father's doubts, along with the slowness of the post between Ireland and Russia, she began her voyage a year later. Martha's outbound journey is not described, posing a notable contrast to her return.

As the Introduction to this chapter showed, Martha satisfied the biographical expectations of her supplement in its early pages by focusing on the sentimentality and familial nature of her special relationship she shared with Dashkova prior to her departure from Russia. Yet this early portion of the narrative lays the groundwork for a move in different direction. Martha focuses heavily on the gossip that assailed Dashkova's reputation both in Russia and internationally; for example, recalling being so 'poisoned' by bad stories that she 'shuddered at the idea' of meeting the noblewoman (II. p. 223). Following on from this, Martha describes in detail the negativity and abuse directed towards the Wilmots from those suspicious of them in Russian society, particularly on the part of Dashkova's daughter Madame Shcherbinina, whose name is omitted. Martha recounts how Shcherbinina spread untrue rumours that Dashkova wished to force her son, 'Prince Daschkaw', to divorce his wife and marry Martha instead – thus making her a legal rather than spiritual member of her own family (II, pp. 253–255). Martha explains how Shcherbinina seamlessly linked her long-standing jealousy of the Wilmots with the growing machinations of war between Russia and Britain. She repeatedly describes Shcherbinina as 'my enemy', framing her own adversarial role as a position into which she is thrust, rather than one that she chooses. In doing so, Martha subtly frames herself as a symbolic figure representing the impossible choices of her own nation drawn into a war not of its own making. By progressively departing from its biographically focused beginning, Martha's supplement gracefully transitions to an in-depth account of her experiences as a British traveller during the Anglo-Russian War. Far from one negating the other, the two contrasting plotlines of the supplement function symbiotically – the sentimentality of the early biographical material effectively camouflaging the historical and political subtext of the latter portion.

Martha's supplement gives her agency not only as Dashkova's companion, but as a commentator on the political conflict amidst which she finds herself at sea, particularly through her narrative of being shipwrecked. Shipwreck narratives were 'common reading fare for the public throughout the eighteenth and nineteenth centuries', replete with the standard entertaining tropes of tragedy and heroisms, exotic lands and encounters, and Christian and moral fortitude.[26] Originating as oral traditions shared between sailors, tales of shipwreck moved onto the page as a unique form of literature in the period, finding popularity with a transatlantic readership.[27] In Britain, accounts of shipwrecks were widely available in print for readers curious about the nation's commercial and military endeavours, appearing in a variety of formats including on the pages of daily newspapers, as full-length bound books capturing scientific travels, or as prefaces and supplements, such as in the case of Martha's text. Personal experiences of shipwreck were also embodied in popular poetry, as in William Falconer's widely reprinted *The Shipwreck* (1762), which was 'was translated, anthologized, and lavishly illustrated through the end of the nineteenth century', and beloved by influential Romantic writers and readers including Burns and Byron.[28] Taken as a symbol of 'national glory', contemporary shipwreck narratives could also communicate 'political concerns about disasters at sea', whether interpreted 'as evidence that the nation was wrong in its policies and priorities' or by recognising that deaths at sea were the 'sad but necessary costs of national glory'.[29] The success and widespread appeal of narratives of shipwreck in the late eighteenth and early nineteenth centuries has been linked to their ability to engage the public in contemporary issues. As a genre, Carl Thompson argues, shipwreck narratives are revealing of 'the construction of British identity in this period, and especially about the emergence of new forms of national and imperial identity'.[30] While Martha's supplement was admittedly composed several years later, she clearly understood the importance of her experience in its immediate aftermath, particularly its capacity to serve as a valuable tool for interpreting her complex experience as a British subject abroad during a time of war.[31]

[26] Cathryn J. Pearce, 'What Do You Do with a Shipwrecked Sailor? Extreme Weather, Shipwreck, and Civic Responsibility in Nineteenth-Century Liverpool', *Victorian Review*, 47:1 (2021), 19–24, 20.

[27] Ann Mitchell-Cook, *A Sea of Misadventures: Shipwreck and Survival in Early America* (Columbia, 2014), p. 4.

[28] 'Introduction', Michael Edson and Bridget Keegan, 'William Falconer: Sailor Poet', *Eighteenth-Century Life*, 47:2 (2023), 3–12, p. 3.

[29] Suvil Kaul, '*Britannia* and the Weight of Empires Past: The Instance of Falconer's *The Shipwreck*', *Eighteenth-Century Life*, 47:2 (2023), 46–65, p. 48.

[30] *Romantic-Era Shipwreck Narratives: An Anthology*, ed. by Carl Thompson (Nottingham, 2007), p. 4.

[31] Thompson notes that the 'cult of the sea grew still more pronounced during the Napoleonic Wars, when for long periods the Navy was the only obstacle preventing a French invasion', leading to an increase in the number of shipwreck narratives in

Comparison of Martha's published writing in her supplement with her unpublished letters and journals reveals a set of authorial strategies. While Martha's voice in the supplement was apparently crafted at least six years later, the earlier contemporary records show more details of her feelings and immediate experiences, which would later be worked up for her narrative. For example, arriving into the port of Karleskrona in Sweden following the events of shipwreck in December 1808, Martha sends a letter to her relative John Eardley Wilmot. 'I am just arriv'd here after a shipwreck & a variety of events,' she writes, promising to share the tale of her journey at the 'beloved fireside' of his home at Bruce Castle 'before new years day or very soon after'.[32] Martha's thirty-three surviving letters to Eardley Wilmot, the majority of which were written in Russia during the height of the Napoleonic conflicts rather than composed after the fact, shed light on her political affinities. While similar sentiments appear in the letters and diaries among her family papers, none are quite as explicit with regard to Martha's own sense of British-Irish identity as an expatriate in face of the rise of Napoleon. The strength of feeling in Martha's letters may be attributed in part to her intended recipient, a Whig and former Member of the House of Commons. The letters are equally politically astute and scathing. Following news of Napoleon's self-declaration as Emperor, Martha expresses disbelief that the 'French nation … are going to reassume all the *despised* distinctions & privileges of Nobility, the nominal cause of all the hated devestation [sic] of so long & so bloody a war'.[33] In another, written in July 1804, Martha despairs over what she sees as the British Empire's lonely position as Europe's protector:

> Alas I fear Eng'd must stand *proudly* alone to oppose the *universal* foe; if her power & success, equals her *brave* attempt, Europe ought to crown her with a thous'd wreathes of Laurel, form'd by the hand of *Gratitude*. Were *wishes*, capable of bearing arms in her cause, I would for one, send her some *Legions*, nor ask the aid of foreign power – Every *vessel* that is taken, goes to my heart, & there are many tongues ready to *wonder* why it is so – would to God it were otherwise, their superiority at *sea* would *too much*, Princess Daschkaw is so *true to the cause*, that her heart goes along with everything in the slightest degree

---

circulation in the earliest years of the nineteenth century, *Romantic-Era Shipwreck Narratives*, p. 6.

[32] Yale University, Beinecke Library, OSB MS 54, Box 3, Folder 151, Martha Wilmot to John Eardley Wilmot, 'Carlescona, 4th Decr 1808', recto.

[33] Beinecke, Martha to Eardley Wilmot (No 4, 19), 'Troitska 23d June 1804 N.S', p. 1v.

favourable [sic] to it, & deplores the reverse, tis pity she has not more to offer.[34]

Martha's language here is intriguing for its desire to intervene in the conflict while also revealing a sense of personal limitations: her 'wishes' are not capable of helping England 'bear arms in her cause'. Martha's engaged awareness of the maritime dimension of British naval efforts to combat Napoleon is laid out in her statement that 'Every *vessel* that is taken, goes to my heart'. These sentiments are echoed by Dashkova's desperate desires to further England's causes, an assertion which cements their shared political affinities. This written declaration of an emotional investment in the conflict, though intended for a sociable familial readership in letter form, foreshadows the later focus on international alliances and naval power in her published travelogue.

Few shipwreck narratives were authored by women in the late eighteenth and early nineteenth centuries from an eyewitness, first-person perspective, with women more often situated in shipwreck accounts as voiceless victims, whose sufferings feature prominently.[35] Yet women's authentic voices were not entirely absent from the discourse of sea narratives. Ann Mitchell-Cook notes that, despite the traditional representation of sea-faring narratives as absent of women's voices in the eighteenth and nineteenth centuries, women did in fact go to sea as the wives of captains or officers, or as passengers – and they wrote about it – whether publishing their narratives or writing informally.[36] Women also wrote about the political dimensions of the sea in other ways, including prominent late eighteenth-century women writers, such as Charlotte Smith, without ever leaving land. Smith's long blank verse poem 'The Emigrants' (1792) deals with the treatment of the refugee crisis in the North Sea created by the aftermath of the French Revolution.[37] Smith subsequently wrote a shipwreck account herself, entitled *A Narrative of the loss of the Catharine, Venus and Piedmont transports*. In the preface to the text, Smith claims to have written the narrative on behalf of 'an unfortunate Survivor from one of the wrecks and her infant Child'. The pamphlet includes a lengthy list of

---

[34] Beinecke, Martha to Eardley Wilmot (No 5, 20), 'Kruglo, 31st July N.S. 1804', p. 2v; emphasis original.
[35] Thompson, pp. 11–12.
[36] See Mitchell-Cook's chapter on women at sea: 'To Honor Their Worth, Beauty, and Accomplishment', pp. 97–112; Mitchell-Cook describes how women's presence on board, and in shipwreck narratives, provided a sense of domesticity to the rugged environment of life on board, as well as a sense of morality.
[37] Charlotte Turner Smith, *The Emigrants, a Poem, in Two Books* (London, 1793).

subscribers, indicating that Smith capitalised on both the interest in the recent shocking wrecks in Dorset as well as her existing literary celebrity to aid the unnamed benefactor.[38]

Into the next century, fictionalised representations of women's shipwreck experiences achieved huge popularity, particularly those that ventriloquised and reimagined the voice of Anglo women travellers experiencing tragedy due to shipwreck in barbaric and exotic lands. For instance, works such as *An Authentic Narrative of the Shipwreck and Suffering of Mrs. E. Bradley ... Written by herself* (1821) were plagiarised to describe a known account of a woman shipwrecked on the Barbary Coast in 1818.[39] Other contemporary strategies for women's literary work on past maritime exploration can be seen in Jane Porter's edited work. In *Sir Edward Seward's narrative of his shipwreck, and consequent discovery of certain islands in the Caribbean sea ... from the year 1733 to 1749, as written in his own diary*, published in 1831, Porter crafts Seward's diaries into a first-person narrative, enabling her to engage with the historical dimensions of imperial power by proxy.[40]

While the scarcity of women-authored shipwreck narratives based on their own experiences makes Martha's supplement in *Memoirs* somewhat unique, it also follows a relatively formulaic structure for the period. Sailing away from Russia, Martha's narrative begins quickly to take shape using what Carl Thompson has described as the 'master narrative' of shipwreck accounts by beginning with an early 'disaster phase', encompassing the wreck itself, which may include sublime experiences such as tempests, or violent scenes of mutiny.[41] Having finally departed after much difficulty, Martha falls asleep on deck, only to be 'suddenly awakened by a most fearful shock' and a crashing that sounds 'like the destruction of the universe' (*Memoirs*, II, 290). Looking up, she sees the outline of a second ship's mast looming above, its sails, rigging, and masts interlaced above the deck. The brig, which had been following the larger ship, had mistaken its course in the dark, 'bearing down ... with the wind in her favour' (II, 290). The

---

[38] Charlotte Turner Smith, *A Narrative of the loss of the Catharine, Venus and Piedmont Transports* (London, 1796).

[39] 'Eliza Bradley', *An Authentic Narrative of the Shipwreck and Suffering of Mrs. E. Bradley ... Written by Herself, etc.* (Boston, 1821).

[40] *Sir Edward Seward's narrative of his shipwreck, and consequent discovery of certain islands in the Caribbean sea: with a detail of many extraordinary and highly interesting events in his life, from the year 1733 to 1749, as written in his own diary*. Edited by Jane Porter (London, 1831).

[41] Thompson, p. 16; Thompson borrows the phrase 'master narrative' from historian George Landow.

terrible force of the impact sends the ship in the opposite direction, where it is 'wrecked by striking upon a rock' (II, 291). Though 'horror-struck', she is surprised at her own reaction: 'I perfectly well remember thanking the Almighty that I was alone, and feeling an elevation of thought which is far above my ordinary frame of mind' (II, 291). She remains calm, resigned to her fate, thanking God that none of her family travelled with her. Mitchell-Cook, Thompson and Kaul all describe how fierce storms and fear for survival can engender evangelical or religious prerogatives in shipwreck narratives, moving towards a message of morality and improvement as a means of justifying the narratives' existence. Martha recounts recently spending much of her time 'under the Divine influence of fervent prayer' – most likely due to her desire to leave Russia safely amidst the outbreak of war. She allows herself to feel hope, which is 'awakened by the idea of being preserved' (II, 291).

The captain of the ship on which Martha sails – an American merchant ship – personifies a stereotypical ideal by assuming the role of the heroic leader.[42] He gives the passengers 'confidence by his courage and presence of mind' (II, 292), fires minute guns throughout the night and has the lifeboats unlashed, but refrains from using them until absolutely necessary. Hoping to save everyone on board, he prevails on 'his crew to drink less freely than they usually do upon such occasions' and, as he is 'greatly beloved', the crew abides by his wishes. The ship carries a valuable load of cargo, and Martha romanticises the potential loss of property. The ship, which was never named prior to the crash of the two vessels, is now referred to as 'poor *Maria*'. Mr Donovan, the merchant property owner, mourns the ship as if he is 'watching the last moments of a dying friend' (II, 292). Martha laments seeing the *Maria* left 'dismantled and disfigured' (II, 292). When morning breaks, the light reveals that the ship is not completely wrecked, though in a 'perilous state': 'what we had supposed to be land during the night proved to be large masses of rock rising out of the sea' that could have hardly served 'to shelter wild beasts' (II, 293). The weather begins to darken and the 'swell of the sea' is frightful. Looking 'around in desolation', Martha 'could not perceive a chance of being saved' (II, 293). Two small boats suddenly approach, having heard the distress call. Thanks to the Captain's persistent ingenuity, relief appears – a reward for the good faith placed in the ship's hierarchical power structure, even in times of crisis.

[42] Although the ship was a private merchant vessel, its American ownership – which Martha understates – is interesting in terms of positioning affinities in the narrative. The United States attempted to remain neutral in the early Napoleonic Wars and was so at the time of the Anglo-Russian War. The country later became bound up in the ensuing conflicts, leading to the War of 1812.

Martha's narrative shifts in focus from calamity at sea to a preoccupation with the rescuers upon the arrival of the boats, which are surprisingly rowed by both men and women. This essentially begins the second part of the narrative, or the 'aftermath' phase.[43] The rowers speak Finnish and identify themselves as inhabitants of 'Stamieux', an island 'twenty versts from Fredericksham' (II, 293).[44] Martha and Mr Haliday, who is serving as her protector and companion, are the only two genteel passengers not involved in crewing the ship. They immediately set off for land with the islanders. By the time they arrive on shore the storm has come into full force, leaving the captain and crew stranded. The islanders refuse to brave the sea again in the storm, leaving Martha to lament her inability to act. After a restless night, Martha sees that the ship and brig have both been spared by the storm, leading her to reflect that 'the islanders were better judges of the matter than we were' (II, 294).

The sound judgement and inherent goodness of the islanders quickly emerges as a central theme of Martha's short residence on Stamieux, which extends to a sense of bodily safety and camaraderie across disparate national identities. When the Captain arrives on shore with 'six brave soldiers in tow', he comes 'acquainted with the horrors sometimes perpetrated in cases of shipwreck', particularly in times of war. He is heavily armed, having told his men that if Martha and Haliday had been harmed 'he would not leave a man, woman, or child alive in the island' (II, 294). They had in fact been well looked after. However, his pre-emptively vengeful assumptions reinforce the risk of enslavement, rape and other dangers that castaways – particularly women – faced on unfamiliar shores, while also underscoring the easy brutality of maritime culture. The scene recalls other European encounters with Pacific Islanders on the other side of the world, with 'prejudices and language difficulties' making it 'almost impossible for the strangers and intruders to interpret correctly the behaviour of the natives'.[45] The risk of 'going native' following shipwreck is a common trope of shipwreck

---

[43] The 'aftermath' phase, according to Thompson (p. 16), further animates horror and suffering, and a later 'improving stage', that offers a space for salvation, reconciliation, and – importantly, a space for a 'propagandist dimension'.

[44] Twenty versts is equal to approximately 13.25 miles; For the purpose of this analysis, I have continued to use Martha's descriptive names. 'Fredericksham' is modern day Hamina in Finland, or 'Fredrikshamn' in Swedish; 'Stamieux' has been identified as the island of Tammio in present-day Finland, also known in Swedish as 'Starnö'. See Yrjö Kaukiainen, 'Wreck-Plundering by East Finnish Coastal People – Criminal Tradition or Popular Culture?', in *Sail and Steam: Selected Maritime Writings of Yrjö Kaukiainen*, ed. by Lars U. Scholl and Merja-Liisa Hinkkanen (St John's, 2004), pp. 151–162, p. 152.

[45] Kaukiainen, p. 160.

narratives concerning Anglo women subjects in the period. Alongside the sexual dangers faced by the shipwrecked woman among native inhabitants, class and national status had to be contended with as well, as 'the shipwreck could destabilize or eliminate a woman's gendered identity, yet what was even more feared, perhaps, was the loss of national and ethnic identity'.[46] For Martha, the inherent risks of 'going native' among the islanders are stripped away by the ingenuity and honour that she encounters among them. Their 'innocence and goodness of heart' makes a welcome surprise for Martha and the ship's entire company (II, 294). This representation of the islanders is important, as it underlines shared sympathies rather than highlighting differences. This strategy stands in contrast to some contemporary, and much more inflammatory narratives, such as the print narratives associated with Eliza Fraser. Fraser's ghost-written experience of shipwreck on an island off the coast of Queensland in Australia appeared in print in 1835, not long before Martha's own narrative appeared.[47] Fraser's account charges brutality against the Aboriginal Badtjala people, including starvation – claims that, despite being disputed by her fellow survivors, had dire consequences, including retaliatory violence and the later dispossession of the tribe – an outcome that underscores the power inherent in women-focused shipwreck narratives written for public consumption.[48]

By contrast, Martha's description of the Stamieux island tribe focuses on what she perceives to be their egalitarian and rational society, qualities that essentially align with her own European sensibilities. Following her arrival, she and Haliday are taken to a hut belonging to the tribe's most respected elder. Though a single room, the expansive dwelling is 'singularly picturesque' and full of simple comforts, such as soft down beds adorned with lace pillowcases. It is in this room, writes Martha, that the 'Mamma' lives, a woman 'surrounded by a numerous tribe [who] was in some measure the queen of the island' (II, 295). The 'Mamma' speaks Russian, allowing Martha to communicate with her. This matriarch and her entire family also know how to read. They are Lutherans and own a much-cherished ancient Bible. Along with these civilised and relatable traits, the islanders seem to

---

[46] Robin Miskolcze, 'Transatlantic Touchstone: The Shipwrecked Woman in British and Early American Literature', *Prose Studies: History, Theory, Criticism*, 22:3 (1999), 41–56, p. 44.

[47] Eliza Ann Frazer, *Wreck of the Stirling Castle. Horrib [sic] treatment of the crew by savages. [An account based on the evidence of Mrs. E. A. Frazer, a survivor. With verses.]* (London, 1835); Thompson suggests that Frazer's narrative was likely constructed by a 'hack' writer using her verbal accounts (Thompson, p. 11).

[48] See *Constructions of Colonialism: Perspectives on Eliza Fraser's Shipwreck*, ed. by Lynette Russell (Wellington, 1999).

possess uniquely enlightened ideas about gender norms. The islanders' matriarchal way of life inspires Martha's imagination, and seemingly safeguards her from the threat of sexual or bodily harm due to their respect for women. Martha and the 'Mamma' share an intense bond during the eight days she remains on the island.[49] Martha attempts to repay the hospitality she receives with a gift from her wardrobe, but is refused, as the 'Mamma' believes that castaways are sent to her by God rather than them being sent to other nearby places inhabited by 'wicked islanders' (II, 298). Here, the women work alongside the men, hauling their boats out of dangerous waters in one moment and returning to their household spinning and knitting in the next. The 'Mamma' tells Martha that 'their habits, manners, customs, and their religion, were such as had existed when they belonged to Sweden; at present they were Russian subjects' (II, 297). The easy alliance between two women, then, becomes clear in the context of shared nationalistic affinities, and echoes Martha's friendship with Dashkova: Russia had invaded Sweden, then a close ally to Britain, earlier in 1808 as a strategic move in the war. The Stamieux islanders became Russian subjects as a result, but had not given up their Swedish identity. Once the ship is adequately repaired to sail for England, Martha describes a tearful goodbye that underlines how both virtue and sentimentality have characterised her time on Stamieux, and that echoes her parting from Dashkova:

> At the moment of bidding her adieu she kissed me with affection, which I most sincerely returned, and her eyes filling with tears, she said, 'May God bless you, my dear child, and guide you safely over the great water; but pity me, for I shall never know it!'[50]

As her narrative soon makes clear, the shared values that allowed Martha to peacefully shelter among the Stamieux islanders, as well as living with Dashkova in earlier parts of the narrative, are not to be taken for granted.

Further experience demonstrates that discord between national affinities could have disastrous consequences to the British traveller at sea. Almost as soon as the ship and brig recommence their journey, they are placed under the power of a completely different sort of islander. Seeking a pilot to navigate perilous waters, the ship sounds its signal from the harbour of the

---

[49] Martha's focus throughout her narrative on female relationships abroad evokes Misty Krueger's view of 'sisterhood' as a recurring theme of eighteenth-century women's travel writing, and one which in turns shapes the woman author's own 'self-representation'. See Misty Krueger, 'Introduction', in *Transatlantic Women Travellers, 1688–1843*, ed. by Misty Krueger (Lewisburg, 2021), p. 16.
[50] *Memoirs*, II, p. 301.

nearby isle of 'Aspo'.[51] When no reply comes from the island, both vessels drop anchor despite dangerous rocks and the party makes its way to shore, discovering a town much larger than the Stamieux village. There, Martha and Haliday lodge in the best cottage but soon become suspicious of the elegant finery furnishing it, finding silver spoons and other items clearly designed for rich travellers accustomed to luxury. 'This told a tale of no very cheering kind', writes Martha. 'We began to think we had got upon one of the wicked islands of which the simple-hearted *Mamma* had heard' (II, 302). Martha does not open her trunks for fear of thievery. The party intends to leave at the earliest chance but is held by shifting wind. Everything on the second island appears different from the first: where before they felt trust and security, here there is an air of anxiety. Day after day, the party remain trapped as winter approaches, with their food and supplies dwindling to alarming levels. When the ice begins to set in, Martha and the rest of the party witness 'convincing proofs that the plunder of wrecks was a sort of livelihood to the inhabitants of Aspo, or at least one of the sweeteners of their lives' (II, 303). Martha documents their shocking profiteering:

> one day as we were walking on the causeway, four ships appeared in the offing, in the utmost distress, with signals flying for pilots to go on board. Every man in the island was a pilot, but neither bribes nor remonstrances could prevail on one to go to the assistance of the unfortunate vessels, which appeared as if they were going to make a tack, which must have been their destruction. The islanders declared that it was the express law of the Emperor of Russia that they should not pilot any vessels into port during the war, of any description; with twenty other things false and inhuman.[52]

The islanders gather to watch the trajectory of the ships. Martha describes them as hardly able to contain their glee. When the first ship breaks through to safety and the others follow suit, Martha and her companions watch in disgust as the Aspo pilots finally set out to guide them in, seeking a fee for their services. Further insult occurs when, after apparently flouting Christian moral values, the islanders gather that evening 'as usual, praying and singing psalms, with every appearance of devotion!' (II, 305).

Martha's description of the Aspo islanders as 'inhuman' is rooted in an eighteenth-century preoccupation with what has recently described

---

[51] Modern day Haapasaari, a former municipality of Finland; Martha refers to the island by an alternate spelling of its Swedish name, Aspö, also called 'Perkelschären' in old maps, according to maritime historian Yrjö Kaukiainen. See Kaukiainen, p. 152.
[52] *Memoirs*, II, p. 304

as 'the golden age of wrecking'.[53] David Cressy's study of shipwrecks and their aftermath in early modern England frames the shore as an arena 'of social conflict, exposing proletarian and seigneurial frictions ... in which the forces of property and propriety were ranged against the moral economy of the poor' (p. 234). Despite the fact that 'coastal dwellers in every era have gathered and redistributed the shipwrecked bounty of the sea', the controversial habit of wrecking was more commonly linked to criminality than the wants of desperate necessity in the period (p. 236). Cautionary pamphlets warned travellers against the dangers of wreckers and relayed tragic stories caused by their malicious activities. One such publication from the period contains a lengthy narrative in verse, titled *The Shipwreck*, published by the Religious Tract Society:

> The raging surf roll'd o'er the dying and dead
> And the rock's craggy cliff was their last lonely bed
> When the life-blood had ceased to flow
> These sights, so afflicting, to wreckers were dear
> Who live by fell rapine and crime
> Whose eyes never shed soft Compassion's sweet tear.[54]

Following the brutal deaths of the majority of the people on board, the unwillingness of the wreckers to intervene and assist the survivors results in the loss of a young sailor, whose death is mentioned in the title evidence of 'inhuman conduct'. Cressy writes of the propensity to label wreckers as 'barbarous' in the period – which he calls a 'crude exaggeration' – a word directly used by the Stamieux 'Mamma' when warning Martha of less-sympathetic peoples on other islands 'by whom shipwrecked persons are treated barbarously' (238; II, 298). In Martha's narrative, the cold-hearted behaviour of the inhabitants of Aspo stands in opposition to her belief in universal humanity, a feeling repeatedly represented through the language of sensibility. This theme surfaces in Martha's improbable relationship with the royal figure of Dashkova, her 'Russian mother', and later again with the 'Mamma', a rural islander. However, it is not universal goodwill that is at stake, but rather a nationalist agenda, as the incongruent malice of the Aspo islanders is negotiated by their nationalistic affinities: by supporting the Emperor of Russia and following his 'express law' to let

---

[53] David Cressy, *Shipwrecks and the Bounty of the Sea* (Oxford, 2022), p. 234.
[54] *The Shipwreck: Showing What Sometimes Happens on our Sea Coasts; also, Giving a Particular Account of a Poor Sailor Boy, who was Refused any Assistance by the Wreckers, and Who Died in Consequence of their Inhuman Conduct* (London, [between 1822 and 1886]), p.10.

ships wreck, the Aspo islanders represent the vindictive enemy forces of the Anglo-Russian conflict. Martha never saw actual evidence of wrecking or plunder, and never fell victim to thievery herself. Reflecting on these circumstances, Kaukiainen notes that Martha's 'prejudicious, and at the same time, naïve and partial' account is not completely unfounded: 'the ill fame' of these islanders as wreck-plunderers was recorded by local and supreme courts of Livonia, Estonia and Finland in the same period.[55] Still, although she 'distinguished – on quite subjective grounds – the people she encountered as either 'unusually charming' or 'wicked', 'it is far more probable that virtues and vices were much more evenly distributed' among the Stamieux and Aspo islanders.[56] After three weeks on the island, the ship and brig finally sail again in the end of November, with a favourable wind, but the remainder of the voyage proves equally treacherous. Martha and her companions see more privateers off in the distance, and the ropes of the ship nearly freeze in brutal weather. 'More than once we imagined ourselves doomed to a Danish or French prison', Martha writes, describing nations aligned with Russia, yet the captain valiantly 'remained on deck, exerting his utmost skill' (II, 306).

On 26 December the party arrive in England at Harwich, having passed safely thanks to the guard of several English frigates. Martha's narrative ends on a relatively anti-climactic note by listing the arrival date and location without giving much away regarding her feelings. Once again, a return to her letters from the period allows for a clearer view of her heightened state of mind on returning to Britain safely after an absence of six years. As she writes to Eardley Wilmot on 27 December 1808 from London, the day after her arrival:

> I write these few lines to tell you that *I am here*. Nor is it *my ghost* which comes from Russia, to tell you these things – the variety of emotions which swell my heart at this instant make a sort of *Fool* of me, but tho' I sometimes anticipate what makes me tremble, when I reflect that for 10 months I know nothing of any of my English or Irish friends, yet please, & a sort of painful extacy is my predominant sensation ... I have written home to mention my arrival, & *that* letter will be the *first* intimation they will have, of my having quitted Moscow, so sudden was everything, & so kindly affectionate was the conduct of my Russian Mother who I have but one consolation in thinking of, &

[55] Kaukiainen argues that in the majority of incidents, it was likely that 'no actual robber was involved – rather, people just collected flotsam which in many instances would have been the only sign that a shipwreck had occurred', p. 153.
[56] Kaukiainen, p. 162.

that is, that I left her in such a state of health, that I trust in god I may one day see her again.[57]

Contrary to the controlled ending of the narrative, here Martha's desire to hold onto the bonds she has formed abroad, placed in opposition with her strong emotions at returning to her family and country, come tumbling out. The intensity of her perilous voyage through a war zone, as well as her joy at her return, has made her 'tremble'. Her desire to find out information about her 'English or Irish friends' and to notify her family of her safety mixes with a longing to return to Dashkova and a focus on the noblewoman's 'kindly' and 'affectionate' conduct. The pull between transnational bonds and the security and identity of home have created 'a sort of painful extacy' that dominates the letter.

While the events of Martha's supplement may seem extraordinary, and perhaps slanted to serve her political message and public identity in print, a nearly contemporary, and more intentionally private, record of her experience corroborates several aspects of the narrative. Written one year after her experience of shipwreck, this brief account is embedded as a journal entry within Martha's Irish tour journal of 1809–10. She begins by writing 'This day year I was shipwreck'd in the Gulph of Finland', and goes on to recount the 'innocent, happy inhabitants of the Island of Stameux' – Britain's then-allies – without mentioning the menacing residents of Aspo Island – who can be presumed as enemies. Instead, Martha focuses on salvation and gratitude for having survived the experience:

> may I never have cause to regret that Life was then spared to me. I shall never forget my feelings at that period. I did not fear to die, for in quitting Russia and the Maternal dear friend who I parted from with so much agony, I have fulfill'd a great duty. I thought, and my mind was in the highest tone of happiness, I saw before me in my own Country amongst my friends a perspective of happiness, where my imagination had full play, this was heightened by recent distress, and the singular circumstances which preceeded [sic] my quitting Russia had raised my mind to such a degree, that it was the very moment to be a Heroine, and see even Death without terror, there are such moments in everybody's life I suppose. Coldly reflecting on what I then pass'd, I shrink fearfully from dangers, which appear'd less terrible at the moment, and I fervently pray, that the life which was then spared, may have been reserved for some good purpose, for had I resigned it then, I

---

[57] Beinecke, OSB MSS 54, Box 3, f.151, 'London, York Hotel, 27 Dec 1808', r–v [emphasis original].

should have died full of hope, full of wishes at least to be virtuous, but perhaps having tasted too few of the bitter dregs, of life's cup, and certainly having had little opportunity to be useful.[58]

Here again, Martha's love for Dashkova is set in opposition to her overwhelming desire to return home to her own country and family, while her lack of fear and sense of being 'Heroine' foreshadow the narrative that she will later write. Seeing her experience as an opportunity 'to be useful', perhaps, to her own family and country, and her gratitude in being able to do so, can also be found in the pages of the supplement. Martha's published narrative in Dashkova's *Memoirs*, then, carefully positions her existing geopolitical affinities in print before the public, allowing her to show how, as a British woman subject abroad in a time of war, she is capable of furthering transnational alliances through intimacy, as well as navigating hostility from known enemies.

Letters from Russia

The page immediately following Martha's supplement is headed 'Letters from Russia, in the Years 1805, 1806, & 1807' (II, p. 308). As with most sections of *Memoirs*, Katherine Wilmot's letters begin with a preface by Martha that places both her role as editor and her affective relationship to the writer of what follows in the foreground. The letters as they appear in the supplement were likely gleaned from the scribal volume created by their sister, Alicia Wilmot, as Martha notes that 'copies were permitted to be taken by her sister' of the letters, 'and they were preserved, along with her own journals'.[59] The disparate nature of the correspondence is due to the fact that 'nothing could possibly be more remote from the contemplation of the writer ... that they should ever be circulated beyond the limits of that intimate known of friends to whom they were addressed'. Therefore, Martha's prefatory statement seeks to gloss the gaps by introducing the author, 'Miss Wilmot, the elder sister of the Editor', whose 'singularly lively imagination' and 'spirit and originality of thought and style ... cannot fail to interest and gratify the reader' (II, pp. 308, 309). While Martha originally intended to take 'only a few extracts of the letters, such as would help convey an idea of what Princess Daschkaw was in the latter years of her

---

[58] Blair Adam House, Wilmot Box 1 Bundle 2, 2/8. Typewritten copy of a second tour in Ireland by Martha Wilmot and her sister Alicia, 'Friday 27th [no month]', p. 7 (n.d.).

[59] *Memoirs*, II, p. 309; RIA MS 12 L 30. See Chapter 2 for more on the preservation of these letters through coterie transcription.

life', further reflection brought the realisation 'that it would hardly be doing justice to the writer, or indeed to the subject they are produced to illustrate, were this intention strictly adhered to' (II, p. 308). Martha's remarks thus prime the reader to enjoy Katherine's talents, while also linking her writing inextricably to Dashkova as 'subject'. At the same time, Martha's editorial interventions in selecting and arranging Katherine's letters for publication clearly highlight some of the themes of Martha's own supplement, which immediately proceeds Katherine's; namely, observations of the transnational political events of which the travelling sisters found themselves a part in Russia. Katherine's supplement in Dashkova's *Memoirs* accordingly draws attention to feudal social relations and the French influence on Russia during the Napoleonic conflicts, alongside traditional epistolary travel writing that reflects on Russia as an exotic location for travel in the period.

Katherine's previous experience as a traveller documenting her time in France between 1801–03 had well-prepared her to capture vivid scenes for her recipients. While each letter is addressed to an individual, with her sisters' initials added in the supplement ('A. W.' for Alicia, 'H. W.' for Harriet), Katherine almost certainly anticipated that her despatches would be circulated beyond the addressee and read aloud to others, as were her earlier French letters. Her correspondence captures small sketches of her time in Russia in the same irresistibly charming narrative voice that characterised her previous epistolary travelogue, which was compiled in her absence and reproduced by her female relatives.[60] Writing to her sister-in-law, confidante, and frequent correspondent Anna Maria Chetwood ('A. M. C.' in the supplement), Katherine shares details of her strange and exotic accommodation at Troitskoe.[61] Taking on a comic voice, she invites Chetwood to 'sit in my room whilst I am going to bed', pointing out the 'five high pillows at the head of my iron bedstead' where she sleeps 'almost upright in my bed, every night of my life, tucked in as tight as a mummy' (II, p. 345). In the corner of the chamber, 'the clumsy boots you see belong to no man'; instead, Katherine has worn them out in the snow along with

---

[60] See Chapter 1 for more on Katherine's Peace of Amien tour; see Chapter 2 for more on her Irish women relatives' efforts to preserve both Katherine and Martha's writing, as well as Martha's extensive fair copy work on Katherine's manuscript travel writing.

[61] Anna Maria Chetwood was also a writer and has been identified by Angela Byrne as the anonymous author of two novels. See Angela Byrne, 'Anonymity, Irish women's writing, and a tale of contested authorship: *Blue Stocking Hall* (1827) and *Tales of My Time* (1829)', *Proceedings of the Royal Irish Academy: Archaeology, Culture, History, Literature*, 119 (2019), 259–281.

the dove-coloured pelisse with its 'sable collar as large as a muff' (II, p. 346). The doors of the room have been covered with additional curtains and the windows with a second frame. The teapot is filled with 'nettle tea' that Katherine is 'ordered to drink for my cough', while the bedside table is strewn with books. 'Is there any harm in having the history of the country one is in to read?' she asks, subtly highlighting her efforts at self-education before signing off playfully: 'now, in the name of patience, good-night to you' (II, p. 346).

Her letters to Alicia Wilmot are similarly infused with the uniqueness of a visit to Russia. Troitskoe is by turns 'a sequestered castle' and 'a wild mansion in the extremities of Europe' (II, p. 347). In December, the 'implacability of winter' manifests itself in 'the blank circumference of snow which encircles our wide horizon' so that 'the shroudings of night and nakedness of day alone diversify our view'. Katherine reassures her sister that 'this sounds, perhaps, more dreary than it really is': while she looks forward to the 'fairy blossoms' of spring, 'now, like other crocuses and daffodils, I submit to the vegetation of a mere bulbous' (II, p. 348). She describes heading out of doors with Martha and Anna Petrovna in 'the kibitka or traineau', which 'resembles in shape an infant's cradle, which is lined with bear-skin'.[62] Katherine paints an amusing picture of their outings, describing herself and her companions as 'enormous bundles; for what with shawls, shubas, and wadded cloaks, it would be difficult to organize us into either shape or form'. Flanked by four male attendants in colourful scarfs ('Gabriel, Petruchio, Theodore and Ivan'), the women 'daily penetrate on our sledges, drawn by three horses abreast' into the 'dark spreading forest' surrounding the 'white stuccoed house'. She captures the sublime terror of the excursion, as 'the opening of the forest is like the charnel-house of nature; every tree rattles like a bleached skeleton – moaning, hollow, gaunt, menacing' (II, p. 349). Yet the experience brings beauty as well, with 'the gliding of the setting sun' creating a 'horizontal beam' that makes 'the ground blaze in sapphires, emeralds, amethysts, opals, and brilliants' (II, p. 350). Local colour in the form of the peasantry on Dashkova's estate further enlivens her description: in the forest, the party passes woodcutters 'whose endless bears, clogged in snow and lengthened by icicles, crackle in responsive measures to their hatchet strokes' (II, p. 350). The labourers hold their caps in their hands as 'the ladies of the castle' ride out of sight. 'Well, are you tired of the forest?', Katherine concludes. She mocks the form of travel

---

[62] Anna Petrovna was another young inhabitant and relation in Dashkova's household. For more on intimate relationships and living arrangements at Troitskoe, see Chapter 2.

letters while also identifying herself as an author of them by concluding 'see what it is to extort truth from travellers' (II, p. 350).

Katherine's letters also prove her to be a keen observer of cultural and political intricacies. In the late eighteenth century, 'by word of mouth and by reading, an increasingly wide section of the British public gained their impressions of a Russia emerging from darkness to take its place among the enlightened nations of Europe'.[63] Katherine's correspondence provides an interesting example of this phenomena of increased contact – one which is mediated by the experience of women writers, and intended for a specifically sociable group of readers to encounter in manuscript rather than printed form. As with her Peace of Amiens letters, Katherine not only notes customs but also criticises what she perceives to be hypocritical behaviour in the context of the unfolding Napoleonic conflicts. 'Russia', she writes, 'is yet barbarous enough to be distinguished for … virtue of hospitality', yet its inhabitants disconcertingly 'seem to imitate the French in everything' (II, p. 335). Katherine laments the lack of authenticity among the 'higher orders', who, in fashioning themselves in accordance to French customs, have lost touch with their own 'national music, the national dancing, as well as the national salutation, the national dress, and the national language', all of which have 'sunk down to the ground, and none but slaves practise them' (II, p. 336).[64] Instead of 'the dignified salutation of former times, that of bowing seriously to one another till their crowns met together', the Russians she meets along her journey kiss her on 'both cheeks with the appearance of transport' (II, p. 335). They 'send one's mind to France' at all times, as 'they cannot eat their dinners without a French cook to dress it; when they cannot educate their children without adventurers from Paris, in the shape of tutors and governesses' (II, pp. 336, 335). As Katherine points out this political hypocrisy, noting that 'there is something childishly silly in railing against Bonaparte and the French … utterly unconscious of degradation to themselves or their country' (II, p. 336). Her depiction paints a complex, if negative, picture of a supposedly Enlightened Russian society at a time of complex international encounters, one that might reinforce stereotypes among the contemporary Irish readers of her letters, as well as the more widely dispersed British and European readers of her published travel letters in *Memoirs* more than thirty-five years later.

---

[63] Cross, p. 28.
[64] 'Slaves' likely refers to the lowest class within Russia's feudal system. On Dashkova's Troitskoe estate, she was Lord to approximately 3,000 feudal peasants. For more on Katherine's interest in the customs of this class, see Chapter 3.

Even as Katherine offers a searing indictment of Russian insincerity, she carefully sets Dashkova apart from such appraisals. Rather than blindly following phony trends, Dashkova's character distinguishes her: 'I know more of hers that any one else's which is diametrically opposite to every species of *singerie*; for if ever there was an original upon the face of the earth, it is herself' (II, p. 337). Martha's expectation, which she states in her editorial preface, that Katherine's letters will be widely read by those seeking information on Dashkova is somewhat prescient. Among the pages of Katherine's letters are several pen portraits of Dashkova, which have over time become the definitive descriptions drawn on by biographers and scholars as proof of the noblewoman's status as a female Enlightenment icon and all-round Renaissance woman, even in later life. As one letter describes her:

> She helps the mason to build walls, she assists with her own hands in making the roads, she feeds the cows, she composes music, she writes for the press ... and yet she appears as if she had her time a burden on her hands. She gives me continually the idea of her being a fairy; and I protest it is not jokingly that I say so, for the impression never quits me for a moment (II, pp. 341–342).

Katherine also notes that Dashkova wears 'an old brown great coat, and a silk handkerchief about her neck worn to rags', which 'she has worn [for] eighteen years ... because it belonged to her friend Mrs. Hamilton'. This mention of Katherine and Martha's aunt, Catherine Hamilton, who originally provided a connection to Dashkova, is important as well, and highlights authentic intergenerational bonds between the sisters and their subject. Katherine's letters give an impression of artlessness and spontaneity, a sense that is helpful in corroborating Martha's appraisal of Dashkova as a benevolent friend and host to the sisters. Katherine describes receiving a letter while travelling towards Troitskoe, 'full of messages of the most affectionate nature from the princess' (II, pp. 316–317). She attempts to give her recipient 'some notion of this dear princess', writing that:

> During supper, Princess Daschkaw frequently talked to me in English, and then translated everything into Russ [for the other guests], embellishing all I said to a marvellous degree; for I was astonished at finding the most common-place observations of mine received, by virtue of my interpreter, with amazement and admiration of countenance on the part of the audience.[65]

---

[65] *Memoirs*, II, p. 338.

While the Wilmots are treated affectionately, as if they are members of Dashkova's family, Katherine notes that 'no man, whatever be his rank, and however covered with decorations, presumes to sit down in her presence without being desired – a permission not always granted' (II, p. 338). Katherine's letters also reference the textual undercurrents of the scribal coterie, the labour from which formed the basis for the book in the readers' hand. Dashkova 'has promised to shew me the Empress Catherine's letters', she writes shortly after arriving at Troitskoe, 'and I have read a good part of the princess's life, written by herself' (II, p. 342). This illustrates Martha's assertion that her sisters' letters are interwoven with important anecdotes on Dashkova, a fact that strengthens the validity of the sisters' supplements while simultaneously bolstering the sense of cohesion among the coterie.

The publication of Katherine's supplement gave her posthumous recognition as a printed author, traveller and as a member of a literary community of women writers. Katherine does not seem to have sought recognition in print in her lifetime, passing up an opportunity for publication with The English Press in preference of active manuscript circulation.[66] However, posthumous authorial praise for Katherine's work, as well as her remembered presence among polite, literary circles, was Martha's long-held wish. In her introduction to *Memoirs*, Martha claims that the publication of her sister's letters will prove the 'powers' she had, 'which, with other solid and amiable qualities and accomplishments, rendered her society much sought and highly valued.'[67] This insistence is echoed in Martha's handwritten postscript to her scribal copy of Katherine's Peace of Amiens travelogue, written sixty-five years after its creation in 1870. Arguing for her sister's brilliance while lamenting her reticence, she writes that Katherine 'thru' life undervalued her own superior talents, and shrunk from the many efforts made at different times to bring them into notice.'[68] The Peace of Amiens travelogue, like much of the material selected for Katherine's supplement, reflects on the unfolding and volatile political situation of Napoleonic Paris, including commentary on the hypocrisy of the social and cultural compromises made in the aftermath of the French Revolution. Martha's efforts to posthumously recuperate her sister's writing on transnational affairs and relationships of her day, as well as her involvement in the coterie, can be seen as largely successful, the printing of her supplement to

---

[66] See Chapter 1 for more on Katherine's association with The English Press, and her strategies for circulating her scribally published travelogue documenting the Peace of Amiens.
[67] *Memoirs*, I, p. xxviii.
[68] RIA MS 12 L 32, postscript, 1870.

Memoirs allowing for a later twentieth-century interest in and recovery of Katherine's writing.[69]

Writing Past and Present Empires

Reflecting on the widespread recovery of women's travel narratives from the eighteenth century that has taken place over the past several decades, Katherine Turner writes that – contrary to superficial beliefs in the scarcity of such narratives – 'the genre ... proved surprisingly accessible for women ... despite cultural expectations that they should stay at home'.[70] The key to understanding this surprising acceptance may lie not only in the uniqueness of women's accounts, but more so in the usefulness of their contributions as records of British interests and experiences abroad. Martha and Katherine's Russian travelogues captured the immediacy of their respective journeys to Russia just after the close of the eighteenth century, a moment that, by the time of publication, lay in the historical record. However, the appearance of *Memoirs of Princess Daschkaw* in 1840 coincided with a period of great further expansion within the British Empire. Queen Victoria's accession to the throne in 1837 set off a new wave of conquest, including settlements in the Eastern and Western Hemispheres, as well as encroachment to existing British colonies including India and throughout the Ottoman Empire. At the same time, the hostilities described in the Wilmots' supplements held enduring relevancy to British readers, particularly in relation to conflicts over expansion between France, Russia and Britain as competing imperial powers. Read within this context, the historical nature of the affinities and conflicts treated in the Wilmots' supplements marks them as important interventions to contemporary political discourse at the time of their publication. The Wilmots' travelogues endure as formidable examples of how eighteenth-century women writers contributed to national dialogues, showing how they used their individual experiences to shape transnational notions of Empire and identity, both past and present.

---

[69] See the bibliography for works on the Wilmot sisters by editors and critics, including Thomas Sadleir, Lady Londonderry, Elizabeth Mavor, Pamela Buck, Angela Byrne, among others.
[70] Katherine Turner, 'Women Writing Travel', *Forum for Modern Language Studies*, 59:2 (2023) 315–319, p. 315.

Conclusion

'In appearing before the public as Editor of these Memoirs, unconnected by the ties of kindred or even of country, it becomes an obligation on my part to give some account of the occasion and manner of their coming into my possession; and in order to do this, so as to satisfy the expectation of those who feel an interest in whatever concerns this distinguished woman, as well as to meet the reasonable demands of every reader of this, her history, it will be requisite to speak a little of so humble an individual as myself. I shall, however, I trust, be pardoned, if at present I touch this subject as lightly as possible; because, for the information of those who may wish for a more copious detail than is suitable to a few prefatory pages, I have ventured, not without great reluctance and great diffidence, to subjoin to the princess's work, a narrative, which I wrote many years ago, of my residence in Russia.'[1]

The Wilmot sisters' story gives a voice to a forgotten, and perhaps prolific, category of women travel writers who first produced work in circulated manuscript form. These women may have engaged in similar forms of writing to the Wilmots while abroad, such as political observations, ethnographic and antiquarian pursuits, as well as translation and editorial work. As Virginia Woolf wrote in 1929, 'I would venture to guess that Anon, who wrote so many poems without signing them, was often a woman.'[2] Scholarship in the ensuing century, and more specifically in the late twentieth and early twenty-first centuries, has recuperated a significant number of both anonymous and forgotten authors.[3] At the same

---

[1] *Memoirs*, I, pp. xvii–xviii.
[2] Virginia Woolf, *A Room of One's Own* (London, 2000), pp. 50–51.
[3] Jacqueline Labbe argued in 2010 that the previous three decades of scholarship have more or less 'overturned' women's absence and occlusion from literary history; this claim has been contested by Jennie Batchelor, whose work on pseudonymous and anonymous women's suggests that 'many works likely written by women may never be definitely assigned to a known author'; *The History of British Women's Writing, 1750–1830*, ed. by Jacqueline M. Labbe (Basingstoke, 2010), IV, p. 1; Jennie Batchelor, 'Anon, Pseud and "By A Lady": The Spectre of Anonymity in Women's Literary History', in *Women's Writing, 1660–1830: Futures and Feminisms*, ed. by Jennie Batchelor and Gillian Dow (London, 2016), pp. 69–86 (p. 72).

time, as Gillian Dow wrote more recently, 'we still need to write literary women's lives because we need – at the very least – to know who these women were, what they wrote and when they wrote it'.[4] This book has demonstrated how we can draw on biographical evidence to look beyond individual achievement, revealing deep networks of women writers and travellers across national and class boundaries. In doing so, it builds on the recent work of initial efforts to map the cultural systems that shaped the circulation of literature, identifying the ways that women's writing from the 'fringes of Europe' contributed to transnational formations of British and European culture in the period.[5] Other recent projects have highlighted women's prolific engagement with print culture beyond the book, identifying how women from across social strata engaged in collective dialogues of literary production as readers and writers, and making their original contributions available online for the first time.[6] This book joins such efforts to reconstruct the textual practices of lesser-known women by examining their networks, as well as by revealing their dynamic literary output across a wide range of genres. Ambitious efforts to recover women's literary history must continue to expand across disciplines, national boundaries and literary-historical periods.

Class distinctions are an equally compelling category to consider in any such future feminist-historical recuperative work, and more work remains to be done in this area. The textual and material evidence discussed in this book reveals that women's literary networks, particularly when connected to provincial and middle-class women, are a significant historical phenomenon than has been largely undervalued by scholarly assessment to date. Their papers – which span many forms, such as journals, loose letters, epistolary travelogues, and a nearly countless range of disciplines including history, antiquarianism, biography and linguistic acquisition – are surely emblematic of middle and upper-middle class women's quotidian habits in the period. Focusing primarily on the efforts of Katherine and Martha

[4] Gillian Dow, 'The "Biographical Impulse" and Pan-European Women's Writing', in *Women's Writing, 1660–1830: Feminisms and Futures*, ed. by Jennie Batchelor and Gillian Dow (London, 2016), pp. 193–213, p. 210.
[5] See, for example, HERA Project, *Travelling Texts 1790–1914: Transnational Reception of Women's Writing at the Fringes of Europe (2013–2016)* <https://www.hivolda.no/Forsking/Forskingsprosjekt/hera-travelling-texts-1790-1914-eu-fp7> [accessed 10 January 2023].
[6] See 'The *Lady's Magazine* (1770–1818): Understanding the Emergence of a Genre' (University of Kent, 2016), which produced an index of 15,000 items in *The Lady's Magazine; or Entertaining Companion for the Fair Sex* (1770–1818) <https://research.kent.ac.uk/the-ladys-magazine/> [accessed 20 October 2023].

Wilmot, in contrast to their upper-class patrons and mentors who more frequently receive critical attention, has the significance of expanding discussions of transgenerational and transnational women's literary networks. In analysing the relationships between middle-ranking and aristocratic women, and the literary opportunities created from this, this book has sought to give greater detail to discussions of the class formation of coteries. First, by placing the Wilmot sisters at the centre of their own nexus, this book has shifted focus onto women travellers who acted as 'companions', granting them a greater agency while actively constructing and negotiating their position. This can be seen, for instance, in Martha's repeated foregrounding of herself as editor of Dashkova's memoirs and – by consequence – of the image of Dashkova, as noted in the opening to these concluding remarks. Likewise, this book has detailed how aristocratic women's public image and literary-social reputation might be interpreted as having been created in large part through the labour of these 'middling' women companions or assistants, such as the Wilmots.

Finally, I have sought to show how both manuscript and printed texts can provide sources for recovering the forgotten or lost voices of middling women from the period. The Wilmot sisters' surviving material and literary archives were kept safe in both institutional and family collections for centuries due to their links to famous figures of their day, and thanks to their own intrepid and prolific travels.[7] Yet their literary remains are perhaps most interesting for what they show about the provincial and transnational exchange of women's writing among women of a middling-rank in the late eighteenth century more generally – suggesting a rich landscape of women's literary practices that thrived across boundaries of provinciality, nationhood or class. While silences will inevitably endure in the absence of earlier preservation, or in the anonymity of editorial work and unattributed authorship, this book has suggested a speculative methodology for reading middle and upper-middle class women's writing from the period within a much wider framework. Taken as a whole, the story of the Wilmot coterie reveals how social networks of women writers and readers functioned across borders and boundaries. I believe that these astonishing records can

---

[7] The sisters' papers were treasured family objects, and were accordingly edited, replicated and shared socially, before being deposited in institutions after the sisters' deaths. The archival afterlife of the Wilmot papers fostered by their descendants also played an invaluable part in securing them a place in posterity. The Wilmots' descendants, whose own literary labour ensured future knowledge of the sisters' achievements, might themselves be considered members of an extended coterie that bridges temporal divides, thereby consecrating a centuries-long lineage of women engaging in literary production.

and should be read as exemplary of other family corpuses that have not been similarly fortunate in surviving, and other women's voices who have been lost to history. Their legacies, I hope, will spur further research into the wide-ranging impact of women's manuscript and non-sole authored texts on cultural geographies of the late eighteenth century – particularly those that may have been forgotten due to neglect, dispersal or simply the distance of time.

Bibliography

Primary Sources (Archival)

Dublin, Royal Irish Academy, Wilmot-Dashkova Collection
MS 12 L 16
MS 12 L 17
MS 12 L 18
MS 12 L 19
MS 12 L 20
MS 12 L 21
MS 12 L 22
MS 12 L 24
MS 12 L 29
MS 12 L 30
MS 12 L 31
MS 12 L 32
MS 12 L 33
MS 12 L 34
MS 12 L 35
MS 12 M 18

Edinburgh, National Library of Scotland, The John Murray Archive
MS 40140

Kelty, Blair Adam House Collection
Bradford/Wilmot Box 2, Item 5.d
Wilmot Box 1, Bundle 2, 2/6
Wilmot Box 1 Bundle 2, 2/8
Wilmot Box 3, 'Original journals of "Kitty" Wilmot'
'Contents of the Letter File of Princess Dashkoff'

London, British Library
Add MS 27879
Add MS 31911
Add MS 41.295.M
Add MS 46612

London, Senate House Library, University of London
MS 704

New Haven, Beinecke Rare Book & Manuscript Library
OSB MS 54, Box 3, Folder 151

New York, New York Public Library
Pforzheimer Collection, S'Ana 0763

Oxford, Bodleian Library, Abinger Collection
MS Abinger c. 7

Paris, Archives de Paris, 'Acte de Société'
D31U3 carton 3

Paris, Archives Nationales
MS Stone 70, F18

Primary Sources (Texts)

Account of the Institution and Progress of the Society of the Antiquaries of Scotland (Edinburgh, 1783–84)

Analytical Review, or History of Literature, Domestic and Foreign, 15 ([London, 1793])

Austen, Jane, *Emma; a Novel. By the Author of Sense and Sensibility, Pride and Prejudice, &c.*, 3 vols (London, 1815)

Authentic Memoirs of the Life and Reign of Catherine II. Empress of all the Russias. Collected from Authentic MS's. Translations, & c. of the Kind of Sweden and Other Indisputable Authorities (London, 1797)

Barbauld, Anna Laetitia, *Works of Anna Laetitia Barbauld. With a Memoir by Lucy Aikin*, 2 vols, 1825. Facsimile ed. by Caroline Franklin (London, 1996), II

Bradford, Rev. William, *Sketches of the Country, Character, and Costume in Portugal and Spain. Engraved and Coloured from the Drawings by W. Bradford with Descriptions of Each Subject* (London, 1809)

— *Correspondence of the Emperor Charles V and his Ambassadors at the Courts of England and France*, ed. by the Rev. William Bradford (London, 1850)

'Bradley, Eliza', *An Authentic Narrative of the Shipwreck and Suffering of Mrs. E. Bradley ... Written by Herself, etc.* (Boston, 1821)

Brooke, Charlotte, *Reliques of Irish Poetry: Consisting of Heroic Poems, Odes, Elegies, and Songs, Translated into English Verse: with Notes Explanatory and Historical* (Dublin, 1789)

Brough, Anthony, *View of the Importance of the Trade between Great Britain and Russia* (London, 1789)
Burney, Charles, *The Present State of Music in France and Italy, or the Journal of a Tour through Those Countries Undertaken to Collect Materials for a General History of Music* (London, 1771)
— *The Present State of the Music in Germany, the Netherlands and the United Provinces or, The Journal of a Tour through Those Countries, Undertaken to Collect Materials for a General History of Music* (London, 1773)
Byron, George Gordon, Baron, *Childe Harold's Pilgrimage. A Romaunt. [Cantos I and II. With Fourteen Other Poems.]* (London, 1812)
Catlin, George, *Letters and Notes on the Manners, Customs, and Condition of the North American Indians* (London, 1841)
Castera, Jean Henri, *Vie de Catherine II, Imperatrice de Russie*, 2 vols (Paris, 1797)
[Caulfeild, Frances Sally] *The Innocents. A Sacred Drama. Ocean, and the Earthquake at Aleppo: Poems* (Bath, 1824)
— *The Deluge: A Poem* (London, 1837)
Charter and Statutes of the Royal Irish Academy: For Promoting the Study of Science, Polite Literature, and Antiquities (Dublin, 1787)
Cook, James, *An Account of the Voyages in the Years MDCCLXVIII, MDCCLXIX, MDCCLXX, and MDCCLXXI*, 3 vols (London, 1773)
Cottin, Sophie, *Élisabeth ou Les Exilés de Siberie; Suivi de La prise de Jéricho, Poème* (Paris, 1806)
Coxe, William, *Travels into Poland, Russia, Sweden, and Denmark: Interspersed with Historical Relations and Political Inquiries* (London, 1784)
Craven, Elizabeth, *A Journey Through the Crimea to Constantinople. In a Series of Letters from the Right Honourable Elizabeth Lady Craven, to His Serene Highness the Margrave of Brandebourg, Anspach, and Bareith* (London, 1789)
Dashkova, Ekaterina, and Martha Bradford, *Memoirs of the Princess Daschkaw, Lady of Honour to Catherine II: Empress of all the Russias Written by Herself: Comprising Letters of the Empress, and Other Correspondence*, 2 vols (London, 1840)
Dashkova, Ekaterina Romanovna, *Memoiren der Fürstin Daschkoff: zur Geschichte der Kaiserin Katharina II* (Hamburg, 1857)
— *Mémoirs de la Princesse Dashkoff, Dame d'Honneur de Catherine II ... avec la Correspondence de cette Impératrice et d'Autres Lettres. Publié sur le Manuscrit Original par Mistress W. Bradfort* (Paris, 1859)
— *Zapiski kniá`gini E. R. Dashkovoĭ, Pisannyiáèiú Samoĭ* (London, 1859)
— Бумаги княгини Е. Р. Дашковой, урожденной Графини Воронцовой *(Mémoires de la Princesse Dashkaw. D'Après le Manuscrit Revu et Corrigé par l'Auteur) [The Original French Version of Princess Dashkova's Memoirs from the Manuscript in the Vorontsov Archives. With Letters and other Documents]* (Moskva, 1881)

— *Записки 1743-1810. Подготовка текста, статья о комментарии Г. Н. Моисеевой* (Leningrad, 1985); *Н. Д. Чечулин, Записки княгини Дашковой* (St Petersburg, 1907); Петр Бартенев (ed.), *Архив князя Воронцова*, 40 vols (St Petersburg, 1870–97)
— *The Memoirs of Princess Dashkova [with Plates, including Portraits]*, trans. and ed. by Kyril Fitzlyon (London, 1958)
— *Литературные сочинения* (Moscow, 1990), pp. 31–262
— *The Memoirs of Princess Dashkova*, trans. and ed. by Kyril Fitzlyon, intro. by Jehanne M Gheith, after. by A. Woronzoff-Dashkoff (Durham NC, 1995)
Diary and Letters of Madame D'Arblay, author of Evelina, Cecilia, & C., Edited by her Niece, Vol. I 1778–1780 (London, 1842)
Edgeworth, Maria, *Maria Edgeworth in France and Switzerland: Selections for the Edgeworth Family Letters*, ed. by Christina Colvin (Oxford, 1979)
Fay, Eliza, *Original Letters from India: Containing a Narrative of a Journey through Egypt and the Author's Imprisonment at Calicut by Hyder Ally* (Calcutta, 1817)
Filmer, Robert, *Patriarcha, or The Natural Power of Kings* (London, 1680)
Frazer, Eliza Ann, *Wreck of the Stirling Castle. Horrib [sic] Treatment of the Crew by Savages. [An Account Based on the Evidence of Mrs. E. A. Frazer, a Survivor. With verses.]* (London, 1835)
Georgi, Johann Gottlieb, *Description de Toutes les Nations de l'Empire de Russie, où l'on Expose leurs Moeurs, Religions, Usages, Habitations, Habillemens et autres Particularités Remarquables ... Traduite de l'Allemand*, 3 vols (St Petersbourg, 1776–80)
Gillray, James, *The First Kiss This Ten Years! – or – the Meeting of Britannia & Citizen François*, BM Satires 9960, in The Catalogue of Political and Personal Satires in the British Museum, ed. by M. Dorothy George and others, 12 vols (London, 1870–1954), VIII (1947)
Maria Graham, *Journal of a Residence in India* (Edinburgh, 1813)
— *Letters on India* (London, 1814
— *Journal of a Residence in Chile, during the year 1822. And a Voyage from Chile to Brazil in 1823* (London, 1824)
— *Journal of a Voyage to Brazil* (London, 1824)
Green, Sarah, *Mental Improvement for a Young Lady, on her Entrance into the World; Addressed to a Favourite Niece* (London, 1793)
Guthrie, Maria, and Matthew Guthrie, *A Tour, Performed in the Years 1795–6, Through the Taurida, or Crimea: the Antient Kingdom of Bosphorus, the Once-Powerful Republic of Tauric Cherson, and all the Other Countries on the North Shore of the Euxine, ceded to Russia by the Peace of Kainardgi and Jassy* (London, 1802)
Guthrie, Matthew, *Dissertations sur les Antiquités de Russie, par M.G.: Rraduites sur son Ouvrage Anglais* (Saint-Petersbourg, 1795)

Hawkins, Laetitia-Matilda, *Letters on the Female Mind, Its Powers and Pursuits. Addressed to Miss H.M. Williams, with particular reference to Her Letters from France*, 2 vols (London, 1793), I

Herder, Johanne Gotfried von, *Volkslieder (Nebst untermischten andern Stücken)* (Leipzig, 1778, 1779)

Hook, Theodore, ed., *Colburn's New Monthly Magazine and Humorist* (1840), III

Johnson, Samuel, *A Dictionary of the English Language* (London, 1755)

— *A Journey to the Western Islands of Scotland* (London, 1775)

Kant, Immanuel, *Towards Perpetual Peace, and Other Writings on Politics, Peace, and History*, ed. by Pauline Kleingold, trans. by David L. Colclasure (New Haven, 2006)

Lafitau, Joseph-François, *Mœurs des Sauvages Ameriquains Comparées aux Mœurs des Premiers Temps*, 2 vols (Paris, 1724)

Lafontaine, August and Isabelle de Montolieu, *Marie Menzikoff et Fedor Dolgorouki: Histoire Russe en Forme de Lettres. Traduit de l'Allemand d'Auguste Lafontaine, par Mme Isabelle de Montolieu* (Paris, 1804)

Lawrence, Hannah, *Historical Memoirs of the Queens of England from the Commencement of the Twelfth Century* (London, 1838–40)

Lecky, Elisabeth, and William Edward Hartpole Lecky, *A Memoir of the Right Hon. William Edward Hartpole Lecky / by his Wife* (London, 1909)

Levesque, Pierre-Charles, *Histoire de Russie, Nouvelle Édition, Corrigée et Augmentée par l'Auteur, et Conduite Jusqu'à la Mort de l'Impératrice Catherine II* (Hamburg, 1800), I

Montagu, Lady Mary Wortley, *Letters of the Right Honourable Lady M—y W—y M—e: Written During her Travels in Europe, Asia and Africa, to Persons of Distinction, Men of Letters & c., in Different Parts of Europe*, 3 vols (London, 1763)

— *The Turkish Embassy Letters* (London, 1993)

— *The Turkish Embassy Letters*, ed. by Teresa Heffernan and Daniel O'Quinn (Peterborough, 2013)

Müller, Gerhard Friedrich, *Ethnographische Schriften I*, Wieland Hintzsche and Aleksandr Christianovich Elert unter Mitarbeit von Heike Heklau, eds. *Quellen zur Geschichte Sibiriens und Alaskas aus russischen Archiven VIII* (Halle, 2010)

— *Sammlung Russischer Geschichte*, 9 vols (St Petersburg, 1732–64)

— *Voyages et Découvertes Faites par les Russes le Long des Côtes de la Mer Glaciale & sur l'Océan Oriental tant vers le Japon que vers l'Amérique: on y a Joint l'Histoire du Fleuve Amur et des Pays Adjacens ... / Ouvrages Traduits de l'Allemand de Mr. G.P. [i.e. G.F.] Muller par C.G.F. Dumas. G. F. Müller, (Gerhard Friedrich)* (Amsterdam, 1766)

Murry, Ann, *The Concise History of the Kingdoms of Israel and Judah; Connected with the History or Chief Events of the Neighbouring States and Succeeding Empires to the Time of Christ* (London, 1783)

— *Mentoria: or, The Young Ladies Instructor, in Familiar Conversations on Moral and Entertaining Subjects. The Fifth Edition* (London, 1791)

Nichols, John Gough, *Autographs of Royal, Noble, Learned and Remarkable Personages Conspicuous in English History* (London, 1829)

Opie, Amelia, 'Recollections of a Visit to Paris in 1802', *The Lady's Magazine, or Mirror of the Belles-Lettres, Fine Arts, Music, Drama, Fashions, &c*, 5 (1831)

— *Memorials of the Life of Amelia Opie, selected and arranged from her Letters, Diaries and other Manuscripts, by Cecilia Lucy Brightwell* (Norwich, 1854)

Paine, Thomas, *Dissertation on the First-Principles of a Government* (Paris, 1795)

Percy, Thomas, *Reliques of Ancient English Poetry, Consisting of Old Heroic Ballads Songs, and Other Pieces of our Earlier Poets, Chiefly of the Lyric Kind Together with Some Few of Later Date*, 3vols (Dublin, 1766)

Pratch, Ivan, and Nikolai L'vov, *Sobraniye Narodnikh Russkikh Pesen* (St Petersburg, 1790)

Rawdon, Elizabeth, Countess of Moira, 'Particulars relative to a Human Skeleton, and the Garments that were found thereon, when dug out of a Bog at the Foot of Drumkeragh, a Mountain in the County of Down, and Barony of Kinalearty, on Lord Moira's Estate, in the Autumn of 1780', *Archaeologia, The Society of Antiquaries of London*, 7 (1785), 90–110

Sandford, Henry, *Thomas Poole and His Friends* (London, 1888), II

Scott, Walter, *Marmion: A Tale of Flodden Field* (Edinburgh, London, 1808)

Shelley, Mary Wollstonecraft, and Charles E. Robinson, *Mary Shelley: Collected Tales and Stories with Original Engravings* (Baltimore, 1976)

Sir Edward Seward's Narrative of his Shipwreck, and Consequent Discovery of Certain Islands in the Caribbean Sea: with a Detail of Many Extraordinary and Highly Interesting Events in his Life, from the Year 1733 to 1749, as Written in his own Diary. Edited by Jane Porter (London, 1831)

Smith, Charlotte Turner, *The Emigrants, a Poem, in Two Books* (London, 1793)

— *A Narrative of the Loss of the Catharine, Venus and Piedmont Transports, and the Thomas, Golden Grove and Æolus Merchant ships, Near Weymouth, ... 18th November [1796]* (London, 1796)

Stodart, M. A., *Female Writers: Thoughts on their Proper Sphere and on their Powers of Usefulness* (London, 1842)

Strickland, Agnes, and Elizabeth Strickland, *Lives of the Queens of England, from the Normal Conquest*, 12 vols (London, 1840–48)

— *Lives of the Queens of Scotland and English Princesses, Connected with the Regal Succession of Great Britain*, 8 vols (Edinburgh, 1852–59)

The Early Married Life of Maria Josepha Lady Stanley, with Extracts from Sir John Stanley's 'Praeterita'. Edited by one of their Grandchildren, Jane H. Adeane (New York, 1899)

The Critical Review: Or, Annals of Literature (London, 1792), X

The Critical Review: Or, Annals of Literature (London, 1797), XIX

The Shipwreck: Showing What Sometimes Happens on our Sea Coasts; also, Giving a Particular Account of a Poor Sailor Boy, who was Refused any Assistance by the Wreckers, and Who Died in Consequence of their Inhuman Conduct (London, [between 1822 and 1886])

Thomson, Katherine, *Memoirs of Sarah, Duchess of Marlborough, and of the Court of Queen Anne* (London, 1839)

Voltaire, *Oeuvres complètes de Voltaire* (Sautelet, 1827)

Vorontsova Archives, Tom. 21, (Moscow, 1880)

Walker Freer, Martha, *The Life of Marguerite D'Angouleme, Queen of Navarre* (Hurst, 1854)

Williams, Helen Maria, *Letters written in France, in the Summer of 1790, to a Friend in England* (Dublin, 1791)

— *A Tour in Switzerland; or, A View of the Present State of the Governments and Manners of those Cantons: with Comparative Sketches of the Present State of Paris*, 2 vols (London, 1798)

— *Correspondance Politique et Confidentielle Inédite de Louis XVI., Avec ses Frères et Plusieurs Personnes Célèbres, Pendant les Dernières Années de son Règne et Jusqu'à sa Mort. Avec des Observations par H. M. Williams*, 2 vols (Paris, 1803)

— *Souvenirs de la Révolution Française*, trans. by C. Coquerel (Paris, 1827)

Wilmot, Catherine, and Thomas U. Sadleir, *An Irish Peer on the Continent, 1801–1803, Being a Narrative of the Tour of Stephen, 2nd Earl of Mount Cashell, as Related by Catherine Wilmot* (London, 1924)

Wilmot, Martha, and Catherine Wilmot, *The Russian Journals of Martha and Catherine Wilmot, 1803–1808 [With plates, including portraits]*, ed. by Edith Marchioness of Londonderry and H. Montgomery Hyde (London, 1934)

Wilmot, Martha, *More Letters from Martha Wilmot: Impressions of Vienna 1819–1829*, ed. by Edith Marchioness of Londonderry and H. Montgomery Hyde (London, 1935)

Secondary Sources

Agnew, Vanessa, *Enlightenment Orpheus: The Power of Music in Other Worlds* (Oxford, 2008)

Agorni, Mirella, *Translating Italy for the Eighteenth Century: Women, Translation and Travel Writing* (Manchester, 2002)

Akel, Regina, *Maria Graham: A Literary Biography* (Amherst, 2009)

Aravamudan, Srinivas, 'Lady Mary Wortley Montagu in the Hammam: Masquerade, Womanliness, and Levantinization', *ELH*, 62:1 (1995), 69–104

Argent, Gesine, Derek Offord and Vladislav Rjéoutski, eds, 'French Language Acquisition in Imperial Russia', in *Вивлиѳѳика: E-Journal of Eighteenth-Century Russian Studies*, 1 (2013), 1–4

Backscheider, Paula, and Catherine E. Ingrassia, eds, *British Women Poets of the Long Eighteenth Century: An Anthology* (Baltimore, 2009)
Bainbridge, Simon, *Napoleon and English Romanticism* (Cambridge, 2005)
Bannet, Eve Tavor, *The Domestic Revolution: Enlightenment Feminism and the Novel* (Baltimore, 2000)
Barchas, Janine, *Graphic Design, Print Culture, and the Eighteenth-Century Novel* (Cambridge, 2003)
Barker, Nicholas, 'In Praise of Manuscripts', in *Form and Meaning in the History of the Book: Selected Essays* (London, 2003)
Batchelor, Jennie, *Women's Work: Labour, Gender, Authorship, 1750–1830* (Manchester, 2014)
— 'Anon, Pseud and "By A Lady": The Spectre of Anonymity in Women's Literary History', in *Women's Writing, 1660–1830: Futures and Feminisms*, ed. by Jennie Batchelor and Gillian Dow (London, 2016), pp. 69–86
— *The Lady's Magazine (1770–1832) and the Making of Literary History* (Edinburgh, 2022)
Batchelor, Jennie, and Cora Kaplan, eds, *British Women's Writing in the Long Eighteenth Century: Authorship, Politics, and History* (Basingstoke, 2005)
— eds, *The History of British Women's Writing* (Basingstoke, 2010)
Batchelor, Jennie, and Gillian Dow, eds, *Women's Writing, 1660–1830: Feminisms and Futures* (London, 2016)
Bigold, Melanie, *Women of Letters, Manuscript Circulation, and Print Afterlives in the Eighteenth Century: Elizabeth Rowe, Catherine Cockburn, and Elizabeth Carter* (Basingstoke, 2013)
Black, Joseph Lawrence, *G. F. Müller and the Imperial Russian Academy of Sciences, 1725–1783: First Steps in the Development of the Historical Sciences in Russia* (Kingston-Montréal, 1986)
Blakemore, Steven, 'Revolution and the French Disease: Laetitia Matilda Hawkins Letters to Helen Maria Williams', *Studies in English Literature, 1500–1900*, 36:3 (1996), 673–691
Blanch-Serrat, Francesca, 'Women Translating Women: Resisting the Male Intellectual Canon in Eliza Hayley's Essays on Friendship and Old-Age, by the Marchioness de Lambert (1780)', *Enthymema* (2023), 78–90
Bohls, Elizabeth A., *Women Travel Writers and the Language of Aesthetics, 1716–1818* (Cambridge, 1995)
Brant, Clare, 'Varieties of Women's Writing', in *Women and Literature in Britain: 1700–1800*, ed. by Vivien Jones (Cambridge, 2000), 285–305
— *Eighteenth-Century Letters and British Culture* (Basingstoke, 2006)
Brown, Hilary, and Gillian Dow, eds, *Readers, Writers, Salonnières: Female Networks in Europe, 1700–1900* (Oxford, 2011)
Burnstein, Miriam Elizabeth, 'Royal Lives', in *Companion to Women's Historical Writing*, ed. by Mary Spongberg (Basingstoke, 2009)
Byrne, Angela, 'The Irish in Russia, 1690–1815; Travel, Gender and Self-Fashioning' (doctoral thesis, National University of Ireland, Maynooth, 2008)

— 'Princess Dashkova and the Wilmot Sisters', in *Treasures of the Royal Irish Academy Library*, ed. by Bernadette Cunningham and Siobhán Fitzpatrick (Dublin, 2009), pp. 248–255
— 'Supplementing the Autobiography of Princess Ekaterina Romanovna Dashkova: the Russian Diaries of Martha and Katherine Wilmot', *Irish Slavonic Studies*, 23 (2011), 25–34
— 'Anonymity, Irish Women's Writing, and a Tale of Contested Authorship: Blue Stocking Hall (1827) and Tales of My Time (1829)', *Proceedings of the Royal Irish Academy: Archaeology, Culture, History, Literature*, 119C (2019), 259–281
— 'Life after Emmet's Death: Sarah Curran's Literary and Friendship circle', *Irish Studies Review*, 30 (2022), 119–135
Buck, Pamela, 'Collecting an Empire: The Napoleonic Louvre and the Cabinet of Curiosities in Catherine Wilmot's Irish Peer on the Continent', *Prose Studies*, 33:3 (2011), 188–199
— 'From Russia with Love: Souvenirs and Political Alliance in Martha Wilmot's The Russian Journals', in *Eighteenth-Century Thing Theory in a Global Context: From Consumerism to Celebrity Culture*, ed. by Ileana Baird and Christina Ionescu (Farnham, 2013), pp. 133–148
— *Objects of Liberty: British Women Writers and Revolutionary Souvenirs* (Newark, 2024)
Bunkers, Suzanne L., and Cynthia A. Huff, eds, *Inscribing the Daily: Critical Essays on Women's Diaries* (Amherst, 1996)
Butler, Marilyn, *Mapping Mythologies: Countercurrents in Eighteenth-Century Poetry and Cultural History* (Cambridge, 2015)
Buzard. James, and Joseph Childers, 'Introduction: Victorian Ethnographies', *Victorian Studies*, 41:3 (1998), 351–353
Chamberlain, Timothy, ed., *Eighteenth-Century German Criticism: Herder, Lenz, Lessing, and Others* (London, 1992)
Chandler, James, 'Critical Disciplinarity', *Critical Inquiry*, 30 (2004), 355–360
Chartier, Roger, *Forms and Meanings: Texts, Performances, and Audiences from Codex to Computer* (Philadelphia, 1995)
Clark, Linda, *Women and Achievement in Nineteenth-Century Europe* (Cambridge, 2008)
Clifford, James, and George E. Marcus, eds, *Writing Culture: The Poetics and Politics of Ethnography* (Berkeley, 1986)
Colbert, Benjamin, *Women's Travel Writing, 1780–1840: A Bio-Bibliographical Database* <www.wlv.ac.uk/btw> [accessed 16 April 2024]
Connolly, Claire, 'A Bookish History of Irish Romanticism', *Rethinking British Romantic History, 1770–1845*, ed. by Porscha Fermanis and John Regan (Oxford, 2014), pp. 271–296
— *Irish Literature in Transition, 1780–1830* (Cambridge, 2020)

Cottam, Rachel, 'Diaries and Journals: General Survey', in *Encyclopedia of Life Writing: Autobiographical and Biographical Forms*, ed. by Margaretta Jolly, 2 vols (Chicago, 2001), I
Craciun, Adriana, *British Women Writers and the French Revolution: Citizens of the World* (Basingstoke, 2005)
— 'What is an explorer?', *Eighteenth-Century Studies*, 45:1 (2011), 29–51
Cressy, David, *Shipwrecks and the Bounty of the Sea* (Oxford, 2022)
Cross, A. G. [Anthony], 'Early British Acquaintance with Russian Popular Song and Music (The Letters and Journals of the Wilmot Sisters)', *The Slavonic and East European Review*, 66:1 (1988), 21–34
— *Anglo-Russica: Aspects of Cultural Relations between Great Britain and Russia in the Eighteenth and Early Nineteenth Centuries: Selected Essays by Anthony Cross* (Oxford, Providence, 1993), pp. 17–18
— 'Poezdka kniagni E. R. Dashkovoi (1776–1780)', I. D. Levin, trans., *XVIII*, 19 (1995), 223–260
Culley, Amy, *British Women's Life Writing, 1760–1840* (Basingstoke, 2014)
Culley, Amy, and Daniel Cook, eds, *Women's Life Writing, 1700–1850: Gender, Genre, Authorship* (Basingstoke, 2012)
Davidoff, Leonore, and Catherine Hall, *Family Fortunes: Men and Women of the English Middle Class 1780–1850* (London, 1992)
Deutsch, Yaacov, *Judaism in Christian Eyes: Ethnographic Descriptions of Jews and Judaism in Early Modern Europe* (Oxford, 2012)
Dow, Gillian, 'The "Biographical Impulse" and Pan-European Women's Writing', *Women's Writing, 1660–1830: Feminisms and Futures*, ed. by Jennie Batchelor and Gillian Dow (London, 2016), pp. 193–213
Dutta, Sutapa, 'Introduction', in *British Women Travellers: Empire and Beyond, 1770–1870*, ed. by Sutapa Dutta (New York and Abingdon, 2020), pp. 1–18
Earle, Peter, *The Making of the English Middle Class: Business, Society and Family Life in London 1660–1730* (Berkeley, 1989)
Edson, Michael, and Bridget Keegan, 'Introduction: William Falconer: Sailor Poet', *Eighteenth-Century Life*, 47:2 (2023), 3–12
Eger, Elizabeth, *Bluestockings: Women of Reason from Enlightenment to Romanticism* (Basingstoke, 2010)
Eger, Elizabeth, and Charlotte Grant, Clíona Ó Gallchoir and Penny Warburton, eds, *Women, Writing and the Public Sphere, 1700–1830* (Cambridge, 2001)
Ezell, Margaret J. M., *Social Authorship and the Advent of Print* (Baltimore, 2003)
D'Ezio, Marianna, 'Literary and Cultural Intersections between British and Italian Women Writers and *Salonnières* during the Eighteenth Century', in *Readers, Writers, Salonnières, 1700–1900*, ed. by Gillian Dow (Bern, 2011), pp. 11–29
Favret, Mary, 'Spectatrice as Spectacle: Helen Maria Williams at Home in the Revolution', *Studies in Romanticism*, 32:2 (1993), 273–295

Felber, Lynette, ed., *Clio's Daughters: British Women Making History, 1790–1899* (Newark, 2007)

Flint, Kate, 'Counter-Historicism, Contact Zones, and Cultural History', *Victorian Literature and Culture*, 27:2 (1999), 507–511

Genette, Gérard, *Paratexts: Thresholds of Interpretation*, trans. by Jane E. Lewin (Cambridge, 1997)

Genette, Gérard, and Bernard Crampé, 'Structure and Function of the Title in Literature', *Critical Inquiry*, 14:4 (1988), 692–720

Georgi, Claudia, 'Maria Graham, Travel Writing on India, Italy, Brazil, and Chile (1812–1824)', in *Handbook of British Travel Writing*, ed. by Barbara Schaff (Berlin and Boston, 2020)

Gleadhill, Emma, *Taking Travel Home: The Souvenir Culture of British Women Tourists, 1750–1830* (Manchester, 2022)

Goodman, Dena, *Becoming a Woman in the Age of Letters* (Ithaca, 2009)

Gowrley, Freya, *Domestic Space in Britain, 1750–1840: Materiality, Sociability and Emotion* (London, 2022)

Griggs, Earl Leslie, *Wordsworth and Coleridge* (New York, 1962)

Groom, Nick, *The Making of Percy's Reliques* (Oxford, 1999)

Guest, Harriet, *Small Change: Women, Learning, Patriotism, 1750–1810* (Chicago, 2000)

Gust, Onni, 'Mobility, Gender and Empire in Maria Graham's Journal of a Residence in India (1812)', *Gender & History*, 29 (2017), 273–291

Habermas, Jürgen, *The Structural Transformation of the Public Sphere*, trans. by Thomas Burger (1989) (Cambridge, 1996)

Havens, Hilary, 'Manuscript Studies in the Eighteenth Century', *Literature Compass*, 16:7 (2019)

HERA Project, *Travelling Texts 1790–1914, Transnational Reception of Women's Writing at the Fringes of Europe (2013–2016)* <https://www.hivolda.no/Forsking/Forskingsprosjekt/hera-travelling-texts-1790-1914-eu-fp7> [accessed 16 April 2024]

Heringman, Noah, *Sciences of Antiquity: Romantic Antiquarianism, Natural History, and Knowledge Work* (Oxford, 2013)

Holcombe, Lee, *Wives and Property: Reform of the Married Woman's Property Law in Nineteenth-Century England* (Toronto, 1983)

Hunt, Lynn, *The Family Romance of the French Revolution* (Berkeley, 1992)

Hyde, H. Montgomery, *The Empress Catherine and Princess Dashkov* (London, 1935)

Ingman, Heather, and Clíona Ó Gallchoir, eds, *A History of Modern Irish Women's Literature* (Cambridge, 2018)

Jarvis, Robin, *Romantic Readers and Transatlantic Travel: Expeditions and Tours in North America, 1760–1840* (Farnham, 2012).

Justice, George L., and Nathan Tinker, eds, *Women's Writing and the Circulation of Ideas: Manuscript Publication in England, 1550–1800* (Cambridge, 2002)

Kaukiainen, Yrjö, 'Wreck-Plundering by East Finnish Coastal People – Criminal Tradition or Popular Culture?', *Sail and Steam: Selected Maritime Writings of Yrjö Kaukiainen*, ed. by Lars U. Scholl and Merja-Liisa Hinkkanen (St John's, 2004), pp. 151–162

Kaul, Suvil, 'Britannia and the Weight of Empires Past: The Instance of Falconer's The Shipwreck', *Eighteenth-Century Life*, 47:2 (2023), 46–65

Kelly, Gary, *Women, Writing and Revolution, 1790–1827* (Oxford, 1994)

— *Anglo-Russica: Aspects of Cultural Relations between Great Britain and Russia in the Eighteenth and Early Nineteenth Centuries: Selected Essays by Anthony Cross* (Oxford, Providence, 1993), pp. 17–18

'Politicizing the Personal: Mary Wollstonecraft, Mary Shelley, and the Coterie Novel', in *Mary Shelley in Her Times*, ed. by Betty T. Bennett and Stuart Curran (Baltimore, 2000)

Kennedy, Deborah, *Helen Maria Williams and the Age of Revolution* (Lewisburg, 2002)

Kennedy, Máire, 'Women and Reading in Eighteenth-Century Ireland', in *The Experience of Reading: Irish Historical Perspectives*, ed. by Bernadette Cunningham and Máire Kennedy (Dublin, 1999)

Kidd, Alan, and David Nicholls, 'Introduction: "The Making of the British Middle Class?"', in *The Making of the British Middle Class? Studies of Regional and Cultural Diversity Since the Eighteenth Century*, ed. by Alan Kidd and David Nicholls (Stroud, 1998), pp. xv–xl

King, Rachael Scarborough, *After Print: Eighteenth-Century Manuscript Cultures* (Charlottesville, 2020)

Kinsley, Zoë, *Women Writing the Home Tour, 1682–1812* (Aldershot, 2008)

Klein, Lawrence E., 'Gender and the Public/Private Distinction in the Eighteenth Century: Some Questions About Evidence and Analytic Procedure', *Eighteenth-Century Studies*, 29 (1995), 95–109

Knott, Sarah, and Barbara Taylor, eds, *Women, Gender and Enlightenment* (Basingstoke, 2005)

Krueger, Misty, ed., *Transatlantic Women Travellers, 1688–1843* (Lewisburg, 2021)

Kuznetsov, Anatoly M., 'Russian Anthropology: Old Traditions and New Tendencies', in *Other People's Anthropologies: Ethnographic Practice on the Margins*,

Labbe, Jacqueline, *The History of British Women's Writing, 1750–1830* (Basingstoke, 2010), IV

Lake, Crystal B., 'History Writing and Antiquarianism', in *The Cambridge Companion to Women's Writing in the Romantic Period*, ed. by Devoney Looser (Cambridge, 2015)

Leerssen, Joep, 'Brooke, Charlotte (c.1740–1793)', *Oxford Dictionary of National Biography* (Oxford, 2004)

Legg, Marie-Louise, 'The Kilkenny Circulating-Library Society and the Growth of Reading Rooms in Nineteenth-Century Ireland', in *The Experience of*

Reading: Irish Historical Perspectives, ed. by Bernadette Cunningham and Máire Kennedy (Dublin, 1999)

Levine, Phillipa, ed., *Gender and Empire* (Oxford, 2007)

Levy, Michelle, *Family Authorship and Romantic Print Culture* (Basingstoke, 2008)

— *Literary Manuscript Culture in Romantic Britain* (Edinburgh, 2021)

Looser, Devoney, *British Women Writers and the Writing of History, 1670–1820* (Baltimore, 2000)

Love, Harold, *Scribal Publication in Seventeenth-Century England* (Oxford, 1993)

Lowenthal, Cynthia, *Lady Mary Wortley Montagu and the Eighteenth-Century Familiar Letter* (Athens, 1994)

Lukowski, Jerzy, and Herbert Zawadazki, *A Concise History of Poland* (Cambridge, 2001)

Maitzen, Rohan Amanda, *Gender, Genre and Victorian Historical Writing* (New York, 1998)

Mavor, Elizabeth, *The Grand Tours of Katherine Wilmot, France 1801–03 and Russia 1805–07* (London, 1992)

Mayo, Robert D., *The English Novel in the Magazines, 1740–1815* (Evanston, 1962)

McAleer, Edward, *The Sensitive Plant: A Life of Lady Mount Cashell* (Chapel Hill, 1958)

McDonald, Christie, 'On the Ethnographic Imagination in the Eighteenth Century', in *French Global: A New Approach to Literary History*, ed. by Christie McDonald abd Susan Rubin Suleiman (New York, 2010), pp. 223–239

Meaney, Gerardine, Mary O'Dowd and Bernadette Whelan, eds, *Reading the Irish Woman: Studies in Cultural Encounter and Exchange, 1714–1960* (Liverpool, 2013)

Mee, Jon, 'Coteries in the Romantic Period', *European Romantic Review*, 27:4 (2016), 515–521

Meehan, Johanna, ed., *Feminists Read Habermas: Gendering the Subject of Discourse* (New York, 1993)

Mills, Sara, *Discourses of Difference: An Analysis of Women's Travel Writing and Colonialism* (London, 1991)

Miskolcze, Robin, 'Transatlantic Touchstone: The Shipwrecked Woman in British and Early American Literature', *Prose Studies: History, Theory, Criticism*, 22:3 (1999), 41–56

Mitchell, Rosemary Ann, '"The Busy Daughters of Clio": Women Writers of History from 1820 to 1880', *Women's History Review*, 7:1 (1998), 107–134

Mitchell-Cook, Ann, *A Sea of Misadventures: Shipwreck and Survival in Early America* (Columbia, 2014)

Mulligan, Maureen, 'Women Travel Writers and the Question of Veracity', in *Women, Travel Writing, and Truth*, ed. by Clare Broome Saunders (New York, Abingdon, 2014), pp. 171–184

Myers, Victoria, David O'Shaughnessy and Mark Philp, eds, *The Diary of William Godwin* (Oxford, 2010)

Nixon, Cheryl, '"Stop a Moment at This Preface": The Gendered Paratexts of Fielding, Barker, and Haywood', *Journal of Narrative Theory*, 32:2 (2002), 123–153

Nussbaum, Felicity A., 'Toward Conceptualizing Diary', *Studies in Autobiography*, ed. by James Olney (Oxford, 1988)

O'Brien, Karen, *Women and Enlightenment in Eighteenth-Century Britain* (Cambridge, 2009)

Ó Gallchoir, Clíona, *Maria Edgeworth: Women, Enlightenment and Nation* (Dublin, 2005)

O'Halloran, Clare, *Golden Ages and Barbarous Nations: Antiquarian Debate and Cultural Politics in Ireland* (Cork, 2004)

O'Loughlin, Katrina, *Women, Writing and Travel in the Eighteenth Century* (Cambridge, 2018)

Palmer, Caroline, '"I Will Tell Nothing that I Did Not See": British Women's Travel Writing, Art and the Science of Connoisseurship, 1776–1860', *Forum for Modern Language Studies*, 51:3, (2015), 248–268

Patell, Cyril R. K., *Cosmopolitanism and the Literary Imagination* (Basingstoke, 2015)

Pearce, Cathryn J., 'What Do You Do with a Shipwrecked Sailor? Extreme Weather, Shipwreck, and Civic Responsibility in Nineteenth-Century Liverpool', *Victorian Review*, 47:1 (2021), 19–24

Pelling, Madeleine, 'Digging Up the Past: Contested Territories and Women Archaeologists in 1780s Britain and Ireland', *Talk, Open Digital Seminar in Eighteenth-Century Studies* (2021)

Peltz, Lucy, 'A Friendly Gathering', *Journal of the History of Collections*, 19:1 (2007), 33–49

Piper, David, *The Image of the Poet: British Poets and their Portraits* (Oxford, 1982)

Prendergast, Amy, 'The drooping genius of our Isle to raise: the Moira House salon and its role in Gaelic cultural revival', *Eighteenth-Century Ireland*, 26 (2011), 95–114

— *Literary Salons Across Britain and Ireland in the Long Eighteenth Century* (Basingstoke, 2015)

Readioff, Corrina, 'Recent approaches to paratext studies in eighteenth-century literature', *Literature Compass*, 18:12 (2021)

Robinson, Charles E., ed., *The 'Frankenstein' Notebooks: A Facsimile Edition of Mary Shelley's Manuscript Novel, 1816–17*, 2 vols (New York, 1996)

Rosenberg, Ruth, *Music, Travel and Imperial Encounter in 19th-Century France: Musical Apprehensions* (New York, 2014)

Rovee, Christopher, *Imagining the Gallery: The Social Body of British Romanticism* (Stanford, 2006)

Russell, Lynette, ed., *Constructions of Colonialism: Perspectives on Eliza Fraser's Shipwreck* (Wellington, 1999)

Said, Edward, *Orientalism* (New York, 1978)

— *Beginnings: Intention and Method* (New York, 1985)

Schechter, Ronald, 'The Jewish Question in Eighteenth-Century France', *Eighteenth-Century Studies*, 32:1 (1998), 84–91

Schellenberg, Betty A., *Literary Coteries and the Making of Modern Print Culture* (Cambridge, 2016)

Schmid, Susanne, *British Literary Salons of the Late Eighteenth and Early Nineteenth Centuries* (New York, 2015)

Sebastiani, Silvia, '"Race", Women and Progress in the Scottish Enlightenment', in *Women, Gender and Enlightenment*, ed. by Sarah Knott and Barbara Taylor (Basingstoke, 2005)

Sloan, Kim, *A Noble Art: Amateur Artists and Drawing Masters c.1600–1800* (London, 2000)

Spongberg, Mary, *Writing Women's History Since the Renaissance* (Basingstoke, 2002)

— 'The Ghost of Marie Antoinette: A Prehistory of Victorian Royal Lives', in *Clio's Daughters: British Women Making History, 1790–1899*, ed. by Lynette Felber (Newark, 2007), pp. 71–96

— *Women Writers and the Nation's Past 1790–1860* (London, 2018)

Stern, Madeleine B., 'The English Press in Paris and Its Successors, 1793–1852', *The Papers of the Bibliographical Society of America*, 74:4 (1980), 307–359

Stone, Daniel, 'Jews and the Urban Question in Late Eighteenth Century Poland', *Slavic Review*, 50:3 (1991), 531–541

Sussman, Charlotte, 'Women's Private Reading and Political Action, 1649–1838', in *Radicalism in British Literary Culture, 1650–1830: From Revolution to Revolution*, ed. by Timothy Morton and Nigel Smith (Cambridge, 2002), pp. 133–151

Sutcliffe, Adam, 'Myth, Origins, Identity: Voltaire, the Jews and the Enlightenment Notion of Toleration', *The Eighteenth Century*, 39:2 (1998), 107–126

Sutherland, John, 'Henry Colburn Publisher', *Publishing History* (1986), 59–84

Sweet, Rosemary, 'Antiquaries and Antiquities in Eighteenth-Century England', *Eighteenth-Century Studies*, 34:2 (2001), 181–206

Tadmor, Naomi, 'The Concept of the Household-Family in Eighteenth-Century England', *Past & Present*, 151 (1996), 111–140

Taruskin, Richard, *Defining Russia Musically: Historical and Hermeneutical Essays* (Princeton, 2000)

Teissier, Beatrice, *Russian Frontiers: Eighteenth-Century British Travellers in the Caspian, Caucasus and Central Asia* (Oxford, 2011)

The Lady's Magazine (1770–1818): Understanding the Emergence of a Genre, ed. by Jennie Batchelor, Koenraad Claes and Jenny DiPlacidi <https://research.kent.ac.uk/the-ladys-magazine/> [accessed 16 April 2024]

Thompson, Carl, 'Journeys to Authority: Reassessing Women's Early Travel Writing, 1763–1862', *Women's Writing*, 24:2 (2017), 131–150
— *Romantic-Era Shipwreck Narratives: An Anthology* (Nottingham, 2007)
— 'Sentiment and Scholarship: Hybrid Historiography and Historical Authority in Maria Graham's South American Journals', *Women's Writing*, 24:2 (2017), 185–206
Todd, Janet, 'Ascendancy: Lady Mount Cashell, Lady Moira, Mary Wollstonecraft, and the Union Pamphlets', *Eighteenth-Century Ireland*, 18 (2003), 98–113
— *Daughters of Ireland* (New York, 2003)
Tomalin, Marcus, *The French Language and British Literature, 1756–1830* (London, 2016)
Turner, Katherine, *British Travel Writers in Europe, 1750–1800: Authorship, Gender and National Identity* (Aldershot, 2001)
— 'Women Writing Travel', *Forum for Modern Language Studies* (2023)
Van Netten Blimke, Linda, *Political Affairs of the Heart: Female Travel Writers, the Sentimental Travelogue, and Revolution, 1775–1800* (Lewisburg, 2022)
Vermeulen, Han F., *Before Boas: The Genesis of Ethnography and Ethnology in the German Enlightenment* (Lincoln, 2015)
Vickery, Amanda, *The Gentleman's Daughter: Women's Lives in Georgian England* (New Haven, 1998)
Wharton, Joanna, *Material Enlightenment: Women Writers and the Science of the Mind, 1770–1830* (Woodbridge, 2018)
Whyman, Susan E., *The Pen and the People: English Letters Writers 1660–1800* (Oxford, 2009)
Williams, Abigail, *The Social Life of Books: Reading Together in the Eighteenth-Century Home* (New Haven, 2017)
Wolf, Alexis, 'Introduction: Reading Silence in the Long Nineteenth-Century Women's Life Writing Archive', *19: Interdisciplinary Studies in the Long Nineteenth Century* (2018), 27
— 'Identity and Anonymity in Lady Mount Cashell's 1798 Rebellion Broadside', *Journal for Eighteenth-Century Studies*, 45:2 (2022), 259–276
Woronzoff-Dashkoff, A., 'Additions and Notes in Princess Dashkova's "Mon Histoire"', *Study Group on Eighteenth-Century Russia Newsletter*, 19 (1991)
— *Dashkova: A Life of Influence and Exile* (Philadelphia, 2008)
Wright, Julia M., '"All the Fire-Side Circle": Irish Women Writers and the Sheridan Lefanu Coterie', *Keats-Shelley Journal*, 55 (2004) 63–72

Index

Alexander I, Emperor of Russia   174, 185
Alexeievna, Elizabeth, Empress Consort of Russia   183–184
Anglo–Russian War   1–2, 131, 174–176, 185–187, 192–200
Antiquarianism   17–18, 94–99, 108–116, 124–9
'Aspo' (Haapasaari)   196–198

Barbauld, Anna Laetitia   29
Barrett, Charlotte   151
Bentley, Richard   142
Blair Adam House   12, 14
Bonaparte *see* Napoleon I
Bradford, Blanche Elizabeth   8, 12, 164, 167
Bradford, Reverend William   8, 136, 142–143, 163–164
  as translator of Memoirs   137–138, 142–143
British Museum   12, 164
Brooke, Catherine Anne Daschkaw   8, 12, 128, 164, 167
Brooke, Charlotte   121, 127–128
Burney, Charles   119
Burney, Frances   150–151

Cadell and Davies Booksellers   109 n.54, 159
Callcott, Lady *see* Graham, Maria
Catherine II, Empress of Russia
  as patron of the arts and sciences   109, 177
  relationship with Dashkova   62–63, 65, 70–72, 143–150, 152–153, 156
Catlin, George   129

Chetwood, Anna   102, 104–105, 201
Chetwood (family)   6, 91–92
Colburn, Henry   141–143
Colburn's New Monthly Magazine   150
Cook, Captain James   119
Cork, literary circle at   6, 73–80, 133
Coterie Culture   19–21, 89–90
Cottin, Sophie   95
Coxe, William   95
Craven, Lady Elizabeth   36, 95, 173, 176n

Damer, Anne Seymour   160
Dashkov, Pavel ('Prince Dashkov')   187
Dashkova, Anastasia *see* Shcherbinina, Anastasia
Dashkova, Princess Ekaterina
  relationship with Catherine II   62–63, 65, 70–72, 143–150, 152–153, 156
  as statesperson   12, 65, 97, 126, 146
  as patron to the Wilmots   10, 67–70, 97, 107, 116, 154
  writing of Memoirs of Princess Daschkaw   63, 80–81, 158
de Montolieu, Isabelle   95–96
Dublin   6, 77

Edgeworth, Maria   48, 171–173
Emmett, Robert   7
English Press, The   34, 48–52
Ethnography   97–98, 101

Falconer, William   188
Feodorovna, Maria ('Mary'), Dowager Empress of Russia   185
France, relations with Britain   29–30

Frazer, Eliza 194

Georgi, Johann Gottlieb 97
Gillray, James 29–30
Glanmire (County Cork) see Cork, literary circle at
Glenbervie, Lord Sylvester Douglas 137, 161, 185
Godwin, William 7, 39, 58–59
Graham, Maria 177, 178–183
  Journal of a Residence in India 179
  Letters on India 180–181
  Journal of a Residence in Chile, during the year 1822 And a Voyage from Chile to Brazil in 1823 181–183
Grand Tour 18, 29, 67, 176, 179
Green, Sarah 52
Green, Mary Anne Everett 140
Guthrie, Matthew 98, 108–113
Guthie, Maria 176 n6

Haapasaari see 'Aspo'
Hamilton, Catherine 7, 62, 100, 126, 159, 187, 204
Hawkins, Laetitia-Matilda 47
Herder, Johann Gottfried 121–122
History as a genre, women's writing of 18–19, 71–72
Holcroft, Fanny 39
Holcroft, Thomas 39, 58–59
Haliday, Dr 108, 193, 194, 196

Imperial Academy of Arts and Sciences 8, 12, 101 n.20, 102, 126, 152
Irish Protestant Sociability 5–6
Irwin, Eyles 91–92
Irwin, Frances Sally (later Caulfield) 91–92

Jews 99–107
Johnson, Samuel 81

'Krouglo' (Kruhlaye) 99–107
Kruhlaye see 'Krouglo'

Lady's Magazine, The 36
Lafitau, Joseph-François 110
Lecky, Elizabeth 12
Lecky, W.E.H 12
Levesque, Pierre Charles 97
Louise of Baden see Alexeievna, Elizabeth

Marindin, Evelyn (née Wilmot-Chetwode) 14
Manuscript Culture 16–17, 73–80, 86–90
Moira, Countess Elizabeth Rawdon 6, 127–128
Montagu, Lady Mary Wortley 113–116
Moore, Reverend Charles 5
Morgan, Elizabeth 159
Morgan, Lady Sydney 142
Moscow, literary circle at 81, 126, 174
Mount Cashell, Lady Margaret King 6, 22, 30–32, 37–39
Mount Cashell, Lord, Stephen 22, 30–32, 37–39
Müller, Gerhard Friedrich 95, 101–103
Murray, John 163–164
Murry, Ann 71–72

Napoleon I, Bonaparte 30, 49, 57, 174, 189–190, 203

Opie, Amelia 36
Orlov, Gregory 152, 170

Paine, Thomas 7, 50
Panin, Nikita 170
Paris, Katherine's visit to 35–40, 44–52, 54–61
Paul I, Emperor of Russia 65, 147, 148, 156, 185

Index

Peace of Amiens 5, 29–30, 205
Penrose (family) 6
Peter I, Tsar of all Russia 67, 101
Petrovna, Anna 105, 202
Percy, Thomas 120, 122
Poland
   Dashkova's lands 97, 99–101, 106
   Jews of 99–107
Porter, Jane 191
Pratch, Ivan 122–123
Prince Dashkov *see* Dashkov, Pavel

Reading Societies 77–78
Royal Irish Academy 11–12, 23, 24, 126–129

Sadleir, Thomas 22, 30 n.5
Saint Petersburg Academy of Arts and Sciences *see* Imperial Academy of Arts and Sciences
Salon culture 39–41
Shcherbinina, Anastasia 68, 174, 187
Scotland, Dashkova's tour of 81–82
Separate spheres 14–16
Seward, Edward 191
Shelley, Mary 142, 155
Shipwreck narratives 190–199
Smith, Charlotte Turner 190–191
Society of Antiquaries of Scotland 98, 109, 110, 113, 128
St Petersburg 102, 109, 122, 168
'Stamieux' (Tammio) 193–196
Stanley, Lady Maria Josepha 30 n.5, 78
Stodart, M.A. 141
Stone, John Hurford 33–34, 45–46, 48–52
Storrington, Sussex 8
Strickland, Agnes 140, 141–142
Strickland, Elizabeth 140, 141–142
Switzerland 57

Tammio *see* 'Stamieux'

Treaty of Amiens *see* Peace of Amiens
Tonci, Salvatore 82, 148–149, 169
Troitskoe, literary circle at 80–86, 124–125

United Irishmen 5, 6, 38

Vienna 8, 26 n.53
Voltaire 105

Walpole, Horace 47
Williams, Helen Maria 33–34, 39–40, 45–59
   Letters Written in France 54–59
Wilmot, Alicia 74–76, 86, 89, 94, 202
Wilmot, Charles 7, 186–187
Wilmot, Captain Edward (father) 5, 10, 37
Wilmot, Edward (nephew) 92 n.112
Wilmot, Elizabeth ('Eliza') 91–92, 132
Wilmot, John Eardley 10, 10 n.16, 109 n.53, 159, 189
Wilmot, Katherine
   biographical overview 2–7, 8
   as author 30–36, 53–61, 200–206
   as editor of *Memoirs* 83, 85, 88, 153
   as translator of *Memoirs* 83–86, 135–137
Wilmot, Martha
   biographical overview 2–6, 7–8
   as author 185–200
   as editor of *Memoirs* 79–80, 133–157, 164–173
   relationship with Dashkova 67–70, 90, 133, 151, 154
Wilmot, 'Mary' (Martha, mother) 5, 73–76, 86, 150–151
Wilmot, Robert (brother) 44–45, 91–92
Wollstonecraft, Mary 38, 39
Woronzow, Simon 8, 161–163

Printed in the United States
by Baker & Taylor Publisher Services